D0225756

OXFORD ENGLISH MONOGRAPHS

Joseph Conrad and the Modern Temper

DAPHNA ERDINAST-VULCAN

CLARENDON PRESS · OXFORD
1991

Oxford University Press, Walton Street, Oxford OX2 6DP
Oxford New York Toronto
Delhi Bombay Calcutta Madras Karachi
Petaling Jaya Singapore Hong Kong Tokyo
Nairobi Dar es Salaam Cape Town
Melbourne Auckland
and associated companies in
Berlin Ibadan

Oxford is a trade mark of Oxford University Press

Published in the United States
by Oxford University Press, New York

British Library Cataloguing in Publication Data
(data available)

Library of Congress Cataloging in Publication Data
Erdinast-Vulcan, Daphna.
Joseph Conrad and the modern temper / Daphna Erdinast-Vulcan.
—(Oxford English monographs) (Oxford historical
monographs)
Includes bibliographical references and index.
1. Conrad, Joseph, 1857–1924—Criticism and interpretation.
2. Modernism (Literature)—Great Britain. I. Title. II. Series.
III. Series: Oxford historical monographs.
PR6005.04Z67 1991
823'.912—dc20 90-26515
ISBN 0–19–811785–X

Typeset by Cambridge Composing (UK) Ltd
Printed and bound in
Great Britain by Bookcraft Ltd
Midsomer Norton, Bath

Acknowledgements

While writing this book I have incurred, as one inevitably and happily does, a multitude of debts of various sorts. The more material ones can easily be taken care of. The difficulty is with those debts of gratitude which can never be fully repaid. My greatest debt, which is bound to remain outstanding, is to my family and friends who have been with me in more than one way all along.

I would like to thank, with all my heart, the scholars and friends who read this work at different stages of its conception and offered valuable advice and encouragement: Dr John Batchelor of New College, Oxford, who followed my toils with invariable kindness; Professor Jacques Berthoud of York University and Professor John Carey of Merton College, Oxford, who supported this project at the later stages; Professor Gabriel Josipovici of Sussex University, whose integrity and friendship gave me faith in my work; Professor Murray Roston of Bar-Ilan University, Israel, who extended wisdom and kindness from afar; Professor Miriam Eliav-Feldon and Dr Joseph Mali of Tel-Aviv University, who offered the benefit of scholarship in other disciplines; my fellow students, Wisla Suraszka and David Medalie, with whom I shared the frequent doubts and the occasional joys of writing; and last but not least, Professor Jon Stallworthy of Wolfson College, Oxford, who was always there for me.

But most of all, I am indebted to Achick, the most generous of men, who, in his magnanimity, refuses to recognize the notion of indebtedness. This book is dedicated, with all my love, to him.

A version of the chapter on *Chance* was published under the title 'Textuality and Surrogacy in Conrad's *Chance*' in *L'epoque Conradienne* (1989); a version of the chapter on *The Arrow of gold* was published under the title 'Conrad's Double-edged Arrow' in *Conradiana* 20, 3 (1988). I am very grateful to the editors for their permission to publish these chapters in the book.

All the references to Conrad's works follow the pagination of the Dent Uniform Edition, 1923–1925.

Contents

Introduction

Many a man has heard or read and believes that the earth goes round the sun; one small blob of mud among several others, spinning ridiculously with a waggling motion like a top about to fall. This is the Copernican system, and the man believes in the system without often knowing as much about it as its name. But while watching a sunset he sheds his belief; he sees the sun as a small and useful object, the servant of his needs and the witness of his ascending effort, sinking slowly behind a range of mountains, and then he holds the system of Ptolemy. He holds it without knowing it. In the same way a poet hears, reads, and believes a thousand undeniable [scientific] truths which have not yet got into his blood.[1]

CONRAD's distinction between the poetic/Ptolemaic outlook, and the scientific/Copernican view of the universe is inscribed within a broader, familiar cultural paradigm: a distinction between pre-modernity and modernity, between a cosmos made to man's measure and a universe which is alien, meaningless, and indifferent. In 1930, six years after Conrad's death, Joseph Wood Krutch published *The Modern Temper*, a painfully lucid perception of the cultural crisis which looms so large in Conrad's work.[2] The central thesis of Krutch's essay is the 'perpetual maladjustment' of humanity: man is the most miserable of nature's creatures precisely because he has managed to transcend nature. He is 'the only one in whom the instinct of life falters long enough to enable it to ask the question "why?"' But this peculiarly human question has become unanswerable since the mid-nineteenth century.

---

[1] Joseph Conrad, 'The Ascending Effort' (1910), in *Notes on Life and Letters* (London: Dent Uniform Edition, 1924), 73–4.
[2] Joseph Wood Krutch, *The Modern Temper* (London: Jonathan Cape, 1930).

The structures which are variously known as mythology, religion, and philosophy, and which are alike in that each has as its function the interpretation of experience in terms which have human values, have collapsed under the force of successive [scientific] attacks and shown themselves utterly incapable of assimilating the new stores of experience which have been dumped upon the world.[3]

The collapse of the myths which had postulated the existence of God, the transcendental authority of the moral order, the privileged position of man within the natural scheme, and the teleological nature of human existence, has turned us into victims of our own consciousness. The intellectual curiosity which has so increased our ability to manipulate and control our physical environment has forced us to surrender the power to mould the universe in our own image. The world of poetry, mythology, and religion, a world born out of man's desires and 'ignorance', has been replaced by the ruthless indifference of nature as science knows it: the 'cozy bowl of heaven' has turned into a 'cold immensity of space'.[4]

There can be little doubt that Conrad, too, was acutely conscious of the collapse of the mythical anthrompomorphic (i.e. Ptolemaic) view of the universe, and its succession by the Copernican vision of a vast indifferent and amoral cosmos. This consciousness is particularly evident in his letters to Cunninghame Graham:

What makes mankind tragic is not that they are the victims of nature, it is that they are conscious of it. . . . We can't return to nature since we can't change our place in it.[5]

Understand that thou art nothing, less than a shadow, more insignificant than a drop of water in the ocean, more fleeting than a dream.[6]

Words fly away; and nothing remains, do you understand? Absolutely nothing, oh man of faith! Nothing. A moment, a twinkling of an eye, and nothing remains—but a clot of mud, of cold mud, of dead mud cast into black space, rolling around an extinguished sun. Nothing. Neither thought, nor sound, nor soul. Nothing.[7]

---

[3] Joseph Wood Krutch, *The Modern Temper* (London: Jonathan Cape, 1930). 40, 9, 12.   [4] Ibid. 7–9.

[5] Letter to Cunninghame Graham on 31 Jan. 1898, in *Joseph Conrad's Letters to Cunninghame Graham*, ed. C. T. Watts (Cambridge: Cambridge University Press, 1969), 70–1.

[6] Letter to Cunningham Graham on 14 Dec. 1897, ibid. 54.

[7] Letter to Cunningham Graham on 15 June 1898, in *The Collected Letters of Joseph Conrad*, ed. Frederick R. Karl and Laurence Davies (Cambridge: Cambridge University Press, 1986), ii. 70 (trans. from French).

But the more interesting point for the purpose of our study is the assumption implicit in Conrad's article that one can, if only for a while, suspend the Copernican and reinstate the Ptolemaic system. This, I would argue, is the ultimate project of Conrad's work, a Sisyphean task for a man whose ideological constructions were to be inevitably demolished by his own temperamental scepticism.

Conrad was never—either literally or figuratively—at home in the world. He remained an exile, an incurable moralist infected with the ethical relativism of his age. Seen in this light, Conrad's work is fascinating precisely for the sheer impossibility of its task, the failure which is immanent in the project of recovery. For it is, indeed, impossible to return to a Ptolemaic universe in a Copernican world, to reinstate myth or metaphysics by a mere exertion, however desperate, of authorial will. But, reading Conrad as we do here, at the close of the century he ushered in, we shall not concern ourselves with the impossible homecoming. We shall study the homesickness and its noble failures.

The first chapter will examine briefly the epistemological, the ethical, and the aesthetic crises, which began to be felt in Europe in the middle of the nineteenth century and culminated at its close, and relate them to the secularization of Western culture, or the 'disappearance of God'. The discussion of this threefold crisis will focus on Nietzsche, the herald of the modern temper, and on Conrad's ambivalent attitude to his cultural legacy. Conrad's extreme susceptibility to the Nietzchean outlook is mostly evident in his letters: he, too, seems at times to regard truth and ethics as brittle man-made constructs; he often views human nature through a Hobbesian prism; and he, too, sometimes projects a cynical view of the role of art as the procurement of sustaining illusions. And yet, as one of Conrad's most astute readers has said, 'we must sometimes force ourselves to remember that the act of creation is not simply the projection of temperament but a criticism and purging of temperament'.[8] I believe that Conrad, a 'homo duplex' as he defined himself, has predicated the best of his work on a purging of his own temperament, a rejection of the Nietzschean

---

[8] Robert Penn Warren, '*Nostromo*', *Sewanee Review*, 59 (1951), 363–91, rpt. in the Introduction to the Modern Library Edition of the novel.

outlook.[9] He could neither accept its celebration of ethical and epistemological relativism, nor endorse its view of the role of art as the supreme lie. His moral heritage, and his desperate personal need for a stable frame of reference, impelled him into a heroic (and foredoomed) struggle with the modern temper.

This study will, therefore, focus on the tension inherent in Conrad's response to modernity: the tension between the writer's temperamental affinity with the Nietzschean conception of culture as a set of fragile illusions imperfectly overlaid on a chaotic, fragmented, and meaningless reality, and his ideological need to reinstate the Ptolemaic (i.e. integrated and anthropocentric) universe. I would suggest that this ambivalence is the key to some of his notorious ambiguities, to the thematic and structural problematics of his work, and to the development of his artistic vision.[10]

Conrad's work, even before what is often regarded as his phase of decline, is singularly uneven. His very best works seem to be riddled with aesthetic contradictions: in *Lord Jim*, which is an exploration of ethical relativism and of the making of a personality, we have a sudden aesthetic transition (accompanying Jim's physical transition to Patusan), where both the narrative mode and the treatment of the protagonist seem to be reduced to the level of adventure stories for boys; in *Nostromo*, an extremely sophisticated literary treatment of historiosophical issues, we have a protagonist who seems to be two-dimensional and crudely outlined against the complexity of his background; *Under Western Eyes* is narrated by a character who often feels (along with some readers) that he may be quite redundant in the novel; in *The Shadow-Line* there is a strong and inexplicable demonic element which violates the realistic proprieties to which the story ostensibly adheres; in *Chance* there is an elaborate network of sub-narrators whose

---

[9] A letter to Kazimierz Waliszewski, 5 Dec. 1903, in *Conrad's Polish Background: Letters to and from Polish Friends*, ed. Z. Najder, trans. Halina Carroll (London: Oxford University Press, 1964), 240.

[10] The notion of 'development' in this context does not imply that there is a linear progression in Conrad's work. One may, in a sense, talk about Conrad's earlier phase as characterized by the 'mythical' mode, and his late phase as featuring the 'textual' mode, but the cases of *Heart of Darkness* and *The Rescue* (the two exceptions in the rough chronological order of the novels discussed here), as well as the exclusion of *The Secret Agent*, which cannot be related to any of these phases, should qualify any pat periodizations of his work.

relations to the plot seem to be entirely contingent; *Victory* starts off with an oblique, ironic narrator, who is simply abandoned when Heist and Lena leave for Samburan, and the narrative slips into a blatantly allegorical pattern.

These problem areas in Conrad's work have often been noted by critics, but the general tendency is to view them as the occasional slips of an otherwise great writer. I would argue that in all these cases the unevenness is not a mere aesthetic fault: it reflects a temperamental and ideological tension which operates both as a theme and as a structuring principle in these texts. I would, therefore, use these fault-lines or 'fissures' in the texts as points of departure for the present discussion, and relate them to the split vision of a *homo duplex*, a modernist at war with modernity.[11]

Conrad first attempts to break away from the modern temper through a regression into the heroic-mythical frame of reference within which the protagonists of *Lord Jim*, *The Rescue*, and *Nostromo* operate. The characters in these novels—insulated in remote exotic settings, away from modern Western civilization—are offered a sanctuary, a space where the heroic-mythical mode of discourse is a viable ethical and aesthetic alternative to the modern outlook. Myth, as we shall see, is not only a matter of setting, scene, or recycled mythological motifs in these novels. It is a mode of discourse, a modality of consciousness governed by the master-trope of metaphor, which functions as a form of mediation between world and consciousness.

The third chapter of the study deals with the failure of metaphysics in *Heart of Darkness*, *Under Western Eyes*, and *The Shadow-Line*. I would suggest that the protagonists in all three works initially set out on a pilgrimage in quest of a metaphysical essence or a transcendental authority. The inevitable failure of the

---

[11] The decision to exclude *The Secret Agent* from a study of Conrad's major novels deserves some explanation: the present study is concerned with 'fault-lines', with unresolved structural and thematic tensions in Conrad's work. These fault-lines are not evident in *The Secret Agent*. Conrad has managed to sustain full control of his material by enclosing it in a barrier of acerbic irony, by removing himself from the text and acting, for once, as the indifferent creator who manipulates his characters with ruthless precision and aesthetic economy. This novel, perhaps the least problematic and the most perfectly crafted of Conrad's works, does not fit into the framework of the present discussion precisely because it is so technically flawless.

quest results in an acceptance of 'doubleness', an assumption of total responsibility, to the point of complete identification with some 'other'. I would view this denial of otherness as an attempt to reverse the role of Cain, the prototype of modern man: the protagonists in the three novels all end up by declaring themselves their brothers' keepers, in recognition of an alternative, albeit precarious, ethical code. The failure of metaphysics can be described as a transition from synecdoche to metonymy, from a mode of semantic transfer which is based on containment to one which relates to contiguity.

The last chapter of this book, entitled 'The Failure of Textuality', deals with three novels often relegated by critics to Conrad's phase of decline: *Chance*, *Victory*, and *The Arrow of Gold*. I believe that this phase does mark a decline in Conrad's work, but would argue that this decline is a failure of vision: Conrad writes in this last phase as a proto-deconstructionist, persistently aware of the absence of any one ultimate truth, afflicted with a Nietzschean view of reality as an indeterminate text, and of all truths as mere interpretations or readings of it. This view of the world as a text seems to be shared by the author and his protagonists at this stage. The characters are constantly aware of their own fictionality. They seem to observe themselves in action, and to assess their own performance in a detached aestheticist manner, which undermines their conviction and strength, making it impossible for them to live up to their knightly roles in their respective stories. Conrad's surrender to textuality is marked by an aporetic, self-defeating mode of discourse.

Our focus on ruptures within the writing, on epistemological scepticism, and on the subversion of ideological essentialism by temperamental scepticism would all seem to call for a deconstructionist approach. Conrad's work is often, indeed, an open invitation to deconstruction, for he, too, has a share in the Nietzschean legacy which nurtures this form of critical discourse, and his writing is constantly engaged in a self-dismantling, self-subversive *mise en abyme*. But Conrad was, as we shall see, a thoroughly didactic artist, primarily concerned with ethical choices in open-eyed defiance of the modern temper and its corrosive relativization of all truths and values. He must have been aware that, as one of his contemporaries put it so well, 'however much life may mock the metaphysician, the problem of conduct remains'.[12] How, then, can one deconstruct Conrad without pushing him down the slippery slope of his own scepticism, back to square one?

A better frame of critical reference for this project may be found in Bakhtin's work, with its focus on the tension between the 'centripetal' and the 'centrifugal' vectors, and its view of internal aesthetic discontinuities as projections of this tension. I believe that this dialogicity which, according to Bakhtin, is a distinct feature of the novel as a genre, may be a key to the dynamics of Conrad's work; that the stylistic and structural fissures in his novels are the front lines of this hostile interaction between the artistic will to meaning and the relativizing forces of his cultural climate.[13]

This tug-of-war is not confined to the split consciousness of the author: it is embodied in the characters who are, in Bakhtin's sense 'ideologues', i.e. the carriers of a point of view, *loci* of perception, voices. This is not to say that Conrad's characters can consciously formulate and articulate their ideologies. On the contrary, with the notable exception of Razumov, they are, for the most part, men of action rather than words, including Marlow, the official authorial surrogate, whose evaluative commentary often recedes into long, enigmatic silences. However, as Bakhtin writes,

the speaking person in the novel is always, to one degree or another, an *ideologue*, and his words are always *ideologemes*. A particular language in a novel is always a particular way of viewing the world, one that strives for a social significance. It is precisely as ideologemes that discourse becomes the object of representation in the novel. . . . The speaking person and his discourse is, as we have said, what makes a novel a novel, the thing responsible for the uniqueness of the genre. But in a novel, of course, the speaking person is not all that is represented, and people themselves need not be represented only as speakers. No less than a person in drama or in epic, the person in a novel may act—but such action is always highlighted by ideology, is always harnessed to the character's discourse (even if the discourse is as yet only a potential discourse), is associated with an ideological motif and occupies a definite ideological position.. . . He lives and acts in an ideological world of his own (and not in the unitary

[12] Irving Babbitt, *Rousseau and Romanticism* (Boston: Houghton Mifflin, 1919), xiv.

[13] 'Discourse in the Novel', in *The Dialogic Imagination*, ed. Michael Holquist, trans. Caryl Emerson and Michael Holquist (Austin, Tex.: Texas University Press, 1981), 259–422.

world of the epic), he has his own perception of the world that is incarnated in his action and in his discourse.[14]

Therefore the elements from which the image of the hero is constructed are not the facts of reality—the reality of the hero himself and of his environment—but rather the significance of those facts for the hero himself, for his self-consciousness. All of the hero's fixed, objective qualities . . . i.e. everything usually employed by the author in creating a concrete and substantive image of the hero—'Who is he?'—. . . [becomes] the object of the hero's own reflection, the subject of his own self-consciousness. . . . We see not who he is but how he perceives himself; our artistic vision focuses not on the reality of the hero, but on the pure function of his perception of that reality.[15]

I would suggest that for Conrad, as for Dostoevsky, there is no objective authorial representation of reality. The mode of representation is entirely subjected to the consciousness of the protagonists themselves, and reality becomes a projection of the hero's perception. The dialogic dynamics of the novels operate, therefore, on more than one level: the form of the novel, the mode of representation, is just as ideologically charged as the explicit or implicit discourse of the protagonists. The structural and aesthetic discontinuities in Conrad's work ought to be studied, then, as extensions of the same ideological dialogues that inform its themes, as projections of the protagonists' perception of their reality rather than authorial, objective representations.

Once we discard the distinction between (and the hierarchic gradation of) the discourse of the author and that of his characters, the question of aesthetic and structural fault-lines takes on a different meaning: it is no longer a matter of an occasional shift or a lapse in the treatment of the material by the author. It is a projection of the consciousness and the perception of the characters themselves which determines the shifting modalities in the text. It is their discourse which superimposes itself on that of the writer.

---

[14] 'Discourse in the Novel', 333–5.
[15] *Problems of Dostoevsky's Poetics*, trans. R. W. Rostel (Ann Arbor, Mich.: Ardis, 1973), 38–9.

1

The Modern Temper

> I had hoped for the impossible—for the laying of what is the
> most obstinate ghost of man's creation, of the uneasy doubt
> uprising like a mist, secret and gnawing like a worm, and
> more chilling than the certitude of death—the doubt of the
> sovereign power enthroned in a fixed standard of conduct
> (*Lord Jim*, 50)

THIS first chapter is devoted to a brief examination of the
'Copernican', or 'modern' cultural context and the ambivalence of
Conrad's response to it.[1] The term 'modern' is, by definition,
semantically unfixed and dependent on the user's vantage point. As
used by Joseph Wood Krutch it simply meant 'contemporary' or
'current': Krutch was offering a diagnosis of the cultural mood, or
Zeitgeist, he had personally experienced and lived through. This
study will use the term 'modern' in reference to a particular
historical-cultural climate, the post-Nietzschean phase of Western
culture. To justify and validate this fixing of an inherently volatile
and relative term, one needs to examine the evolution of this phase
in Western cultural history.

   Cultural historians usually trace the roots of modernity to the

---

[1] Conrad's place within the contemporary cultural-historical context has already
been discussed in several critical studies, the most recent of which are *A Preface to
Conrad* by Cedric Watts (London: Longman, 1982); *Consciousness and Time* by
Torsten Pettersson (Abo: Abo Akademi, 1982); *Joseph Conrad and the Ethics of
Darwinism* by Allan Hunter (London: Croom Helm, 1983); and *Joseph Conrad
and Charles Darwin* by Redmond O'Hanlon (Edinburgh: Salamander Press, 1984).
The present study, however, is concerned mainly with Conrad's ethical and aesthetic
rejection of the modern temper, and this introductory chapter is designed to
highlight only those issues which later form the thematic core of the novels
discussed.

scientific discoveries of the seventeenth century, and the subsequent advent of the Enlightenment, the 'emancipation of secular Reason from Revelation', which opened the way for the development of science and produced the belief in man's reason and his ability to control and regulate his world through secular systems. The earlier phases of modernity held on to a quasi-religious belief in Reason and Progress, a comforting faith which had initially run concurrently with and mitigated the withdrawal of God from the universe. By the end of the nineteenth century, however, when science had finally triumphed, this faith was almost completely eroded. The price paid for the emancipation from metaphysics was the abolition of the concept of a divinely ordered universe, of the anthropomorphic view of man's place within that universe, and of what was hitherto conceived in terms of 'spirit' and 'soul'. By the mid-nineteenth century, the process of secularization was concluded.[2]

The world became soulless, and only on this presupposition could modern science evolve. No miracles and no mysteries, no divine or diabolical interventions in the course of events, were conceivable any longer. . . .

To be sure, it took time before the consequences of this new universe were unfolded. Massive, self-aware secularity is a relatively recent phenomenon. It seems however, from our contemporary perspective that the erosion of faith, inexorably advancing in the educated classes, was unavoidable. Faith could have survived, ambiguously sheltered from the invasion of rationalism by a number of logical devices, and relegated to a corner where it would seem both harmless and insignificant. For generations, many people could live without realizing that they were the denizens of two incompatible worlds, protecting, by a thin shell, the comfort of faith while trusting in Progress, Scientific Truth and Modern Technology. The shell was to be eventually broken, and this was ultimately done by Nietzsche's noisy philosophical hammer. His destructive passion brought havoc into the apparent spiritual safety of the middle classes, and demolished what he believed to be bad faith among those who refused to be witnesses to 'the death of God.' In passionately attacking the spurious mental security of

---

[2] C. S. Lewis described the process as 'the de-christianization of Europe' and defined the period beginning in the mid-19th century as the 'Post-Christian era'. 'De descriptione temporum', an Inaugural Lecture delivered at Cambridge in 1955, repr. in *They Asked for a Paper* (London: Geofrey Bles, 1962); Norman Stone rightly points to the parallel secularization of Jewish thought which accounts for some of the most significant cultural upheavals of modernity, in *Europe Transformed: 1878–1919*, Fontana History of Europe (London: Fontana Press, 1983), 389–411.

people who failed to realize what really had happened, he was successful because it was he who pursued everything to the end: the world generates no meaning and no distinction between good and evil; Reality is pointless, and there is no other hidden reality behind it; the world as we see it is the Ultimatum, it does not try to convey a message to us, it does not refer to anything else, it is self-exhausting and deaf-mute.[3]

But the onset of radical scepticism, proclaimed by 'Nietzsche's noisy philosophical hammer', not only exposed and undermined the spiritual complacency of the age, but also turned—as scepticism invariably does—against the certainties of the very age which had produced it. It is at this point that the notion of modernity undergoes a radical semantic shift, making an about-turn which almost reverses its meaning: the Arnoldian version of modernity, which was largely the product of Enlightenment premises, turns into a 'disenchantment with culture itself', a mood of pervasive scepticism, relativism, and despair.[4]

The 'Counter-Enlightenment' which had previously been a shrill dissenting note in the harmony of Reason and Progress had, by the late nineteenth century, suddenly assumed a prophetic significance in the writings of the 'destroying fathers', as Gerhard Masur calls them. These godfathers of our century, thinkers and artists like Schopenhauer, Kierkegaard, Nietzsche, Dostoevsky, and Baudelaire, had diagnosed the death of traditional systems and patterns of thought and 'bequeathed to us a "landscape of ruins"'.[5] The following discussion would attempt to chart this 'landscape of ruins', which, I believe, is Conrad's cultural habitat.

A significant feature of this phase of modernity is its namelessness: cultural historians have studied the period in depth, but have not yet coined a term to designate and define it, or, indeed, to distinguish it from the preceding phase of modernity. In the introduction to his fascinating study of *fin de siècle* Vienna, Carl E.

---

[3] L. Kolakowski, 'Modernity on Endless Trial', *Encounter*, 66/3 (Mar. 1986), 9–10.

[4] Lionel Trilling, 'On the Teaching of Modern Literature', in *Beyond Culture: Essays in Literature and Learning* (London: Secker & Warburg, 1966), 3–30; for a discussion of this turning point in the semantic development of the term, see M. Bradbury and J. McFarlane, 'The Name and Nature of Modernism', in *Modernism*, ed. Bradbury and J. McFarlane (first published in 1974; Sussex: Harvester Press, 1978), 19–55.

[5] Gerhard Masur, *Prophets of Yesterday: Studies in European Culture 1890–1914* (London: Weidenfeld & Nicolson, 1963), 40.

Schorske writes of the difficulties he encountered when he set out to construct a course in modern European intellectual history. The broad categories used by nineteenth-century intellectuals to chart the development of their own era could not sustain a conceptual framework for an understanding of the 'post-Nietzschean culture', with its 'ubiquitous fragmentation', and its refusal to lend itself to any 'dialectical integration into the historical process as previously known'. Another notable attempt to establish a coherent conceptual framework for the same cultural crisis has been made by H. Stuart Hughes in his study of social thought in Europe at the time. Hughes does suggest a broad definition of the intellectual trends of the period, describing them as varieties of an 'anti-positivistic approach', but he, too, cautiously avoids any definite labels, as does John A. Lester, who deals with the effect of the same cultural crisis on British literature.[6]

One common denominator which does emerge from various descriptions of the period is the relativistic and sceptical outlook which has pre-empted all absolute truths and values. A younger contemporary of Conrad, the Spanish philosopher José Ortega y Gasset, defined the 'question of truth' as 'the root of the modern theme': 'Belief in truth is a deeply rooted foundation of human life; if we were to remove it life is [sic] converted into an illusion and an absurdity.... Relativism is, in the long run, scepticism, and scepticism ... is in itself a theory of suicidal character.'[7] The implications of the Darwinian revolution in biology, Lyell's geological revolution, and Lord Kelvin's second law of thermodynamics (better known as the law of entropy), paved the way for the scientific developments of the early 1900s—the theory of relativity, the quantum theory, and the theories of statistics and probability—and shook the foundations of science itself with their introduction of unfixity and chance as the very principles which govern the ostensibly immutable laws of nature. These new scientific developments yielded a sense of acute epistemological uncertainty. It could

[6] Carl E. Schorske, *Fin-de-Siècle Vienna* (first published in 1961; London: Weidenfeld & Nicolson, 1980), Introduction, xix; H. Stuart Hughes, *Consciousness and Society: The Reorientation of European Social Thought 1890–1930* (London: McGibbon & Kee, 1959), 33–66; John A. Lester, Jr., *Journey through Despair: Transformations in British Literary Culture 1880–1914* (Princeton: Princeton University Press, 1969).

[7] *The Modern Theme*, a series of lectures delivered in 1921–2, trans. by James Cleugh (London: W. C. Daniel Co., 1931), 28–9.

no longer be assumed that 'somewhere within or behind or beyond the world of observable experience there was an eternal and credible truth, a truth concordant to, at least consistent with the human spirit and its aspirations', or that 'man possessed a capacity of at least dimly perceiving that truth'. Man seemed to be 'helplessly enmeshed by inhuman and impersonal forces in a world he never made and could not control, caught up in a life of no purpose, neither human nor ethical nor divine', and solipsistically 'locked within his own world of sense impressions'.[8]

Another concomitant of the death of the Absolute, probably far more devastating than the epistemological crisis, was felt in the realm of ethics. The optimistic positivism of the Enlightenment, the belief in man's ability to set up secular ethical systems, was gradually superseded by an awareness of moral and social disorientation, an awareness which is still very much with us towards the close of the twentieth century. The demolition of the metaphysical-religious foundations of ethics by scepticism, empiricism, and relativism had left a vacuum of moral authority. Man-made, secular ethics (as advocated by the utilitarians, or by the pragmatists, for example) had proven to be inadequate. Morality in this deaf-mute world was perceived as yet another man-made system, as ephemeral and fragile as any other human construct. Conrad and his fellow disinherited moralists were all too aware of this.

What prevails in the region of the natural law is endless change and relativity; therefore the naturalistic positivist attacks all the traditional creeds and dogmas for the very reason that they aspire to fixity. Now all the ethical values of civilization have been associated with these fixed beliefs; and so it has come to pass that with their undermining by naturalism the ethical values themselves are in danger of being swept away in the everlasting flux. Because the individual who views life positively must give up unvarying creeds and dogmas 'anterior, exterior, and superior' to himself, it has been assumed that he must also give up standards. For standards imply an element of oneness somewhere, with reference to which it is possible to measure the mere manifoldness and change.[9]

A third parameter of the disappearance of the Absolute is most directly related to the role of the artist, but the questions arising

---

[8] Lester, *Journey through Despair*, 20–1, 24, 35.
[9] Irving Babbitt, *Rousseau and Romanticism*, xii.

out of what can be viewed as an aesthetic crisis are, as we shall see, closely linked to the epistemological and the ethical parameters of that 'post-lapsarian' modernity with which we are concerned. The aesthetic crisis of modernity has been most movingly and brilliantly presented by Erich Heller in his easy 'The Hazard of Modern Poetry'.[10] Heller traces the predicament of modernity back to sixteenth-century Marburg and to the theological dispute between Luther and Zwingli about the nature of the Eucharist. For Luther, the bread and the wine were 'the thing itself', the blood and the body of Christ; for Zwingli, they were 'mere symbols'. This theological dispute, as presented by Heller, is the paradigm of the modern predicament, the separation of the real from the symbolic.

This increasing rift between reality, reduced to a collection of empirically observable phenomena, and meaning, now relegated to the realm of the merely symbolic, has impoverished them both: 'Robbed of its real significance, what did the symbol signify? Robbed of its symbolic meaning, what did reality mean?' Living with the awareness of man's fundamental insulation in subjectivity and the absence of a sovereign source of moral authority, the modern writer is 'disinherited' and powerless. Art, exiled into the realm of the merely symbolic and banished from the serious business of 'real life' into the realm of entertainment, can no longer infuse reality with meaning or recreate it as it once had done. A similar exposition of the predicament of the artist in a Godless universe is offered by J. Hillis Miller, who uses the same paradigm:

The Eucharist was the archetype of the divine analogy whereby created things participated in the supernatural analogy they signified. Poetry in turn was, in one way or another, modelled on sacramental or scriptural language. The words of the poem incarnated the things they named, just as the words of the Mass shared in the transformation they evoked. . . . Poetry was meaningful in the same way as nature itself—by a communion of the verbal symbols with the reality they named.[11]

Heller discusses a few of the 'disinherited minds' in modern Germany, thinkers and writers who have had to face and grapple with the disappearance of God and the devaluation of the symbol.

---

[10] Erich Heller, *The Disinherited Mind*, 4th edn. (first published in 1952; London: Bowes & Bowes, 1975), 261–300.

[11] *The Disappearance of God*, 2nd edn. (first published 1963, Cambridge, Cambridge University Press, 1975), 3, 6.

The range of their individual responses to the crisis—the stoical resignation of Burkhardt, Nietzsche's desperate joy, Spengler's prophetic wrath, Rilke's quest for an absent God, and the nightmarish vision of Kafka—marks the territory of Conrad's exile. He, too, was among the disinherited.

The most interesting figure for a study of Conrad's work in this gallery of 'destroying fathers', or 'disinherited minds', as respectively presented by Gerhard Masur and Erich Heller is that of Nietzsche, the 'seismograph of modern Europe'.[12] It is not by accident, Heller writes, that Nietzsche's preoccupation with values 'often took the form of a seemingly aesthetic problem—the problem of the relationship between poetry and truth.'[13] The relatedness of this ostensible preoccupation with aesthetics and truth to problems of ethics is all the more significant in view of Nietzsche's place among the godfathers of modernity. Other 'destroying fathers' who had peered into the abyss—Schopenhauer, Kierkegaard, and Dostoevsky—recoiled and found refuge in the metaphysics of despair, but Nietzsche was the first thinker who took the headlong plunge, refused all metaphysical consolations, and pursued the implications of the death of the Absolute to their ultimate conclusions. He paid for this integrity of vision, if one may legitimately speculate, with his sanity.[14]

Nietzsche's response to the modern temper is one of invincible and cruel lucidity. Refusing to leave a single stone unturned in his exploration of the wasteland left to man after the death of God, he seems almost eager at times to precipitate the demolition of the old

[12] J. P. Stern, *Nietzsche*, Fontana Modern Masters, ed. Frank Kermode (London: Fontana Press, 1978), 22. The 'devastatingly explosive impact of Nietzsche' on the decade of the nineties is discussed by James McFarlane in 'The Mind of Modernism', *Modernism*, 77–79.

[13] Heller, *The Disinherited Mind*, 268, 275.

[14] If one views the psychological need for significance as essential, one may well argue that Nietzsche's mental breakdown was the inevitable conclusion of a philosophical outlook which defies that need and exposes the fictionality of all truths and values. On 6 January 1889, a few days before he was put in a mental asylum, Nietzsche wrote a letter to Jacob Burkhardt, his admired colleague at Basle: 'Dear Herr Professor, when it comes to it, I too would very much prefer a professional chair in Basle to being God; but I did not dare to go as far in my private egoism as to refrain for its sake from the creation of the world'. (First published in Edgar Salin, *Jakob Burkhardt und Nietzsche*, 1938; repr. in Heller, *The Disinherited Mind*, in Heller, 83.) I believe that this letter does, in a sense, justify the conjunction of Nietzsche's philosophy and his mental breakdown.

edifice, to strip mankind of its protective myths, and to expose it to the ruthless freezing blasts of its cultural winter.

Whither is God?... *We have killed him*—you and I.... What were we doing when we unchained this earth from its sun? Whither is it moving now? Whither are we moving?... Are we not straying as through an infinite nothing? Do we not feel the breath of empty space? Has it not become colder?... Do we smell nothing yet of the divine decomposition? Gods, too, decompose. God is dead.[15]

The total character of the world ... is in all eternity chaos, in the sense not of a lack of necessity but of a lack of order, arrangement, form, beauty, wisdom and whatever other names there are for aesthetic anthropomorphisms ... Let us beware of attributing to it [i.e. the universe] heartlessness and unreason or their opposites.... None of our aesthetic and moral judgments apply to it.... Let us beware of saying that there are laws in nature. There are only necessities: there is nobody who commands, nobody who obeys, nobody who transgresses.[16]

There are no moral facts whatsoever. Moral judgment has this in common with religious judgment that it believes in realities which do not exist. Morality is only an interpretation of certain phenomena, more precisely a *mis*interpretation. . . . *Morality is merely sign-language, merely symptomatology.*[17]

If we had not welcomed the arts and invented this kind of cult of the untrue, then the realization of general untruth and mendaciousness that now come to us through science—the realization that delusion and error are conditions of human knowledge and sensation—would be utterly unbearable. *Honesty* would lead to nausea and suicide. But now there is a counterforce against our honesty that helps us to avoid such consequences: art as the *good* will to appearance.... As an aesthetic phenomenon existence is still *bearable* for us.[18]

Conrad, like other intellectuals at the time, was familiar, at least superficially, with the work of Nietzsche, who had become a household name by the end of the nineteenth century. Some of the philosopher's most ardent readers and the people who helped

[15] F. Nietzsche, *The Gay Science*, trans. Walter Kaufmann (first published in 1882; New York: Vintage Books, 1974), section 125. Emphasis in source.

[16] Ibid., section 109.

[17] F. Nietzsche, *Twilight of the Idols*, trans. R. J. Hollingdale (first published in 1889; Harmondsworth: Penguin Books, 1968), 'The "Improvers" of Mankind', section 1. Emphasis in source.

[18] *The Gay Science*, section 107. Emphasis in source.

disseminate the Nietzschean vogue—i.e. Garnett, Gosse, Gals-
worthy, Wells, and Arthur Symons—were Conrad's closest friends
or members of his literary circle, and there are several explicit
references to the Nietzsche in his letters.[19] However, it is not my
intention in this study to demonstrate any direct influences of the
philosopher on the writer, but rather to follow up a direction
already pointed to by Edward Said, 'a common tradition of which
Nietzsche . . . is in many ways the apogee'. Said notes some points
of similarity between Conrad and Nietzsche in their treatment of
language as 'a tyrannical epistemological system', in their 'discovery of the inevitable antitheses everywhere to be found in human
existence' and in their belief that 'the world is devoid of anything
except spectacular value'.[20] He also points to the striking verbal
resemblance between Conrad's famous letter on the 'knitting
machine' and the last section in Nietzsche's *The Will to Power*.

This world: a monster of energy without beginning, without end; a firm,
iron magnitude of force that does not grow bigger or smaller, that does
not expend itself but only transforms itself; . . . enclosed by 'nothingness'
as by a boundary.[21]

There is a—let us say—a machine. It evolved itself (I am severely scientific)
out of a chaos of scraps of iron and behold! it knits. . . . And the most
withering thing is that the infamous thing has made itself; made itself
without thought, without conscience, without foresight, without eyes,
without heart. . . . It knits us in and it knits us out, it has knitted time,
space, pain, death, corruption, despair and all the illusions—and nothing
matters. I'll admit however that to look at the remorseless process is
sometimes amusing.[22]

[19] For a study of Nietzsche's growing reputation in England at the time see
David S. Thatcher, *Nietzsche in England 1890–1914* (Toronto: University of
Toronto Press, 1970). Thatcher, who is mainly concerned with the concept of the
'superman', does not mention Conrad, but his introductory chapter and the chapter
on 'Nietzsche and the Literary Mind' provide a great deal of circumstantial evidence
supporting my argument. For references to Nietzsche in Conrad's correspondence,
see Conrad's letters to Helen Sanderson on 22 July 1899; to Garnett (in response to
the latter's essay on Nietzsche) on 24 Oct. and on 9 Nov. 1899; and to Ford on 23
July 1901. In *Collected Letters*, ii. 188, 209, 218, 344.
[20] Edward Said, 'Conrad and Nietzsche', in N. Sherry, ed., *Joseph Conrad: A
Commemoration* (London: Macmillan, 1977), 66, 71, 72.
[21] Quoted ibid. 73.
[22] Letter to Cunninghame Graham, 20 Dec. 1897, in *Conrad's Letters to
Cunninghame Graham*, 56–7.

As we shall see in the last section of this study, the resemblance between Conrad and Nietzsche goes much deeper and further than that. At this stage, however, it is sufficient to note their strong temperamental affinity and their similar response to the modern predicament. The following extracts from Conrad's letters, which often read like passages out of Nietzsche's work, indicate, more than any biographical evidence, their common territory in the modern wasteland. Conrad, no less than Nietzsche, is fully aware of the epistemological and ethical implications of the death of God; he, too, is a 'disillusioned moralist' in the age of relativism; and he, too, often affects a pose of detachment and voices his despair in notes of ruthless sarcasm and contempt.[23]

Let us pray to the potbellied gods, to gods with more legs than a centipede and more arms than a dozen windmills ... As long as we don't pray to the *gods made in man's image* we are sure of a most glorious perdition. Don't know though. I wouldn't give two pence for all its glory—and I would pray to a god made like a man in the City ... for a little forgetfulness. Say half an hour.[24]

There is no morality, no knowledge and no hope; there is only the consciousness of ourselves which drives us about in a world that whether seen in a convex or a concave mirror is always but a vain and fleeting appearance.[25]

Life knows us not and we do not know life—we don't even know our own thoughts. Half the words we use have no meaning whatever and of the other half each man understands each word after the fashion of his own folly and conceit. *Faith is a myth and beliefs shift like mists on the shore*; thoughts vanish; words, once pronounced, die; ... As our peasants say: 'Pray, brother, forgive me for the love of God.' And we don't know what forgiveness is, nor what is love, nor where God is. Assez.[26]

I have come to suspect that the aim of creation cannot be ethical at all, I would fondly believe that its object is purely spectacular.[27]

This susceptibility to the modern temper which Conrad had shared with Nietzsche—the Hobbesian view of human nature, the devastating cosmological pessimism, the nihilistic view of faith and

---

[23] See Masur, *Prophets of Yesterday*, 90.

[24] Letter to Cunninghame Graham on 26 Aug. 1898, in *Conrad's Letters to Cunninghame Graham*, 101, my emphasis.

[25] Letter to Cunninghame Graham on 31 Jan. 1898, ibid. 71, my emphasis.

[26] Letter to Cunninghame Graham on 14 Jan. 1898, ibid, 65, my emphasis.

[27] *A Personal Record* (London: Dent, 1923), 92, my emphasis.

knowledge as man-made illusions, and the desperate vision of the artist as the procurer of comforting untruths—might have driven him, too, to madness or suicide or, at the very least, to silence. But Conrad's work is not merely a reflection of the modern temper: it is an active revolt against it. His condemnation of 'the mad individualism of Niet[z]sche' is at the same time a refutation of the Nietzschean element in himself, an affirmation of his moral heritage.[28] Nietzsche had pursued the implications of the death of God to their ultimate conclusion, the end of all eternal truths and values, and 'baptized the ensuing vacuum in the name of nihilism';[29] Conrad set out on a foredoomed quest for the 'sovereign power enthroned in a fixed standard of conduct'.

Conrad's attempt to reinstate a Ptolemaic universe, a universe essentially endowed with human coherence and value, against the indifference and amorality of the Copernican universe he inhabited, demanded an enormous 'leap of faith' across the abyss of modernity which lay at his feet. He responded to it with all the religious fervour of the unbeliever:

A wrestle with wind and weather has a moral value like the *primitive acts of faith on which may be built a doctrine of salvation and a rule of life*. At any rate men engaged in such contests have been my spiritual fathers too long for me to change my convictions.[30]

It must not be supposed that I claim for the artist in fiction the *freedom of moral Nihilism*. I would require from him many *acts of faith* of which the first would be the cherishing of an undying hope; and hope, it will not be contested, implies all the piety of effort and renunciation ... What one feels so hopelessly barren in declared pessimism is just its arrogance.[31]

In the famous preface to *The Nigger of the Narcissus*, often taken as the ultimate expression of his artistic credo, Conrad writes: 'The artist speaks ... to the latent feeling of fellowship with all creation—and to the subtle but invincible conviction of solidarity that knits together the loneliness of innumerable hearts.' Here, then, is Conrad's other voice, negating his own nihilism, alluding to acts of faith in the age of disbelief, to a knitting together of

---

[28] A letter to Helen Sanderson on 22 July 1899, in *Collected Letters*, ii. 188.

[29] Masur, *Prophets of Yesterday*, 93.

[30] A letter to William Blackwood on 26 Aug. 1901, in *Collected Letters*, ii. 354, my emphasis.

[31] 'Books' (1905) in *Notes on Life and Letters*, 8, my emphasis.

innumerable hearts against the senseless *perpetuum mobile* which 'knits us in and knits us out'. Mankind may be doomed to extinction, but

when the last aquaduct shall have crumbled to pieces, the last airship fallen to the ground, the last blade of grass have died upon a dying earth, man, indomitable by his training in resistance to misery and pain, shall set this undiminished light of his eyes against the feeble glow of the sun. The artistic faculty, of which each of us has a minute grain, may find its voice in some individual of that last group, gifted with a power of expression and courageous enough to interpret the ultimate experience of mankind in terms of his temperament, in terms of art.[32]

Conrad might have been thinking of himself as that individual who would interpret the ultimate experience of mankind, when he wrote to Garnett 'I will not hold my tongue',[33] or when he made Marlow, his surrogate, defy the chaos at the heart of darkness with the simple assertion 'I have a voice, too, and for good or evil mine is the speech that cannot be silenced' (*Heart of Darkness*, 97). This may have been what he had in mind when he wrote to Graham 'I am allowed nothing but *fidelity to an absolutely lost cause*, to an idea without a future'.[34]

This romantic conception of writing as an act of redemption and the moral responsibility of the writer may have been, as Najder and Busza argue, an inseparable part of Conrad's Polish romantic heritage, which he perceived as a willingness to 'go to battle without illusions', to fight, indeed, for lost causes.[35] But one could also argue, as Lukacs does, that all good literature attempts to restore the lost unity of life and meaning, by saying 'and yet!' to life. The most essential creed of literature, the belief in the immanence of essence in life, is set in the novel as 'a demand against life' even as the author is painfully aware that 'it is only a demand and not an effective reality'.[36] This, I believe, is particularly true of Conrad.

[32] 'Henry James: An Appreciation,' in *Notes on Life and Letters* (1904), 13–14.
[33] *Collected Letters*, i. 262.
[34] A letter to Cunninghame Graham, 8 Feb. 1899, in *Collected Letters*, ii. 160–1 (translated from the French), my emphasis.
[35] Najder, *Conrad's Polish Background*, 15–16; Andrzej Busza, 'Conrad's Polish Literary Background', *Antemurale*, 10 (1966), 109–256. See Conrad's letter to Edward Garnett, in October 1907, in *Letters from Conrad 1895–1924*, ed. and intr. Edward Garnett (London: Nonesuch Press, 1928), 216.
[36] Georg Lukacs, *The Theory of the Novel*, trans. Anna Bostock (first published in 1920; London: Merlin Press, 1971), 85.

Conrad's relationship with modernity is, then, a complex one. There can be little doubt of his temperamental constitution: an exile who had sought out and explored the condition of 'extraterritoriality' (as Steiner might put it), fully aware of the ultimate implications of epistemological and ethical relativism, and afflicted with a suspicion of the futility of art, Conrad was very much a man of the post-Nietzschean age. But he was, at the same time, deeply hostile to the spirit of modernity, precisely because he understood it so well. He had no share in Nietzsche's exhilarated sense of liberation from the metaphysical bondage.

Conrad is concerned with nothing less than Salvation. But, far from an affirmation of the 'few simple truths' that Conrad scholars have all too often snuggled against, his undertaking is a foredoomed rejection of modernity. His high moral seriousness, his desperate need to construct an ethical and aesthetic system to counteract the menace of nihilism within and without, is the need of the deracinated for a fulcrum, a foothold in a world which is slipping away.

2

The Failure of Myth

The novel is the epic of a world that has been abandoned by
God. (Lukacs, *The Theory of the Novel*, 88).

CONRAD'S 'fidelity to a lost cause' and the 'act of faith' to which
he had committed himself in his need to counteract the implications
of modernity are initially realized through what I would call the
'epic-mythical mode' in his work, a willed regression to a pre-
modern frame of ethical and aesthetic reference. The relationship
between the epic and the novel has been explored—from diametri-
cally opposite positions—by Lukacs and Bakhtin. The remarkable
similarity between these two Russian contemporaries, and the utter
divergence of their attitudes, deserves a more detailed study, but
their views of the epic are of particular interest for our present
purposes. Both Lukacs and Bakhtin discuss the difference between
these two genres as an essential difference of outlook. 'The world
of the epic', writes Bakhtin, 'is the national heroic past: It is a
world of "beginnings" and "peak times" in a national history, a
world of fathers and founders of families, a world of "firsts" and
"bests"'; 'In the epic world view, "beginning", "first", "founder",
"ancestor", "that which occurred earlier", and so forth are not
merely temporal categories but *valorized* temporal categories, and
valorized to an extreme degree.'[1] The novel, by contrast, deals with
historical reality and life-size characters.

[The epic hero] is a fully finished and completed being ... He is,
furthermore, completely externalized. There is not the slightest gap
between his authentic essence and its external manifestation ... He is

---

[1] Bakhtin, 'Epic and Novel' in *The Dialogic Imagination*, 13, 15.

entirely externalized in the most elementary, almost literal sense: every-thing in him is exposed and loudly expressed: his internal world and all his external characteristics, his appearance and his actions all lie on a single plane ... Such traits account for his limitations and his obvious woodenness under conditions obtaining in a later period of human existence.[2]

A similar observation, albeit with a different attitude, is made by Lukacs, who relates the treatment of character in both genres to the significant difference between the ethical frameworks which govern the epic and the modern age.

The epic hero is, strictly speaking, never an individual. It is traditionally thought that one of the essential characteristics of the epic is the fact that its theme is not a personal destiny but a destiny of a community. And rightly so, for the completeness, the roundness of the value system which determines the epic cosmos creates a whole which is too organic for any part of it to become so enclosed within itself, so dependent upon itself, as to find itself an interiority—i.e. to become a personality. The omnipotence of ethics, which posits every soul as autonomous and incomparable, is still unknown in such a world.[3]

The price to be paid for this epic quality is, therefore, a certain oversimplification or flattening of the characters. As we shall see, the stereotyped characterization of the protagonists, who are cast into the mould of the epic-mythical hero, has been pointed out by critics as a major artistic weakness in the Patusan section of *Lord Jim*, in *The Rescue*, and in *Nostromo*. Why, then, does Conrad choose to regress to an archaic, essentially unsophisticated, form of literature? How does this regression serve his struggle with the ethical and aesthetic predicament of the modern temper?

The answers to these questions may be found in what Lukacs nostalgically calls the 'integrated' nature of the epic-making socie-ties. The 'age of the epic', as presented by Lukacs, is an integrated, and therefore a happy world, in that it does not yet recognize the rift between the individual and the community, the self and the world, the soul and the deed:

The world of meaning can be grasped, it can be taken in at a glance; all that is necessary is to find the *locus* that has been predestined for each

---

[2] Bakhtin, 'Epic and Novel', 34–5.
[3] Georg Lukacs, *The Theory of the Novel*, trans. Anna Bostock (1920; London: Merlin Press, 1971), 66.

individual. Error, here, can only be . . . a failure of measure or insight. For knowledge is only the raising of a veil, creation only the copying of visible and eternal essences, virtue a perfect knowledge of the paths . . . For man does not stand alone, as the sole bearer of substantiality, in the midst of reflexive forms: his relations to others and the structures which arise therefrom are as full of substance as he is himself, indeed they are more truly filled with substance because they are more general, more 'philosophic', closer and more akin to the archetypal home: love, the family, the state. What he should do or be is, for him, only a pedagogical question, an expression of the fact that he has not yet come home.[4]

A similar view of the age of the epic has been recently proposed by the philosopher Alasdair MacIntyre who sets the ethics of the 'heroic age' against the ethical predicament of modernity.[5] The heroic society, as it appears in the Icelandic or Irish sagas or in the Homeric epic, is one where 'every individual has a given role and status within a well defined and highly determinate system of roles and statuses', and the virtues are those qualities which are necessary to sustain the community. 'Morality and social structure are in fact one and the same'.[6]

This last point brings out the division between a system of ethics which relates to the community rather than the individual as its point of reference, and views the survival of the community as the supreme criterion for defining the virtues. This perception of the virtues as instrumental for communal survival rather than inherently valuable and the view of the individual as defined by his role and by the excellence of his performance are, of course, alien to modern Western tradition, which places a high premium on individual freedom of choice, and on an a priori distinction between good and evil. It is not surprising, therefore, that with the collapse of transcendental sanctions and a priori ethical distinctions, brought about by the secularization and individualization which underlie the evolution of modernity, there emerges a sense

---

[4] Georg Lukacs, *The Theory of the Novel*, trans. Anna Bostock 32–3.

[5] Alasdair MacIntyre, *After Virtue: A Study in Moral Theory*, 2nd edn. (1st edn. 1981; London: Duckworth, 1985). For a fuller discussion of MacIntyre's theory see my section on *Lord Jim*.

[6] Ibid. 122–3. The question of the actual historical existence of the heroic societies portrayed in the Homeric epics or the Icelandic sagas is, as MacIntyre rightly argues, irrelevant. What we are concerned with is the role of these narratives as 'the historical memory, adequate or inadequate, of the societies in which they were finally written down' (ibid. 112).

of nostalgia for that very distant cultural past perceived as an age of cohesion and moral certainty.[7]

This sense of nostalgia, the need to break away from the ethical relativism of modernity, leads Conrad to the 'mythical' mode of his work. In this mode he attempts to recreate, or duplicate, the social structure of a heroic community and its implicit ethics in an attempt to find refuge from an essentially individualistic and relativistic socio-ethical framework. He can only do that by enclosing his characters and cutting them off from the modern world. The 'fellowship of the sea' provides him with a ready-made model of an insulated community where the individual is defined by his role in the struggle for communal survival and the virtues are those qualities which would help sustain his community at the moment of crisis.

The prototype of epic virtue is old Singleton in *The Nigger of the Narcissus*, inarticulate and invincible, perceived by the narrator as 'a learned and savage patriarch, the incarnation of barbarian wisdom, serene in the blasphemous turmoil of the world' (6). It is Singleton who, alone of the crew, remains unmoved by Wait, whose imminent death throws the crew into a state of panic and near mutiny. The oracular equanimity of the old man is set against the subtleties of the situation which upset the crew to the point of losing 'all certainties' (43). Significantly, it is he who stands at the helm, steering the ship through the storm, a beacon of seamanly virtue at the ultimate trial of the community (86–9). But Old Singleton is a thoroughly flat character. He seems to have no interiority, no self-consciousness at all. 'Singleton lived untouched by human emotions. . . . We were disturbed and cowardly. That we knew. Singleton seemed to know nothing, understand nothing'

---

[7] Interestingly, Nietzsche too, notwithstanding his insistence on the need to rejoice in man's ascent beyond good and evil, sounds distinctly nostalgic in his references to the ancient Greeks and their 'morality of custom': 'Morality is nothing other (therefore *no more!*) than obedience to customs, of whatever kind they may be; customs, however, are the *traditional* way of behaving and evaluating. In things in which no tradition commands there is no morality; and the less life is *determined* by tradition, the smaller the circle of morality. The free human being is immoral because in all things he is determined to depend upon himself and not upon a tradition.' (*Daybreak*, 9) Nietzsche too juxtaposes the individualistic morality of Christianity with the 'morality of custom' practised by the ancient Greeks, a morality which originates in the idea that 'the community is worth more than the individual' (*Assorted Opinions and Maxims*, 89).

(42). And while this heroic obtuseness may be what enables him to withstand the 'blasphemous turmoil of the world', it is also aesthetically reductive and highly problematic in a modern text.

In a letter to Cunninghame Graham, who had probably felt the flattening effect which inevitably follows the use of the epic hero as a prototype and suggested the creation of a 'Singleton with an education', Conrad writes:

I think Singleton with an education is impossible. But first of all—what education? If it is the knowledge how to live my man essentially possessed it. He was in perfect accord with his life. . . . Would you seriously, of malice prepense, cultivate in that unconscious man the power to think. Then he would become conscious—and much smaller—and very unhappy. Now he is simple and great like an elemental force. Nothing can touch him but the curse of decay—the eternal decree that will extinguish the sun, the stars one by one, and in another instant shall spread a frozen darkness over the whole universe. Nothing else can touch him—he does not think. Would you seriously wish to tell such a man: 'Know thyself'. Understand that thou art nothing, less than a shadow, more insignificant than a drop of water in the ocean, more fleeting than the illusion of a dream. Would you?[8]

The same is true, one feels, for Conrad's other heroes of the sea-tales, Captain McWhirr of *Typhoon*, and Captain Beard of 'Youth'. They are 'in perfect accord with their lives', because they are unconscious; they are as great as elemental forces in their inarticulate strength and simplicity, because they have not been touched by the curse of that civilized, self-destructive intelligence which would have made them aware of their utter insignificance in a meaningless universe. But these strong, silent, 'elemental' men were the products of a mind which, as established in the previous chapter, was nothing if not susceptible to the modern temper and afflicted with the doubting, self-destructive consciousness these protagonists are spared. Conrad's withdrawal into the insulated heroic society of the 'fellowship of the sea' (both in life and in literature) could not have endured as a sanctuary from the modern temper for long.

The three novels discussed in this section—*Lord Jim*, *The Rescue*, and *Nostromo*—are more interesting for the purpose of

---

[8] A letter to Graham on 14 Dec. 1897, *Conrad's Letters to Cunninghame Graham*, 53–4.

this study precisely because they are unlike Conrad's hermetically sealed sea-tales, because the regression to the heroic-epic mode must be elaborately worked out and—most important of all—be seen to collapse with the invasion of modernity, and the failure of the hero. The dialogic quality of these novels is derived from the tension between the epic outlook and the modern one.

The epic ingredients common to these novels are not difficult to detect: the insulation of the characters in exotic settings away from modern Western civilization; the political and military rivalries which trigger the action and endow the narrative with an epic scope; the superhuman, semi-divine stature of protagonists, their heroic feats, and the dependence of a whole community on their performance of their respective roles as leaders, can all be seen as 'generic markers' which invest these characters with the aura of epic heroes. But Jim, Lingard, and Nostromo are fallen epic heroes. After being presented at various points in their respective stories as legendary leaders of communities, as saviour figures, they fail to live up to their heroic stature. By placing their private ethical choices over and above those which are required of them by their respective social roles, they bring about the disintegration of their communities and the collapse of the epic-heroic narrative mode which has sustained them.

Jim, Lingard, and Nostromo are all eventually pulled down from the level of epic to that of the novel. The epic hero is 'a fully finished and completed being . . . hopelessly ready-made. He is all there, from beginning to end he coincides with himself, he is absolutely equal to himself. He is, furthermore, completely externalized, there is not the slightest gap between his authentic essence and his external manifestation.' The protagonist of the novel is 'either greater than his fate, or less than his condition as a man' as 'one of the basic internal themes of the novel is precisely the theme of the hero's inadequacy to his fate or his situation'.[9] What we have in these works, then, is a process of 'novelization', a shift from an epic mode to a modern one. The fact that this 'novelization' of the discourse is related to the failure of the protagonist is, of course, highly significant. Conrad, one feels, would have shared the nostalgia of Lukacs, for that distant, integrated (and entirely hypothetical) world of the epic.

[9] Bakhtin, 'Epic and Novel', 34, 37.

But the collapse of the heroic epic narrative is in itself only a symptom of a yet more significant failure—it is the failure of the mythical frame of reference, which finds its narrative formulation in the epic, but ranges far beyond it in its cultural significance. Critical studies dealing with these aspects of Conrad's work have been informed by an archetypal approach or by Frye's theory of mythical displacement.[10] The present discussion would focus on mythicity as a *mode of discourse* rather than a repertoire of recycled or displaced mythical motifs and archetypes, on the significance of the quasi-epic elements in Conrad's work, and on mythicity as a voice which operates dialogically against the voice of modernity in the text.

The study of myth by anthropologists and philosophers has produced a wide diversity of opinions regarding its definition, its origins, its functions, and the mental processes it reflects.[11] I believe that, whether one views myth as a reflection of specific human preoccupations, a validation of social structures and norms, a pre-scientific exploration of the relation between culture and nature, or an articulation of religious rituals, it remains essentially a narrative vehicle of imposing meaning on experience, of assigning to man a place within a comprehensible scheme.

Studied alive, myth . . . [is] a narrative resurrection of a primeval reality, told in satisfaction of deep religious wants, moral cravings, social submissions, assertions, even practical requirements. Myth fulfills in primitive culture an indispensable function: it expresses, enhances, and codifies belief: it safeguards and enforces morality; . . . Myth is thus a vital ingredient of human civilization; it is not an idle tale, but a hard-worked active force; it is not an intellectual explanation or an artistic imagery, but a pragmatic charter of primitive faith and moral wisdom. . . . These stories are to the natives a statement of primeval, greater, and more relevant reality, by which the present life, fates, and activities of mankind are determined.[12]

But the need for a mythical arrangement of the world is not a 'primitive', archaic cultural phenomenon. The study of myth is no

---

[10] Cf. Claire Rosenfield, *Paradise of Snakes: An Archetyal Analysis of Conrad's Political Novels* (Chicago: University of Chicago Press, 1967).

[11] For a typology of the functions of myth, see G. S. Kirk, *Myth* (Cambridge: Cambridge University Press, 1970), 252–86.

[12] B. Malinowski, *Myth in Primitive Psychology* (1926), reprinted in *Magic, Science and Religion* (New York: W. W. Norton, 1955), 101, 108.

longer confined to the domain of the exotic 'other', and its universality has by now been widely acknowledged by thinkers as widely apart as Roland Barthes and L. Kolakowski.[13] In *The Presence of Myth*, Prof. Kolakowski cogently treats myth as a reflection of man's refusal to accept the arbitrary, random quality of reality, and his need to see the world as a continuum, to 'domesticate' empirical reality and endow it with meaning. The whole of human endeavour is aimed, according to Kolakowski, at overcoming the 'indifference of the universe', a task which can be accomplished only through the imposition of a mythical—philosophical or religious—significance on reality.

The need for integration, the need to view essence as immanent in existence, which is at the core of myth, generates a mode of discourse which does not recognize the split between subject and object, meaning and reality, essence and existence. This view of the myth-making mentality has been fully expounded by Ernst Cassirer in *The Philosophy of Symbolic Forms*. Myth, according to Cassirer, is not allegorical or symbolic but *tautological*: the 'separation of the ideal from the real', the 'disinction between a world of immediate reality and a world of mediate signification', the 'opposition of "image" and "object"' which characterize the modern consciousness, are alien to it. 'Where we see mere "representation", myth, insofar as it has not yet deviated from its fundamental and original form, sees real identity. The "image" does not represent the "thing": it *is* the thing; it does not merely stand for the object, but has the same actuality, so that it replaces the thing's immediate presence.'[14]

This identity of 'image' and 'thing' brings us back to Heller's description of the split between the 'symbolic' and the 'real', a split which began with the theological debate over the Eucharist and has endured ever since as the primal curse of the modern, disinherited mind. Conrad's reversion to a mythical mode of discourse entails not only a return to a pre-modern ethical framework, but

---

[13] Roland Barthes, *Mythologies* (1957; London: Jonathan Cape Ltd., 1972). I will return to Barthes's conception of myths in my discussion of *Nostromo*; Prof. Kolakowski's *The Presence of Myth* (1966) has not yet been translated into English. The citations in this study are based on the Hebrew translation by Eliezer Ha'cohen (Tel Aviv: Sifiyat Poalim, 1971).

[14] Ernst Cassirer, *The Philosophy of Symbolic Forms*, trans. R. Manheim (New Haven, Conn.: Yale University Press, 1955), ii. 38.

an attempt to close this gap between meaning and reality through a reinstatement of the poetic idiom of myth, to recover, as Eric Gould might put it, the mythicity of literature.[15] A similar formulation of the mythical mode of discourse has been suggested by Northrop Frye. Following the eighteenth-century philosopher, Giambattista Vico, Frye perceives human history as a succession of 'ages' which produce different types or modes of writing. The mythical age produces a 'hieroglyphic' or 'poetic' use of language, which does not recognize the separation between subject and object, so essential in our culture. Frye refers to the mode of discourse which dominates in this phase of culture as 'metaphorical', bearing a strong sense of 'identify of life or power or energy between man and nature'.[16]

One aspect of the mythical mode of discourse is, as we shall see, the uninhibited animistic treatment of nature. The sun, the forest, the mountain, and the ocean are treated as active agents in the epic narrative. This anthropomorphic or animistic framework, which the modern outlook might deprecate as a pathetic fallacy, recreates the mythical sense of participation, an essential unity of man and nature.

Another aspect of mythicity is the attitude to magic, the 'feeling that subject and object are linked by a common power or energy [sometimes called *mana*]. . . . The articulating of words may bring this common power into being; hence a magic develops in which verbal elements, "spell", and "charm", and the like, play a central role. A corollary of this principle is that there may be a potential magic in any use of words. Words in such a context are words of power or dynamic forces.'[17] This aspect of myth appears in the three novels in the use of a magic object: Stein's ring in *Lord Jim*, Hassim's ring in *The Rescue*, and the silver in *Nostromo*. The magic object is not only identified with, but seems to generate an abstract quality, so long as the protagonist operates within the mythical mode. With the invasion of the modern temper and the abdication of the myth by the protagonist, the object seems to lose its power or, as happens in *Nostromo*, to reverse the direction of

[15] Eric Gould, *Mythical Intentions in Modern Literature* (Princeton, NJ: Princeton University Press, 1981).

[16] Northrop Fyre, *The Great Code: The Bible and Literature* (1981; London: Ark Paperbacks, 1983), 7.

[17] Ibid.

its *mana*, and cast a curse on its owner. This aspect of the demythologizing process can be described as a 'tokenization' of the 'totem': the totem, an object which was endowed with real, animistic power, becomes a token, a mere symbol, a stage property rather than an active agent in the narrative.

Many of the features of the mythical mode of discourse are encapsulated in 'Karain', a story chronologically placed between the first phase of *The Rescue* (1896–8) and *Lord Jim* (1899–1900), which illuminates that important phase of Conrad's word, both in its representation of the mythical mode and in its withdrawal from it.[18] The figure of Karain can be seen as the prototype of Lingard or of Jim in Patusan; he is the essential mythical hero, an embodiment of heroic virtues, larger than life, holding the life of his people in his hands:

They were Karain's people—a devoted following. Their movements hung on his lips; they read their thoughts in his eyes; he murmured to them nonchalantly of life and death, and they accepted his words humbly, like gifts of fate. (4)

He indicated by a theatrical sweep of his arm along the jagged outline of the hills the whole of his domain; and the ample movement seemed to drive back its limits, augmenting it suddenly into something so immense and vague that for a moment it seemed to be bounded only by the sky. (4–5)

He seemed too effective, too necessary there, too much of an essential condition for the existence of his land and his people to be destroyed by anything short of an earthquake. He summed up his race, his country, the elemental force of ardent life, of tropical nature. . . . He appeared utterly cut off from everything but the sunshine, and even that seemed to be made for him alone. . . . He gave them wisdom, advice, reward, punishment, life or death with the same serenity of attitude and voice. He understood irrigation and the art of war. . . . He could conceal his heart; had more endurance; he could swim longer, and stir a canoe faster than any of his people. (7–8)

He dispensed justice; near him a youth improvised in a high tone a song that celebrated his valour and wisdom. (16–17)

---

[18] 'Karain' was included in *Tales of Unrest* in the Dent Collected Edition. The mythic elements in 'Karain' have been noted by Wray C. Herbert in 'Conrad's Psychic Landscape: The Mythic Element in *Karain*,' *Conradiana*, 8/3 (1976), 225–32. Herbert, however, proposes yet another psychological interpretation of the reversion to myth as a recovery of the unconscious.

Like a true mythical figure, Karain commands the faithfulness not only of his people but also that of nature, and of inanimate things. He speaks of future victories to the sword, which seems to vibrate in response (18–19); and his agony after the death of the shaman is accompanied by 'ragged edges of black clouds' and 'invisible thunderstorms' which finally erupt when he can no longer contain his fear (20–21).

Karain's story is—like that of Lingard and Jim—a version of the story of Cain, a man guilty of fratricide, haunted by guilt and remorse, and its denouement is also brought about by a charm, a jubilee sixpence which is the equivalent of the ring of friendship in *Lord Jim* and in *The Rescue*. But Karain's story has a different ending. The charm in his case—ostensibly a cheap trick played on a superstitious, 'primitive' native—does perform its redemptive function. It exorcizes the ghost of Pata Matara and reinstates Karain in his mythical role. To understand his divergence of the story from the two long novels for which it may have served as a preliminary study, one must be fully aware of the relationship between the narrative frame and the protagonist who is held captive within it.

The relationship between the mythical and modern modes of perception in *Lord Jim* and in *The Rescue* is markedly different from that in 'Karain'. Unlike Jim or even Lingard, Karain is clearly not 'one of us', and the narrative frame of the story erects a clear-cut division between this likeable but primitive other, and the modern, civilized outlook of the white people, drawn together to form a cohesive cultural unity by the first-person plural of the narrative. The neatness of this division accounts for the greater atavistic power of Karain's portrayal as the prototype of the mythical hero, which—unlike that of Jim or Lingard—is unadulterated with echoes of an alien idiom.

Karain has come to the white men in his flight from the ghost of his friend because, in his agony and fear, he wished to cross over to their world, to their haven of unbelief where things unseen cease to exist. Karain's 'leap' out of 'the stockade' (24) is a distinct anticipation of Jim's leap out of the Raja's stockade in Patusan, but its direction is reversed. While Jim leaps into a mythical mode of existence which enables him to create a new world and a new identity for himself by the power of his word, Karain wishes to escape into the 'civilized' world where material facts alone have power, where men 'understand all things seen, and despise all else' (44).

Hollis is the only white man aboard who seems to understand the cultural implications of Karain's move. He realizes that it would be impossible for Karain to take the leap into civilized society, and helps him instead by reaffirming the mythical mode of perception. He produces a gilt jubilee sixpence engraved with the Queen's image, and gives it to Karain as a charm, saying: 'This is the image of the great Queen, and the most powerful thing that white men know' (49). The gilt coin thus serves a dual purpose: it is, on the one hand, an ironic comment of the whites who—even at the height of their materialist disbelief—ascribe magic powers to mere tokens and invest them with totemic significance. The other, and more important, function of the charm derives from its significance as a reaffirmation of the power of the mythical mode of perception, its ability—to use the expression of Prof. Kola-kowski—to domesticate an alien universe and overcome its indifference.

Hollis undertakes the task of the writer and becomes a surrogate for Conrad himself, when he tries to make Karain see, to make him believe in the reality of the fiction (the spurious charm) through the power of his lies: 'This is no play; I am going to do something for him. Look serious. Confound it!. . . Can't you lie a little . . . for a friend!' (46); 'Don't look thunderstruck, you fellows. Help me to make him believe—everything's in that' (50). Like his author, Hollis, too, transforms the fiction into a living myth. In making Karain believe in the charm, he makes it work for him. Once re-established, the mythical idiom is echoed by the sympathetic response of the sea: 'The water all around broke out as if by magic into a dazzling sparkle' (51). The sense of participation or unity between Karain and his world is restored, and he departs, free of his ghost, leaving the white men in their haven of unbelief.

The concept of *presence* rather than *representation* which is characteristic of mythical thinking extends not only to what we could recognize as images and symbols but to language itself. 'Myth and language are inseparable and mutually condition each other. Word and name magic are, like image magic, an integral part of the magical world view. But in all this the basic presup-position is that word and name do not merely have a function of describing or portraying but contain within them the object and its real powers. Word and name do not designate and signify, they are and act'.[19] The significance of the protagonists' names and titles—Lord Jim, King Tom (Lingard), and Nostromo ('Our man')—clearly relates their bearers to a mythical conception of word and name magic. These titles are integral to their essence, and when they prove unworthy of their roles in their respective communities, they not only abdicate their titles, but give up something of their selfhood as well.

MacIntyre significantly notes that 'the chief means of moral education' in heroic cultures is the telling of stories. The teller of the tales is more than a mere entertainer: he is entrusted with the sacred task of transmitting an ethical code.[20] Conrad's attempt to recover the mythical idiom is, therefore, not merely a nostalgic escape from the predicament of modernity, but an attempt to rescue art from its captivity in the realm of entertainment, to restore the magic power of the word, and to reinstate the artist in his once-sacred role.

A. *LORD JIM*

The following discussion of *Lord Jim* will focus on the problematic structural rift in the novel, the transition from the story of the *Patna* and its consequences (chapters 1–21) to the story of Patusan (chapters 22–45). Conrad himself had referred to this transition as a 'plague spot' in the novel,[21] an epithet which was later followed by an almost unanimous, if qualified to various degrees, critical dismissal of the second part as a regrettable artistic lapse. Thus, when Ian Watt discusses the 'intractable contradiction between the basic terms of [Conrad's] previous [i.e. *Patna*] and his present [i.e. Patusan] narrative assumptions', he registers 'a sense of reduced complexity and rapid confluence of the narrative elements', and John Batchelor argues that the Patusan part of the novel has 'a curiously simple moral polarity, a brightly coloured "flatness" . . . It is as though the end of *Lord Jim* were drawn from a part of Conrad's mind different from, and shallower than, the consciousness that has created the bulk of the novel.'[22]

---

[19] Cassirer, *Symbolic Forms*, 40.
[20] MacIntyre, *After Virtue*, 121.
[21] In *Letters from Conrad*, ed. E. Garnett, 172.
[22] Ian Watt, *Conrad in the Nineteenth Century* (London: Chatto & Windus,

A somewhat crude but useful distinction can be made between 'first generation' and 'second generation' critics of the novel.[23] The former group, including eminent scholars like Thomas Moser and A. J. Guerard, largely avoids the ethical problematics of the novel, the unresolved questions posed by the first part, and posits a stable ethical code by which Jim's story is to be judged. Moser's pioneering study is symptomatic of this approach in its definition of Conrad's ethic as founded on the 'simple principles' of fidelity, stoic humanism, and solidarity with the community in a godless universe, a moral hierarchy which, according to Moser, is 'implicit on every page'.[24]

The critics of the latter group, including T. Tanner, C. B. Cox, J. Hillis Miller, and others, regard the novel as a distinctly modernist expression. Having registered the effect of extreme ethical relativism where moral judgement is well-nigh impossible, these 'second generation' critics present the open-endedness of the moral dilemmas in the first part of the novel as its ultimate stance. The 'meaning' of the novel is thus construed as the Absence of Meaning, the invalidation of all metaphysical, epistemological, and ethical certainties.[25]

My own view is that, while the novel is undoubtedly foregrounded against the spiritual and ethical malaise of modernity, it is not merely a reflection of the modern temper but an active, if desperate, attempt to defeat it by a regression to a mythical mode of discourse. This regression, effected by the transition to Patusan, is at the core of the structural rift in the novel.

The second issue which emerges from the first part of the novel as an axis of critical interpretation is the character of Jim himself.

1980), 307–8; John Batchelor, *The Edwardian Novelists* (London: Duckworth & Co., 1982), 46.

[23] This classification of critical approaches does not pretend to do justice to the complexity and particular insights of the interpretations under discussion, but as the purpose of this discussion is to suggest an alternative approach, I have chosen to resort to this schematic mode of presentation.

[24] Thomas C. Moser, *Joseph Conrad: Achievement and Decline* (Hamden, Conn. Archon Books, 1966), 10–49.

[25] Tony Tanner, 'Butterflies and Beetles—Conrad's Two Truths', *Chicago Review*, 16 (Winter-Spring 1963), 123–40. Repr. in the Norton Critical Edition of *Lord Jim*, ed. by Thomas C. Moser (New York: W. W. Norton & Company, 1968), 447–62; C. B. Cox, *Joseph Conrad: The Modern Imagination* (London: J. M. Dent & Sons, 1974), 19–44; J. Hillis Miller, *Fiction and Repetition* (Oxford: Basil Blackwell, 1982), 22–41.

Guerard describes Jim as 'a rather adolescent dreamer and "romantic" with a strong ego-ideal, who prefers solitary reveries of heroism to the shock and bustle of active life. . . . He has a strong visual imagination and vividly foresees the worst. . . . He differs from other introverted dreamers chiefly in the degree of his Bovarysme; he can literally confuse reality and dream at times. . . . He tries to live his dream.' Thomas Moser relates Jim to a long line of Conradian heroes: romantic egoists, dreamers who idealize their self-deceptions and distort reality in their obsession with the fixed idea of their own greatness. Berthoud also defines Jim as 'unfit for reality' because he has 'exchanged his real self with an ideal self' and attributes his jump from the *Patna* to a 'prolonged habit of self-deception'.[26]

These analyses of Jim's character and his sense of identity are founded on a neat distinction between facts and ideas, truth and fiction, reality and illusion, 'real' self and self-ideal, where the first term in each pair of opposites is a reflection of a desired standard, and the second is a form of deviation. I believe that such a distinction, however essential as a working hypothesis in everyday life, is seriously questioned in the novel: through Marlow's distinction between the 'facts' and the 'truth' in Jim's case (56); by his realization of 'the convention that lurks in all truth and . . . the essential sincerity of falsehood' (93); by his participation in 'the spirit of his [Jim's] illusion' (109) and his reluctant admission of his own part in 'the fellowship of . . . illusions' (128).

Marlow, ostensibly the spokesman for solid British common sense and decency, is forced to recognize the optical illusions that turn the most ostensibly tangible sights and sounds into deceptive phantoms (113–15, 135); the grey area between what is 'a lie' and what is 'not true' (130); and the inadequacy of the judgement of that 'expert in possession of the facts' (146), the admirable French Lieutenant. His final acknowledgement of the universal need for 'some such truth or some such illusion—I don't care how you call it, there is so little difference, and the difference means so little' (222), is a painful diagnosis of a state of epistemological uncertainty which is so closely linked to the problem of ethical indeterminacy.

---

[26] A. J. Guerard, *Conrad the Novelist* (Cambridge, Mass.: Harvard University Press, 1958), 140–1; Moser, *Achievement and Decline*, 30–3; Jacques Berthoud, *Joseph Conrad: The Major Phase* (Cambridge: Cambridge University Press, 1978), 72–3.

The relationship of these two aspects of the novel is significant: MacIntyre argues that 'man is in his actions and practice, as well as in his fictions, essentially a story-telling animal. He is not essentially, but becomes through his history, a teller of stories that aspire to truth. . . . We enter human society . . . with one or more imputed character-roles into which we have been drafted—and we have to learn what they are in order to be able to understand how others respond to us and how our responses to them are apt to be construed. . . . Mythology, in its original sense, is at the heart of things.'[27] According to the narrative view of the self, 'the story of my life is always embedded in the story of those communities from which I derive my identity'. The predicament of modern ethics results, according to MacIntyre, from 'the lack of any such unifying [narrative] conception of a human life' and from its conception of ethics as distinct from and prior to the social context (the narrative) of the individual.[28]

MacIntyre's theory clearly suggests that one's sense of identity and the ethical code by which one chooses to live are both the products of a fictional self-perception (i.e. as assumption of a certain role in a hypothetical narrative). This theory, which defies the traditional distinction between the spheres of ethics and psychology, is illuminating for a reading of *Lord Jim*. The structural rift in the novel, the fault-line between the *Patna* and the Patusan sections, marks the willed effort of the character to enter another story, as it were, to construct his identity and find a new ethical orientation in a different textual sphere.

Jim is leading a fictional life. Like other Conrad characters (John Kemp in *Romance* and M. George in *The Arrow of Gold*) he constructs his identity in a literary context, viewing himself as a protagonist in an imaginary story. The ethical code he must obey is embedded in the generic conventions of the narrative (the courage of the hero in impossible circumstances), and Jim's self-assigned role in the fiction provides him with a psychological and a moral point of reference. His decision to become a seaman was

[27] *After Virtue*, 216.
[28] Ibid. 221–5. A narrative view of the self has been presented by post-modern theorists, such as Lyotard and Butor, but MacIntyre's theory is more relevant to the present discussion because narrative, for him, is not a fictional-and-therefore-fictitious construct. It is a form of ethical, as well as epistemological, mediation between consciousness and world which can be validated by the protagonists' acts.

occasioned by 'a course of light holiday literature' (5), and his image of himself as a seaman is nurtured on adventure stories: 'He saw himself saving people from sinking ships. . . . He confronted savages on tropical shores, quelled mutinies on the high seas, and in a small boat upon the ocean kept up the hearts of despairing men—always an example of devotion to duty, and as unflinching as a hero in a book' (6). The use of the adjective 'unflinching' in this introductory passage and at the very end of Jim's story when, with an 'unflinching glance', he faces his death, is, as noted by one of the critics, a framing device designed to illuminate Jim's entire life as conceived by a single vision.[29]

But as MacIntyre so convincingly argues in his definition of man as 'a story-telling animal', this process (whereby identity is derived from a role in a narrative view of human life) is not necessarily a pathological peculiarity. We all construe our sense of identity in terms of our role in the narrative we are part of, and this fictional identity is not necessarily fictitious as long as one can maintain some measure of congruence between the fictional ego-ideal and one's actual conduct. Marlow himself is forced into an admission of the universal need for some sort of 'moral *posture*' (41, my emphasis), for some sort of sustaining faith which may be either truth or illusion (222). When an individual realizes, as Jim does after his jump from the *Patna*, that the fictional role has become manifestly fictitious, that it is no longer tenable, he or she is bound to experience an identity crisis.

In the situation on board the *Patna* as perceived by the officers, the sinking of the ship within a few moments from the apparently fatal collision seemed to be inevitable. Marlow himself is impelled to admit: 'Frankly, had I been there I would not have given as much as a counterfeit farthing for the ship's chances to keep above water to the end of each successive second. . . . Their escape would trouble me as a prodigiously inexplicable event . . .' (97–8). The only force that could have made Jim stay on board would have been an indomitable adherence to his heroic ego-ideal. His illusion (or ego-ideal) has failed to sustain him when all other potential supports of his identity—the eye of others, the possibility of action, the light of day—have been snatched away from under his feet.

[29] J. E. Tanner, 'The Chronology and the Enigmatic End of *Lord Jim*', *Nineteenth-Century Fiction*, 21/4 (1967), 379.

His problem is not, as suggested by some, that his illusion is overwhelmingly strong, but simply that it is *not strong enough*.

I would like, at this point, to introduce the concept of 'identi-fiction' to denote a literary text or genre on which a fictional character construes his or her identity. The use of the term might, I hope, indicate the distinction between a generic model which reflects the intentions of the author, and a text or a genre which serves as a point of reference for the characters themselves in the definition of their identity and the management of their lives. Emma Bovary, whose identi-fiction is the sentimental novel, is an obvious case in point, but, as already suggested, I believe that a certain degree of *bovarysme* is universal. Emma and Jim are merely extreme cases.

Jim's initial identi-fiction was the Stevensonian adventure story. It had failed him on the *Patna*. His subsequent choice of the heroic epic as a prototext of the Patusan episode in his life can best be understood in terms of MacIntyre's theory again. MacIntyre examines the features of heroic societies in an attempt to understand the Aristotelian formulation of the virtues which is based on the moral order of the (fictional?) heroic age. The virtues in heroic societies— courage, fidelity, friendship—are important not merely as qualities of individuals, but as qualities necessary 'to sustain a household and a community':

Morality and social structure are in fact one and the same in heroic societies. There is only one set of social bonds. Morality as something distinct does not yet exist. Evaluative questions *are* questions of social fact. It is for this reason that Homer speaks of *Knowledge* of what to do and how to judge. Nor are such questions difficult to answer, except in exceptional cases. For the given rules which assign men their place in the social order and with it their identity also prescribe what they owe and what is owed to them and how they are to be treated and regarded if they fail and how they are to treat and regard others if those others fail. Without such a place in the social order, a man would not only be incapable of receiving recognition and response from others; not only would others not know, but he himself would not know who he was.[30]

MacIntyre's comment on the difference between modern society and the heroic society is particularly relevant to Jim's case:

---

[30] MacIntyre, *After Virtue*, 123–4.

There is thus the sharpest of contrasts between the emotivist self of modernity and the self of the heroic age. The self of the heroic age lacks precisely that characteristic which we have already seen that some modern philosophers take to be an essential characteristic of human selfhood: the capacity to detach oneself from any particular standpoint or point of view, to step backwards, as it were, and view and judge that standpoint or point of view from the outside. In the heroic society there is no 'outside' except that of the stranger. [The freedom of choice of values on which modernity prides itself would appear] from the standpoint of a tradition ultimately rooted in heroic societies . . . more like the freedom of ghosts—of those whose human substance approached vanishing point—than of men.[31]

By moving to Patusan, Jim becomes part of another story, as it were. This new identi-fiction, which is closely modelled on the heroic epic, offers him a new context of psychological and ethical orientation. He turns away from the individualized ethos of modernity, the 'ghostly freedom of choice', offered by the multiplicity of voices in the first part of the story, towards the heroic mythical narrative, a fictional genre which is predicated on the ethos of communality.

The heroic-epic model of the Patusan section of *Lord Jim* has been noted by Tony Tanner, who argues that the collision of the two sections is ironical in that even as it presents the passing of the heroic ideals in an 'elegiac light', it refuses to take them at their face value. In support of his view of the novel as a modernist reflection of an epistemological and ethical uncertainty, Tanner aptly quotes Ulrich, the unheroic hero of *The Man without Qualities*, who speaks of the unrequited yearning for a 'narrative order' in life.[32] I would suggest that Jim's transition to Patusan is, indeed, the last stop in his quest for a 'narrative order', but the terms of this narrative order, the heroic-epic or mythical prototext ought to be accepted as valid so long as the fiction is upheld by Jim himself. Only by a willing suspension of our modern disbelief, by a re-enactment of Jim's transition into the mythical mode, can we accommodate the different ethical and aesthetic assumptions of the Patusan section.

Patusan is described by Marlow as 'a distant heavenly body', 'a star of the fifth magnitude' where Jim can find 'a totally new set of

---

[31] MacIntyre, *After Virtue*, 126–7.
[32] Tony Tanner, *Conrad: Lord Jim*, Studies in English Literature no. 12, ed. D. Daiches (London: Edward Arnold Publishers, 1963), 8–12.

conditions for his imaginative faculty to work upon', leaving his 'earthly failings behind him' (218). The local people regard Jim as a 'creature of another essence' (229), and the folk stories that evolve around his feats of courage and cunning are patterned on the mythical model, ascribing supernatural powers to the hero in his dealings with his enemies and with nature itself: 'There was already a story that the tide had turned two hours before its time to help him on his journey up the river' (242–3); 'As to the simple people of the outlying villages, they believed and said (as the most natural thing in the world) that Jim had carried the guns up the hill on his back—two at a time' (266).

Jim himself seems to accept this mythical version of himself without the slightest touch of self-consciousness. His description of his flight from the Rajah's stockade employs the same epic hyperbole: 'He . . . went over "like a bird" . . . The earth seemed fairly to fly backwards under his feet' (253). He seems to act upon that mythical concept of himself when he visits the Rajah's camp and drinks the coffee which might be poisoned, as if he were, indeed, immune to poison (251–2). When Marlow tells him of the legends that have evolved around his victory over Sherif Ali, he denies them earnestly, as if they were not incredible in themselves (266–7).

Marlow, amused but slightly irritated by Jim's unconscious propagation the myth, views that 'subtle influence of his surroundings' as 'part of his captivity' (266). But Marlow himself seems to be drawn into the spirit of this illusion just as he was by Jim's experience on board the *Patna*. His own description of Jim is couched in the idiom of the very myth he ridicules: 'He had heroic health' (244); 'he . . . burst into a Homeric peal of laughter' (267). Marlow's scepticism seems to waver before the magic of Jim's conviction: when Jim shows him the moon rising behind the two hills Marlow smiles at the note of 'personal pride' with which he relates to the sight, 'as though he had had a hand in regulating that unique spectacle'. But immediately afterwards he qualifies his irony: 'He had regulated so many things in Patusan! Things that would have appeared as much beyond his control as the motions of the moon and the stars' (221). Marlow himself describes Jim as 'the heir of a shadowy and mighty tradition' (244), 'a figure set up on a pedestal, to represent in his persistent youth the power, and perhaps the virtues, of races that never grow old' (256). Jim embraces the heroic virtues: physical courage, fidelity, cunning, and friendship (261, 305)—the virtues which are essential for the maintenance of the community. He creates the community of Patusan as a mythical heroic society, and is, in turn, created by his role in this society, given a new identity and a new name.

A significant illustration of the difference between the modern and the mythical modes of discourse which constitute the *Patna* and the Patusan parts of Jim's story respectively is the relationship between Jim and the natural world. In the first part, nature is perceived as indifferent or viciously hostile to Jim. The *Patna* sails 'under a sky scorching and unclouded, enveloped in a fulgor of sunshine that killed all thought, withered all impulses of strength and energy' (15); the menace of the storm seems to have 'a sinister violence of intention . . . a purpose of malice . . . an unbridled cruelty . . .' (10–11). When Jim tells his story to Marlow, racked with remorse and shame, 'the rain pattered and swished in the garden; a water-pipe (it must have had a hole in it) performed just outside the window a parody of blubbering woe with funny sobs and gurgling lamentation, interrupted by jerky spasms of silence . . .' (178), in cruel mockery of Jim's anguish.

This relationship with nature is reversed in Patusan. As I have already noted, it is not only the local myth, spun by the natives, which invests Jim with supernatural powers (242, 266–7, 270). Marlow, too, observes that Jim is 'in complete accord with his surroundings—with the life of the forest and with the life of men' (175). Jim's downfall is sympathetically responded to by nature, to a degree that would induce one to invoke the 'pathetic fallacy', were it not so appropriately keyed up to Jim's archetypal stature: 'There was a gloom as if enormous black wings had been spread above the mist that filled its depth to the summits of the trees. The branches overhead showered big drops through the gloomy fog' (401); 'The sky over Patusan was blood-red, immense, streaming like an open vein. An enormous sun nestled crimson amongst the tree-tops, and the forest below had a black and forbidding face' (413). It is only through a mythical arrangement of our universe— a meaningful narrative order—that we can overcome its essential randomness and indifference.[33]

Another aspect of the mythical mode of discourse, as established in the introductory section, is the feeling that subject and object

[33] L. Kolakowski, *The Presence of Myth*, chaps. 7–8.

are linked by a common power or energy, that words have the power to generate reality (hence the importance of spells, vows, and curses), and that objects can be the vehicles of abstract qualities. The distinction between the mythical or metaphoric idiom, which accommodates the concept of *mana* (a magic power which fuses the subject and the object), and the modern mode of discourse which is predicated on a clear-cut distinction between meaning and reality, is illuminating when applied to the history of the ring which had brought Jim into the heart of the community of Patusan, and which is, perhaps, the most significant evidence of what happens to him.

In the world of Patusan, where the poetic or metaphoric is the culturally ascendant language, *the ring is friendship*. It is, in this sense, a charm through which, as in a myth or a fairy-tale, Jim is gifted with the quality of friendship. But as I hope to have established, Jim cannot fully surrender himself to the terms of his own fiction, and the incompleteness of his vision results in a transition to the metonymic phase. In the metonymic phase, *the ring is 'put for' friendship*. It is no longer a totem, animated by magic and endowed with a potent power, but a token, a mere symbol. In the latter phase Jim's heroic virtues are not immanent and immutable qualities: They are predicated on his willed application of the metonymic relationship, on his 'putting' the ring for friendship. The ring may lose its precarious magic power when he fails, if only for a moment, in his indomitable belief in its power. Indeed, the massacre of Dain Waris and his people, who have trusted to the magic of the ring, is perceived as 'a failure of a potent charm' (351), and Jim will have to fulfil his vow and pay with his life in order to reinstate the power of his word.

Another prototext of the Patusan chapters is the Old Testament story of the Garden of Eden. Jim's rebirth from the mud in Patusan enacts a phylogenetic rebirth. Marlow tells Stein that Jim is 'the youngest human being now in existence' (219). Jim has symbolically drowned his identity when he jumped from the *Patna*, and after a few years in the limbo of the coast, he is now sent to Patusan to be reborn as Adam, the man without a history. He wakes up, covered with mud and 'alone of his kind' (254) as Adam was when he was created. He meets the woman who is the 'refuge from his loneliness' (300) and names her Jewel, as Adam had named Eve (277–8).

The establishment of the Old Testament story as a prototext of the Patusan episode alerts the reader to the possible existence of a serpent in Jim's Garden of Eden. The obvious suspect is Cornelius, who is constantly described in reptilian terms: '*creeping* across in full view with an inexpressible effect of *stealthiness*, of dark and secret *slinking*' (285); 'perpetually slinking away' (324); '*crushed like a worm* . . . his obsequious shadow *gliding* after mine . . .' (326, my emphases). The most poignant evidence of Cornelius's position in this Garden of Eden is Marlow's comment about the man's hatred for Jim: 'After all it was a kind of recognition. You shall judge of a man by his foes . . .' (325). The recognition is not merely the immediate antipathy of the crooked man towards the hero—it seems to be a recognition of the ancient rivalry between Adam and the serpent. But this profusion of signals which mark Cornelius as the serpent is not vindicated by the plot. Cornelius's hatred of Jim and his devious manipulations do play a minor part in Jim's downfall, but he has no hand in Jim's fatal decision to let Brown go. He only takes advantage of the disintegration of the Patusan fiction, for which Jim alone is responsible.

The description of Gentleman Brown, the direct catalyst of the process, is also loaded with metaphysical-demonic connotations: 'Brown was a latter day buccaneer . . . but what distinguished him from his contemporary brother ruffians . . . was the arrogant temper of his misdeeds and a vehement scorn for mankind at large . . .' (352); 'Brown, as though he had been really great, had a satanic gift of finding out the best and the weakest spot in his victims' (385). But the demonic attributes of Brown are brought into play only by the encounter with Jim and his power of posing as Jim's secret sharer. Shortly before the encounter he is described as a shabby adventurer, a man who, in spite of his glorious notoriety in the past, is clearly headed for failure, and the peculiar story about his love for the missionary's wife who had died in his arms (353) adds a touch of humanizing pathos to his hatred for mankind. Brown is not innately endowed with demonic powers. He attains his demonic stature by his power over Jim.

The real serpent in Jim's Garden of Eden is his own weakness, the wavering of his faith in his own fiction. Earlier in the novel Marlow speculates on that weakness: 'The commonest sort of fortitude prevents us from being criminals in a legal sense: it is from weakness unknown, but perhaps suspected, as in some parts

of the world you would suspect a *deadly snake in every bush*—
from weakness that may lie hidden, watched or unwatched . . . not
one of us is safe (42–3, my emphasis). Jim's weakness is not, as
has been argued by critics, his tendency to live in a fictional realm,
but his inability to bring himself to a total surrender to the fiction.

In terms of the biblical prototext, Jim is made to relinquish his
identity as Adam and forced back in the role of Cain. Jim was cast
into the role of Cain after his desertion of the *Patna*: 'He was
running. Absolutely running, with nowhere to go to' (155); ' ". . .
The earth would not be big enough to hold his caper" ' (196). In
Patusan he tried to cast off the role of Cain, after having enacted
the archetypal punishment, and to regain the wholeness of Adam.
Paradoxically, his sympathetic identification with Brown and his
inability to kill him or let him die will bring about the death of
Dain Waris, his adopted brother, and the collapse of the heroic
code.

The allusion to Cain has been noted by critics, but has led them
to look for an Abel to match the ostensible biblical story.[34] I believe
that the significance of the story lies elsewhere: one must remember
that it is Cain who is the forefather of civilization. Abel had no
progeny, and his literal murder is, therefore, a literary and cultural
ending as well. Cain is the man who had lived on and later founded
a city. Civilization is, therefore, Cain's estate by extension. Jim
tries to regain the wholeness of Adam in the garden of Eden, but—
being human and therefore of Cain's offspring, as Gentleman
Brown's apearance brings home to him—he is doomed to fail. He
cannot erase the mark of Cain.

With the intrusion of time and memory, in the person of
Gentleman Brown, into the mythical (i.e. a historical and atem-
poral) world of Patusan, the fiction created by Jim in an attempt to
redeem himself from the role of Cain, is shattered. There are
indications, however, even before Brown's arrival, that Jim's escape
into the mythical mode is destined to fail, that his own history and
the history of his race must eventually disrupt the fictional fabric
of Patusan.

Marlow's scepticism about Jim's proposal to 'begin with a clean
slate' overshadows the entire Patusan episode with its prophetic

---

[34] Daniel R. Schwarz, *Conrad: 'Almayer's Folly' to 'Under Western Eyes'*
(London: Macmillan Press, 1980), 90.

echo: 'A clean slate, did he say?' As if the initial word of each our destiny were not graven in imperishable characters upon the face of a rock' (186). Marlow's foreboding, his awareness of the inevitability of Jim's failure, colours his description of Patusan with an overtone of heavy sadness: 'A brooding gloom lay over this vast and monotonous landscape; the light fell on it as if to an abyss. The land devoured the sunshine . . .' (264); 'In the darkened moonlight the interlaced blossoms took on shapes . . . as though they [were] . . . destined for the use of the dead alone. . . . The lumps of white coral shone round the dark mound like a chaplet of bleached skulls . . .' (322). Jim himself is impelled to admit, even at the height of his success, that he cannot seal himself off in the Patusan fiction: ' "I have not forgotten why I came here. Not yet!. . . they [the people of Patusan] can never know the real, real truth . . ." ' (305). This, then, is the source of Jim's weakness, his 'snake in the grass'.

Patusan is, as noted by critics, a work of art. It is recalled by Marlow as a motionless painting, 'fixed and revealed forever', partaking of 'that stillness and permanence which is the prerogative of a work of art'.[35] It is, in a sense, Jim's own creation, a story of which he is both the author and the protagonist. Marlow's initial description of Jim's inarticulateness is reversed at the end of his story, when he acknowledges the artistic powers of his former protégé:'. . . you must remember he was a finished artist in that peculiar way, he was a gifted poor devil with the faculty of swift and forestalling vision. The sights it showed him had turned him into cold stone' (96); 'He . . . had that faculty of beholding at a hint the face of his desire and the shape of his dream, without which the earth would know no lover and no adventurer' (175). It is this faculty of vision which paralyses Jim on board the *Patna*, but later impels him to attain greatness. Marlow's homage to Jim as an artist is rendered in the very same terms which Conrad himself has used in his artistic manifesto, the famous Preface to *The Nigger of the Narcissus*. Jim is an artist because he can make

[35] Tony Tanner, *Lord Jim*, 49; Schwarz, *Conrad*, 80–2. However, even those critics who have credited Jim with the creation of Patusan, have accounted for his artistry in purely aesthetic terms. The relegation of Patusan to a closed aesthetic sphere establishes a disparity between ethics and aesthetics, a disparity which goes against the grain of Conrad's convictions, and obscures the significance of the second part of the novel.

Marlow see: 'His few mumbled words were *enough to make me see* the lower limb of the sun . . . the tremble of a vast ripple . . .' (122–3, my emphasis); 'It's extraordinary how he could cast upon you the spirit of his illusion. I listened as if to a tale of black magic. . . . he said "They shouted"—and involuntarily I pricked up my ears for the ghost of that shout that would be heard directly through the false effect of silence' (109–10). The 'real', 'objective' silence around the narrator and his listener turns into a false effect by the power of Jim's shared vision.

The regression to the heroic-epic narrative model and to the mythical mode of discourse in the Patusan part of *Lord Jim* is, then, a projection of the protagonist's perception of himself, his own ideological and aesthetic construction of his world. Jim's enactment of the evolutionary process and his rebirth in Patusan take him back to the earliest form of narrative in human history, the heroic epic. Patusan is, for him, not merely a physical haven, but an aesthetic and ethical space, a different narrative mould for his shattered self.

The power of the word which is predominant in the mythical phase, turns into a double-edged weapon in Jim's hands. Jim has, in a mythical sense, created the community of Patusan with his word alone. 'Those people had trusted him implicitly. Him alone! His bare word. . . . His word decided everything' (268–9). 'His word was the one truth of every passing day' (272). But, as Marlow cryptically observes, 'the imprudence of our thoughts recoils upon our heads; who toys with the sword shall perish by the sword' (342). In Jim's case one might well be tempted to rephrase this oracular comment as 'who toys with the *word* shall perish by the *word*'. Jim uses his *mana*, the power of his word, to persuade the people of Patusan to let Brown go. 'He . . . told them . . . that he had never deceived them. . . . Had his words ever brought suffering to the people?' (392). His rash vow does eventually recoil on him. He perishes, like a true biblical or mythical hero, by his own word.

B. *THE RESCUE*

The Rescue is the last novel in a peculiar trilogy, comprising three novels set in the Malay archipelago and dominated to various extents by the figure of Tom Lingard. The first novel in the trilogy, *Almayer's Folly* (1895), is the last in the fictional chronology, and

Lingard features in it only as a memory of past greatness and forfeited hopes for Almayer, his deluded, decadent adopted son-in-law. The second novel, *An Outcast of the Islands* (1986) goes further back in time, to the beginning of Lingard's decline and the collapse of his trading empire. Lingard still appears as a powerful figure in this novel, but is eventually betrayed by Willems, another renegade son-figure. *The Rescue* (begun in 1896 and finished in 1920), chronologically the latest and fictionally the earliest novel, may have been an attempt to go back to the glorious beginning, to trace the breakup line to its very source. The 'writing backwards' of the trilogy is, in this sense, a project of recovery, an attempt to redeem the present by the power of the past.

But the attempt to recover the mythical vision is defeated once again in *The Rescue*, where the struggle between the mythical and the modern modes of perception operates as a subtle but forceful subtext. If the Patusan episode in *Lord Jim* represents, as suggested earlier, a successful, albeit temporary, withdrawal into the epic narrative which enables Jim to establish a stable identity for himself, *The Rescue* is fraught throughout with echoes of the inevitable failure of the mythical vision. Whereas Jim's mythical retreat in Patusan is sustained for a while by the protagonist's artistic powers, the narrative of Lingard's tale is infected with intimations of failure at its very outset.

The adumbrations of Lingard's failure are evident in what I would call the 'contrapuntal dynamics' of the novel, where the same image operates simultaneously and dialogically in two opposite directions, suggesting that the conflict in the novel is, in fact, between two rival modes of human perception. It is important to note that the 'contrapuntal dynamics' which will presently be demonstrated, operate *before* Lingard meets the Europeans and falls in love with Edith Travers (thus subjecting himself to an overt conflict of loyalties). The conflict which brings about Lingard's defeat is present in his story from its very beginning.

The resemblance of Jim in the Patusan episodes of *Lord Jim* and Lingard in *The Rescue* lies mainly in their mythical stature and in their respective roles as artists, creators of their own world. Tom Lingard, like Jim in Patusan, becomes a legendary figure for the local people, and he, too, seems to reinforce the myth by recklessly exposing himself to danger as if he were magically immune to it. Wasub tells the crew of the *Lightning* that 'no wind can ever hurt this ship. . . . Have you heard him shout at the wind—louder than the wind? I have heard . . . I have often heard him cry magic words that make all safe . . . for the charms he, no doubt, possesses protect his servants also' (47–8, compare to *Lord Jim*, 250–1). When Lingard begins his exploration of the unknown coast, he appears to Hassim 'a white man of great stature with a beard . . . like gold' who 'strolls' on the beach unarmed, like a creature that cannot be killed or hurt, but is able to hurl men about 'as the wind hurls broken boughs' (69–70, compare to *Lord Jim*, 266–7). Conrad's portrayal of a mythical figure is far bolder and more explicit in Lingard's case, but his mythical stature is systematically counteracted and threatened by an undercurrent of hostility in the writing.

Lingard's first appearance on board the ship is depicted with crimson and gold, the colours of royalty and of the sun itself: 'The master of the brig . . . took a long *lingering* look round the *horizon*. . . . The clipped beard glinted vividly when he passed across a narrow strip of sunlight, as if every hair in it had been a wavy and attenuated *gold wire*. . . . The eyes, as if glowing with the light of a *hidden fire*, had a *red glint* in their greyness that gave a scrutinizing ardour to the steadiness of their gaze' (9–10, my emphases); 'The sun was no more than a degree or so above *the horizon* . . . a mere *glowing red disk* . . . shot out on the polished and dark surface of the sea a track of light, straight and shining, resplendent and direct; *a path of gold and crimson and purple*. . . . At last only a vestige of the sun remained, far off, like a red spark floating on the water. It *lingered* and, all at once—without warning—went out . . .' (14, my emphases). The proximity of these passages, and the precedence of Lingard's description, create a hyperbolic effect which harmonizes with Lingard's semi-divine stature, for whereas one would expect the sun to be the source of all crimson and gold in a more chaste and traditional metaphor, in these passages it is Lingard who seems to lend his regal colours to the sun.

But even in this description with its overwhelming suggestion of Lingard's semi-divine mastery of his world, there are already some dissonant overtones. The sun is 'falling'; the water takes on 'a tint, sombre, like a frown; deep, like the brooding meditation of evil'; the sunset is perceived in terms of defeat, and the light is 'vanquished' by the sea, 'extinguished' by 'a treacherous hand'.

Lingard, who had been watching the sun linger (the puns on Lingard's name are too obvious to be politely ignored by the fastidious reader), misses the last moment of its descent into 'a glorious death', an omission suggesting that he will not be able to sustain his role as a sun-god, that his own end will not be modelled on the glorious death of the sun. The archetypal pattern of the death and resurrection of the sun is invaded by the terminality and ultimate smallness of human life.

Lingard's semi-divine stature is further reinforced by bold clusters of biblical and Jovian images: like God out of the burning bush he defines his identity in its own terms ' "I am what I am" ' (323). He communicates with his followers and guides their actions from afar, by a pillar of fire and smoke: 'an invisible fire belched out steadily the black and heavy convolutions of thick smoke, which stood out high, like a twisted and shivering pillar against the clear blue of the sky' (57). Lingard's 'coat-of-arms', which he proudly shows to his visitors, is a circular shield on whose 'red field' is represented 'in relief and brightly gilt' a 'shaft of conventional thunderbolts darting down the middle between the two capitals T. L.' (32). The name of his brig is 'lightning'. Like Jove himself, he seems to own the sea (50), and to manipulate the elements for his own purposes: he is believed to command the faithfulness of the sea and the wind (198), and feels himself bound to reciprocate the trust of the elements: 'There was something to be done, and he felt he would have to do it. It was expected of him. The seas expected it; the land expected it. Men also' (87).

Lingard's apparent control of the elements, and his readiness to respond to what he believes is the call of the land and the sea, is indicative of the mythical phase, as defined by Frye, Cassirer, and others, when there is virtually no distinction between subject and object. But this sympathetic symbiosis which establishes a mythical-metaphoric context for Lingard's story, is undermined by suggestions of the hostility or indifference of the elements even before the overt dramatic conflict of loyalties emerges and precipitates his downfall. Lingard's voice is 'unable altogether to master the enormous silence of the sea (18), the storm seems to 'annihilate' his vision of the shore 'under the hooked darts of flame . . . the wrath and fire of Heaven', making him 'uneasy' as he stands watching it, 'deafened and blinded, but also fascinated, by the swift visions of an unknown shore . . .' (80). The alteration of vision and blindness which affect Lingard as he watches the thunderstorm, carries an ominous suggestion of the potential for destruction inherent in the divine powers he has abrogated unto himself. The Jovian thunderbolts will eventually be directed at his own head (171, 430); the pillar of fire and smoke by which he had guided his people will turn into 'smoke and flame . . . shapeless ruins', first in Lingard's imagination (229), and then in reality when the *Emma* is blown up by Jorgenson leaving a 'great smoky cloud that hung solid and unstirring above the tops of the forest, visible for miles . . .' (442).

The mythical phase both in *Lord Jim* and in *The Rescue* is also marked by a different quality of time. The linearity of human existence as measured by clock-time is superseded by a mythical, almost static conception. Jim drops the watch he has been trying to repair 'like a hot potato' before he makes the second jump which lands him in the mythical sphere of Patusan (*Lord Jim*, 254). Lingard in his mythical phase is similarly defiant of temporality. Travers, the obtuse representative of civilization and the ideal of progress, is primarily concerned with the waste of time (126, 138) and obsessively keeps on winding his broken watch, which cannot tell the time (336–7), while Lingard keeps a broken watch in his drawer as if he were impervious to the passage of time and to the imminence of the end (361). It is significant that when Lingard's mythical mode of perception collapses, the broken watch will be used by Jorgenson to calculate the time for setting up the explosion of the *Emma*. Lingard is to be destroyed, both literally and figuratively, by the reinstatement of clock-time.

The most noteworthy point of resemblance between the mythical phases in *Lord Jim* and *The Rescue* is the power of the protagonist's words. Jim's role as an artist in the creation of Patusan and the sanctification of his word have already been noted. Lingard, who makes his first entrance as 'a voice from down below' (8), and like a deific being seems to exert his will by the power of his words and his name alone (133, 191–2, 298), shares the same artistic omnipotence, and he, too, is doomed when his word is broken. The significance of Lingard's role as a 'Prospero figure, a magician-artist' and a surrogate of Conrad himself has been noted by D. Schwarz in his study of Conrad's fiction, but it seems to me that in his quest for continuity in the later works, Schwarz forces a false note of optimism upon the conclusion of the novel, when he argues that 'Lingard—albeit temporarily, for finally he too fails—is able to write his significance on this world'.[36] As in the case of Jim, the power of Lingard's word, which is very real while he remains enclosed in the mythical mode of perception, begins to fail when his world is invaded by the Europeans, for while the arrival of Travers's party and Lingard's infatuation with Edith Travers are by no means the cause of Lingard's downfall, they act as a catalyst in bringing to light the conflict which has so far been only subtly implicit in the contrapuntal elements cited above. The exact nature of this conflict is the subject of the present discussion.

The immediate and explicit enmity between Lingard and Mr Travers sets up a slightly misleading framework for the dramatic conflict in the novel. Travers feels 'inexplicably elated at the thought of defeating the secret purposes of the man' as though it were 'of profound importance to his career' (127). He regards Lingard's very existence as a 'disgrace to civilization' (147), and carries on with a downpour of 'official verbiage' about his own 'position' and 'the social aspect of such an incident', proclaiming that 'if the inferior race must perish, it is a gain, a step toward the perfecting of society which is the aim of progress' (147–8). Travers is obviously a puppet figure representative of the corrupt West, whose prime motives are personal ambition and vanity (152, 455) hypocritically clothed in the glib rhetoric of imperialism.

But Travers's obtuseness and his ultimate insignificance in the development of the plot disqualify him as Lingard's antagonist. A conflict in which the parties are so unevenly matched in stature and significance could not have sustained the plot, and readers who have credited Travers with the role of the opponent are not doing justice either to the subtlety of Conrad's art or to the seriousness of its issues.[37] I would suggest that Lingard's inner opponent, the 'enemy within himself' (329), is embodied in the person of Edith Travers whose appearance brings out the underlying cross-current in the narrative, a cross-current which will eventually submerge Lingard himself.

On the surface of the narrative it seems that Edith Travers,

[36] Daniel R. Schwarz, *Conrad: The Later Fiction* (London: Macmillan Press Ltd., 1982), 119.

[37] Eloise Knapp Hay in *The Political Novels of Joseph Conrad* (Chicago: University of Chicago Press, 1963), chap. 3, 83–107; Gary Geddes in *Conrad's Later Novels* (Montreal: McGill-Queen's University Press, 1980), chap. 5, 145–71.

awoken from her apathetic acquiescence in the role of the elegant hostess by the life force of Lingard, who has nothing in common with the mankind she knows (149), has chosen to align herself with him and cast off the 'growth of centuries' (167), the hollow conventions amidst which she has had to perform her role. Her husband accuses her of being 'perfectly primitive' at heart (270), of talking 'like a pagan', of looking 'heathenish' in the oriental costume she has put on, and of having 'lost all sense of reality, of probability' (352).

Lingard's influence on Edith derives mainly from the magic power of his words. 'His tale was as startling as the discovery of a new world. She was taken along the boundary of an exciting existence . . .' (162); 'The story appealed to the audacity of her thoughts, and she became so charmed that she forgot where she was' (163); 'She felt alive in a flush of strength, with an impression of novelty as though life had been the gift of this very moment' (165). She believes that she will end by 'surrendering' to the forces of the 'magic circle' within which she finds herself enclosed (285), and takes up the mythical idiom along with the oriental costume, sandals and veil: 'I hope you will never regret that you came out of your friendless mystery to speak to me, King Tom. How many days ago it was!' (307).

But the accelerated contrapuntal process which follows the meeting of Lingard and Edith turns into a confrontation between these two characters and what each of them stands for. Edith's repeated assertions of her strength and luck (254, 255, 287) which could have been taken as an affirmation of their being 'made for each other' (310), are, in fact, an unconscious challenge of Lingard's power, a challenge which he fails to recognize or answer. Edith's surrender to the magic of Lingard's words is temporary and incomplete, for she, too, has the capacity of 'magic words' as both D'Alcacer and Lingard perceive (142, 161), and Lingard's 'mastery of expression' (211) has to give way before her own articulateness and the scepticism of the other Europeans: 'he could tell them nothing because he had not the means. . . . Their coming . . . deprived him in a manner of the power of speech' (121–2); 'He simply hung on Mrs. Travers' words as it were only for the sake of the sound' (255). The most significant sign of Lingard's surrender is his loss of faith in his own words, the invasion of scepticism into the mythical realm he has created for himself: 'The sadness of defeat pervaded the world. . . . "And then for these charm-words of mine. Hey? Turn danger aside? What? But perchance you would die all the same. Treachery is a strong magic, too . . ." ' (202).

The failing power of Lingard's words is only a symptom of the greater issue that is at stake between Edith and himself—the mode of perception that will emerge triumphant when the subtle duel, or dialogue, they are engaged in is over. The power of words to create a world and to sustain it is typical, as suggested earlier, of the mythical phase which Lingard, as a semi-divine figure, the wielder of thunder, the legendary ruler of the sea, represents. But Lingard's power is sustained by the implicit belief of his followers and of himself in the power of his words, which collapses before the scepticism of the Europeans:

Lingard, unconscious of everything and everybody, contemplated the sea. . . . It had lulled him into a belief in himself, in his strength, in his luck. . . . He had said all he dared to say—and he perceived that he was not believed. This had not happened to him for years. It had never happened. It bewildered him as if he had suddenly discovered that he was no longer himself. He had come to them and had said: 'I mean well by you. I am Tom Lingard—' and they did not believe! Before such scepticism he was helpless, because he had never imagined it possible. . . . He imagined himself sweeping their disbelief out of his way. . . . He did not even need to lift his hand against them! All he had to do was shut his eyes now for a day or two. . . . Let their disbelief vanish, their folly disappear, their bodies perish . . . (128–9)

One must remember that Lingard is not being merely childish in his belief that he can make the Europeans disappear simply by shutting his eyes. If he had shut his eyes, they would probably have been slaughtered by the natives, and their disturbing presence would have disappeared at no inconvenience to himself. But Lingard cannot, by shutting his eyes, ward off the subtle invasion of scepticism into his own mode of perception, when he unknowingly leaves himself exposed to destruction by taking the enemy in.

Edith, the 'enemy', is no less a victim than Lingard is, and his downfall, which she cannot help bringing about, is undoubtedly her own as well. Being the 'flower' (140) of a civilization which operates on the 'principle of reality', she cannot dispense with the polarity of reality and dream, fact and illusion, truth and fiction, not even when she is genuinely swayed by the power of Lingard's voice and believes that she has surrendered to it. 'She saw herself standing alone, at the end of time, on the brink of days. . . . And there was such finality in that illusion, such an accord with the trend of her thought that when she murmured into the darkness a faint "so be it" she seemed to have spoken one of those sentences that resume and close a life' (151).

One would suppose that Edith's *fiat* ('so be it') marks the closure of her former existence and the beginning of a new phase under the spell of Lingard's power, but the very same portentous formula is to be ironically repeated after Edith's decision to suppress the message of the ring, a decision which will ruin Lingard and shatter his world: when D'Alcacer proposes that she should suppress anything she does not understand, she listens to him, and after a long, significant silence turns away 'with a gesture that seemed to say: "So be it" ' (407).

Edith's apparent surrender to the mythical mode, to the 'genius of the place' and the power of Lingard's word, is contrapuntally interwoven with glimpses of her own mode of perception, the 'civilized', 'realistic' mode. Her aestheticism, which has been noted by various critics, is another product of the civilized mode of perception which splits experience into the categories of the factual and the fictional, the real and the illusory, the object of knowledge and the stuff of dreams.[38] Even as Edith believes that she has actually surrendered to the power of Lingard's idiom, she perceives the experience in terms of fiction: 'She thought of herself as of some woman in a ballad . . .' (216); 'She advanced between the two men dazed, as if in a dream. . . . Everything was still, empty, incandescent, and fantastic (288); 'Mrs. Travers felt more than ever as if walking in a dream . . .' (299); 'Mrs. Travers . . . had the sensation of acting in a gorgeously got up play on the brilliantly lighted stage of an exotic opera . . .' (295); '[Daman] delighted Mrs. Travers not as a living being but like a clever sketch in colours, a vivid rendering of an artist's vision . . .' (297).

The irreconcilable difference between Edith's and Lingard's modes of perception is nowhere clearer than in their seemingly incongruous talk of the opera, in which Edith insists on the unreality of 'real' events: '. . . the morning when I walked out of Belarab's stockade on your arm, Captain Lingard, at the head of

---

[38] Schwarz, *The Later Fiction* chap. 7, 105–24; Bruce Johnson, *Conrad's Models of Mind* (Minneapolis: University of Minnesota Press, 1971), chap. 10, 177–20.

the procession. It seemed to me that I was walking on a splendid stage in a scene from an opera, in a gorgeous show fit to make an audience hold its breath. You can't possibly know how unreal all this seemed, and how artificial I felt myself.' When Lingard tells her of an opera he saw, she says: 'How it must have jarred on your sense of reality. . . . It must have appeared to you like the very defiance of all truth. Would real people go singing through life anywhere except in a fairy tale?' She seems to believe that Lingard is in possession of some truth or reality to which she has no access.

But Lingard, still clinging to his own, metaphoric, mode of perception at this early stage of their confrontation, refuses to accept her distinctions: 'These people didn't always sing for joy . . . I don't know much about fairy tales. . . . I assure you that of the few shows that I have seen that one was the most real to me. More real than anything in life . . . It carried me away. But I suppose you know the feeling.' To which she replies, 'No, I never knew anything of the kind . . .' (300–2).

Edith's concluding remark is particularly revealing: 'Do you know the greatest difference there is between us? It is this: That I have been living since my childhood in front of a show and that I never have been taken in for a moment by its tinsel and its noise or by anything that went on on the stage' (305). She does not pursue this intended comparison any further, but its implication seems to be that Lingard has either not been living in front of a show or that, unlike her, he *had* been taken in by the tinsel and the noise.

Readers of the novel who have suggested that Lingard is enmeshed in an illusion, would probably accept the latter interpretation of Edith's comment.[39] My own feeling is that, as in the case of Jim in Patusan, the fiction one chooses to model one's life on is not necessarily fictitious or illusory so long as one is prepared to act upon it. Lingard's failure is occasioned by the subtle intrusion of Edith's scepticism into the mythical conception on which he had created himself and his world. When he stops believing in it, it does become unreal.

The only person on Edith's 'stage' who seems to realize the nature of the drama is D'Alcacer, who, by placing himself in the margins of human existence as a detached spectator after having

---

[39] T. Moser, *Joseph Conrad: Achievement and Decline*, 153; Paul L. Wiley, *Conrad's Measure of Man* (Madison: University of Wisconsin Press, 1954), 135.

decided that 'his contest with fate was ended' (123), has gained the insight which is the privilege of those who are no longer fully alive. But this type of insight, however superior to the obtuseness of Mr Travers, is still delimited by the position which D'Alcacer has set himself in, the position of a non-participant. His complete under-standing of Edith Travers's passive disenchantment with life (122) reflects the fundamental affinity between them: 'These two talked about things indifferent and interesting, certainly not connected with human institutions, and only slightly with human passions' (124).

Both D'Alcacer and Edith respond to the mythical quality of Lingard's world (150, 152), and D'Alcacer is 'fine enough to be aware that these two [i.e. Edith and Lingard] seemed to understand each other in a way that was not obvious even to themselves' (310). But his understanding fails to go beyond that point. Edith's ostensible departure from their common ground leaves him baffled and wondering (310). Although he seems to recognize and respect the essential greatness of Lingard, whom he half jokingly calls 'The Man of Fate', he remains encased in his role as an observer, when he insists on the man's *otherness*, and reduces his complexity by defining him as a 'simple and romantic person' (313): 'What can he know about people of our sort? It is when I reflect how little people of our sort can know of such a man, that I am quite content to address him as Captain Lingard' (312).

Lingard's 'great visions' are, for D'Alcacer, 'a world of dreams' which may be fatally dangerous. He fears that Edith, too, may be 'the prey of dreams' in her surrender to Lingard's visions (314–15); for a moment she is seen as 'a figure in a faded painting', to which he responds with a dumb sense of wonder approaching 'a feeling of awe' (316), just as Lingard would seem to him like 'a masculine rendering of mournful meditation' as one might see on 'the sculptures of ancient tombs' (411). This aestheticist appreciation of Lingard's world, and the qualified sympathy that he is prepared to give it, mark D'Alcacer as Edith's unconscious accomplice in the undoing of the mythical mode.

D'Alcacer's detachment wavers momentarily only at the thought of his approaching death, but he immediately checks this unwonted display of human weakness with an almost Wildean observation: 'he was surprised as his own emotion. He had flattered himself on the possession of more philosophy. He thought that this famous sense of self-preservation was a queer thing, a purely animal thing. "For, as a thinking man", he reflected, "I really ought not to care"' (345). This, in brief, is the philosophy by which he lives, the quiescent, sterile uprootedness of the intellect which Conrad saw as the plight of the West. The collaboration of D'Alcacer in Lingard's fall is not effected merely by his advice to Edith to suppress anything she does not understand (i.e. the ring), but—as in the case of Edith—by the subtle infusion of his idiom into Lingard's world, as we shall later see.

The question of D'Alcacer's position as a commentator and the measure of his insight lead to the question of genre, for it is D'Alcacer who defines the story as a romance: ' "If she [Imada] is a princess, then this man is a knight", he murmured with conviction. "A knight as I live! A descendent of the immortal hidalgo errant upon the sea"' (142). D'Alcacer's allusion to Don Quixote relegates Lingard's enterprise to the realm of heroic 'day-dreams', both admirable and slightly ludicrous, which are inevitably destined to be defeated by gross reality. The same view is echoed by Edith when she dreams of Lingard as a knight 'in chain-mail armour . . . walking away from her in the depths of an impossible landscape' (458). For her, too, the knight and the princess are both part of the opera (300), the 'dream' (259), and the 'fairy-tale' (301).

We have seen how, when the outcome of the conflict between them is still undecided, Lingard refuses to accept the fictionality which Edith is trying to impose on his life. In his own inarticulate way he resists her analogies, and defends his enterprise from the invasion of her idiom: 'I don't know much about fairy tales . . . Fairy tales are for children, I believe,. . . But that story . . . was the most real to me. More real than anything in life' (301); of Imada, whom Edith calls 'this figure of your dream', and of her brother, he says, 'they are no dream to me' (259–60). It seems, then, that the generic identity of the story is being debated by the characters themselves. The dramatic conflict boils over from the picture onto the frame. In a true dialogic manner, the characters' consciousness seems to operate on a plain parallel to that of the author.

Critical evaluations of *The Rescue* have, for the most part, been predicated on its being a romance, as proclaimed by its subtitle, by a number of allusions to the code of chivalry, and to the ostensible presence of love and adventure in the plot. This generic tag has led to an almost unanimous critical dismissal of the novel as a minor, market-orientated work.[40] I would argue that Conrad's relationship with the genre of romance is rather more complex than is commonly accepted, and that the title—like many other Conrad titles—is an open and disturbing question rather than a straightforward designation.[41]

The relatedness of myth—which I hope to have established by now as a central mode in the novel—and romance (which the novel at times pretends to be) goes back to the earliest known stages of cultural evolution. Susanne Langer relates myth and fairy tale to the symbolic function of dream and fantasy. The difference between these forms of expression, which are made of 'the same material', is in their function. The fairy tale is 'irresponsible; it is frankly imaginary and its purpose is to gratify wishes. . . .' It is 'a personal gratification, an expression of desires and of their imaginary fulfillment, a compensation for the shortcomings of real life, an escape from actual frustration and conflict'. Myth, on the other hand, 'whether literally believed or not, is taken with religious seriousness'. It is 'a recognition of natural conflicts, of human desire frustrated by non-human powers, hostile oppression, or contrary desires; it is a story of the birth, passion, and defeat by death which is man's common fate. Its ultimate end is not wishful distortion of the world, but serious envisagement of its fundamental truths; moral orientation, not escape'.[42]

Northrop Frye proposes a similar distinction between what he calls 'the mythical' and 'the fabulous': 'The difference between the mythical and the fabulous is a difference in authority and social function, not in structure.'[43] The truth of myth is not the truth of correspondence to facts, of verifiability by reference to the real world: it is a truth which derives from a social bond, an acceptance of the authority of the narrative. The fabulous is defined by being

---

[40] Moser, *Achievement and Decline*, 144–55; A. J. Guerard, *Conrad The Novelist*, 84–93; Bruce Johnson, *Conrad's Models of Mind*, 177–204; Leo Gurko, *Joseph Conrad: Giant in Exile* (New York: Macmillan, 1962), 228–34.

[41] Conrad's complex treatment of romance as a genre is to be explored in detail in Chapter 4 below, which deals with *Chance, Victory*, and *The Arrow of Gold*.

[42] Susanne Langer, *Philosophy in a New Key: A Study of the Symbolism of Reason, Rite and Art* (3rd edn.; first published in 1942; Cambridge, Mass.: Harvard University Press, 1969), 175–6.

[43] Northrop Frye, *The Secular Script: A Study of the Structure of Romance* (Cambridge, Mass.: Harvard University Press, 1976), 16.

untrue in the former sense, and therefore considered inferior in the Platonic and Christian frame of reference.

The generic distinction which is based on the function of the material rather than on any of its inherent qualities is clearly applicable to the present analysis: Edith's fairy-tale and D'Alcacer's romance are opposed to Lingard's mythical idiom, because, in spite of the manifest similarity in their structure and content, they are devoid of any social significance, and serve merely as vehicles for personal escape and gratification, while Lingard's mythical role is tied in with the establishment of a certain social order, with his obligation towards a community.

We have seen, then, that D'Alcacer's interpretation of the story as a romance cannot be accepted at face value, that it is very much the product of the sophisticated, jaded aestheticism which D'Alcacer shares with Edith Travers, and that it is, in fact, actively rejected by Lingard himself. And yet D'Alcacer does seem capable of recognizing Lingard's innate greatness and is finally drawn out of his self-assigned role as an observer of the drama into an act of participation. He warns Lingard of the fatality of his love for Mrs Travers, although it is manifestly in the interests of his own survival that Lingard should be manipulated by this passion. He tells him of the underlying bond of understanding between Mrs Travers and her husband, who, in spite of their emotional alienation are 'quite fit to understand each other thoroughly' (410), and rightly predicts that Edith 'will always remain in the fullest possession of herself' (410).

D'Alcacer defines Mrs Travers with an almost cruel acuteness as belonging to a rare species of women for whom 'men toil on the ground and underground and artists of all sorts invoke their inspiration', who are 'the gracious figures on the drab wall which lies on this side of our common grave', who 'lead a sort of ritual dance, that most of us have agreed to take seriously'. That 'ritual dance' is 'a very binding agreement with which sincerity and good faith and honour have nothing to do. Very binding. Woe to him or her who breaks it. Directly they leave the pageant they get lost' (411–12). The oxymoron implicit in D'Alcacer's warning is extremely apt: centuries of acculturation have brought about the degeneration of ancient ritual, which is an enactment of man's need for significance and the origin of myth, into a pageant which has nothing to do with faith or sincerity, but which is the only mode of existence possible in the urbane, civilized, and hollow world of the Europeans.

It is significant that when D'Alcacer remembers Mrs Travers in her role as an elegant hostess, he thinks of her drawing room as an ocean: 'He saw her in the luminous perspective of palatial drawing rooms, in the restless eddy and flow of a human sea, at the foot of walls high as cliffs, under lofty ceilings that like a tropical sky flung light and heat upon the shallow glitter of uniforms, of stars, of diamonds, of eyes . . .' (140). The blatant use of the sea metaphor serves a double ironic purpose: it trivializes the mythical signific- ance of the sea in Lingard's mode of perception, and suggests that if Lingard is master of the elements, a demigod in his natural environment, so is Edith Travers in hers. In depicting Edith as a high priestess of the ritual dance of society by using the sea as a vehicle, Conrad seems to suggest that the implicit conflict between Lingard and Edith will not only end up in the latter's defeat but also in the debasement of his vision, its assimilation into the pageant which Edith unwittingly conducts.

The subtle conflict between the modes of perception represented by Lingard and Edith is all the more painful, because Lingard's defeat is, in fact, Edith's final abandonment to a life of empty gestures and hollow words. For a short while, when she seems to be on the verge of surrender, she suddenly comes alive as the 'fiction', as she has so far seen it, overshadows her former reality: 'She saw, she imagined, she even admitted now the reality of those things [i.e. the Shore of Refuge and its inhabitants, who had previously delighted her as the picturesque figures of fairy tales] no longer a mere pageant marshalled for her vision with barbarous splendour. . . . She became aware of the empty Cage [the impro- vised quarters of the Europeans on board Lingard's brig] . . . The whole struck her as squalid and as if already decayed, a flimsy and idle fantasy' (367). When driven by her passion to go after Lingard with the torch in her hand, Edith feels as if she is being moved 'by enchantment' like 'a half-conscious sleeper' (391). When driven by her passion to go after Lingard with the torch in her hand, Edith feels as if she is being moved 'by enchantment' like 'a half-conscious sleeper' (391). Guided by Lingard's voice 'somewhere from the sky', she lets go of her own mode of perception, or voice, for an instance of bliss: 'She seemd to feel the very breath of his words on her face. It revived her completely. . . . As his great voice had done a moment before, his great strength, too, seemed able to fill all space in its enveloping and undeniable authority. Every time she tried to stiffen herself against its might, it reacted, affirming its fierce will, its uplifting power' (394–5).

But as much as she wishes to enter the romance or the fairy tale (as she sees it), and to be rescued by the knight, Edith knows that she is incapable of forgetting herself in a story (302). Her surrender to the power of the story is short-lived as it is intense:'. . . she felt stealthily over the ground for one of the sandals which she had lost. Oh, yes, there was no doubt of it, she had been carried off the earth, without shame, without regret. But she would not have let him know of that dropped sandal for anything in the world. That lost sandal was as symbolic as a dropped veil. But he did not know of it. He must never know' (396). The symbolic sandal is, of course, related to the magic slipper of the fairy-tale, which redeems Cinderella from her bondage at her stepmother's house. But Edith Travers is no Cinderella. She refuses to accept the redemptive and reviving power of Lingard's mode of perception, which remains, after all, a fiction for her.

Edith's resubmission to the reality principle, and her regained 'possession of her personality' are paradoxically associated with lying. She lies about the reason for her coming to him, the mission she had been entrusted with while 'feeling her personality, crushed to nothing in the hug of those arms, expand again to its full significance' (397); she confronts him boldly only after having veiled her face, ostensibly for the sake of 'proprieties' (399). The link between Edith and her husband, whose convenient weapon against unacceptable experiences is 'shamming' (347, 456) is thus re-established. She has realigned herself with him.

Lingard's fall from the mythical state is evidenced in the declining power of his words, in his inability to sustain his own voice in the dialogue, and his gradual conversion into the mode of perception which Edith represents. His surrender is consummated on the morning following their night together, when he feels his existence to be divorced from life. 'It was as to being alive that he felt not so sure. He had no doubt of his existence; but was this life—this profound indifference, this strange contempt for what his eyes should see, this distaste for words, this unbelief in the importance of things and men? He tried to regain possession of himself, his old self which had things to do, words to speak as well as to hear'

(430–2). The loss of his power of words, the gnawing scepticism about the magic with which he had created himself and his world, lead him to view his life as an illusion, a mere shadow. He refuses to acknowledge the reality of the imminent disaster or to put up a fight against those 'shadows of the water' which are, in fact, Tengga's boats (437). Even at the last moment he has to resist the impulse to join Edith and D'Alcacer in their remote and superior vantage point, to 'dominate the tumult, let it roll away from under his feet—the mere life of men, vain like a dream and interfering with the tremendous sense of his own existence . . . Even the sense of self-preservation had abandoned him' (436–7). The contempt for 'mere life' and the loss of the instinct of self-preservation, the aestheticist reversal of reality and dream, are clearly echoes of the idiom of the other world into which Lingard has been initiated by Edith Travers and D'Alcacer.

On the level of plot, the immediate cause of the collapse of Lingard's world is Edith's suppression of the message of the ring, which Conrad's critics have, for the most part, treated—both in *Lord Jim* and in *The Rescue*—as a conventional stage property of the exotic adventure story that the surface of the tale pretends to be. One notable exception is an essay by R. Caserio entitled '*The Rescue* and the Ring of Meaning'.[44] Caserio presents an interpretation of the novel as an anti-imperialistic romance, and a reevaluation of the concept of realistic representation and the romance as a genre, viewing the novel as a 'dramatized *ars poetica*' of Conrad's work, a 'justification of the romance element present in his work since *Almayer's Folly*'. Romance, Caserio argues, is 'the sign of Conrad's defence of the representational nature of his novels and of their truth to the world', whereas imperialism 'accepts romance in only two reduced forms: as exclusively different from reality, or as a sign of universal indeterminacy'. Following Scott's paradigm of the rescue event as 'a necessary recourse against the new Imperialism on the part of persons who have become victims of modern ungenerous authority', Conrad asserts, according to Caserio, the truth of romance as a representation of life 'even as it differs from life' and from the notion of reality as fostered by imperialism. 'Conrad sees representation as the only

---

[44] In Ross C. Murfin, ed., *Conrad Revisited: Essays for the Eighties* (Alabama: University of Alabama Press, 1983), 125–49.

entry to a reality otherwise shadowed by appearances . . . This gap between two levels of the real . . . between appearance and essence . . . gives Conrad the rescuer of representation the opportunity to match different things in a way that shows the truth of identity emerging within the appearance of difference'. When the ring which 'stands for Conrad's representational art' turns into a 'dead talisman' *The Rescue* becomes 'a tale of the withdrawal of novelistic representation from the world', 'an emblem of the hateful trivializing of the function of writing'.[45]

I have tried at some length to do justice to an extremely elaborate argument with which I do not entirely agree, but which seems to offer a valuable insight of the nature of the process I have attempted to outline. I would differ with Caserio's rather loose usage of the term 'Imperialism', and the assumption that the novel is anti-imperialistic in its thrust. I believe that this political orientation is invalidated by the eulogy to the bold, dreaming adventurers, the pioneers of colonialism, of whom Lingard is descended (3–4).[46] I would also question Caserio's ready response to the generic seduction of the title which, as I have indicated, appears to be questioned by the characters themselves. These reservations notwithstanding, it seems to me that Caserio has rightly perceived the problematics of representation in the novel. I have suggested earlier that the mythical mode of perception does not recognize the distinction between art and life as the realist mode does, that the power of words to create and sustain a world is derived from this sense of unity, or *mana* as Frye would call it, between subject and object, man and nature, word and world. The 'mythicity' of language, as Gould would call it, is an attempt to close the semiotic gap, to eliminate the division between signified and signifier. The reduction of metaphor to a mere figure of speech reduces the potency of artistic vision, turning it into a spectacle for the entertainment of a clever, sophisticated, and half-dead audience.

As in *Lord Jim*, the loss of the mythical idiom is a loss of the

[45] Ross C. Murfin, ed., *Conrad Revisited: Essays for the Eighties* 126, 128–9, 134, 139, 127.

[46] A similar reservation would apply to other readings of *The Rescue* as an anti-imperialistic novel, as proposed by John A. McClure in *Kipling and Conrad: The Colonial Fiction* (Cambridge, Mass.: Harvard University Press, 1981); and Benita Parry in *Conrad and Imperialism: Ideological Boundaries and Visionary Frontiers* (London: MacMillan Press Ltd., 1983).

power of metaphor. The distinction between reality and illusion, fact and fiction, knowledge and imagination, which strips Lingard's words of their power to create a world and dominate it, establishes a rift between tenor and vehicle, subject and object: the ring which had carried the power of friendship and loyalty in the history of Lingard's relationship with Hassim turns into a mere object, a token which can be divested of its significance and magic power before the scepticism of the subject. As in *Lord Jim*, the failure of the ring is symptomatic of the failure of its owner: the 'charm' of the ring which 'was strong enough to draw all the power of the white man' (379), a power which Jorgenson believed would 'compel Lingard to face [his commitment to Hassim and Imada] . . . without flinching' (388), turns into 'a dead talisman' in Edith's hands (467), not only because she has suppressed its message, but because Lingard would have been impervious to its charm even if it had been produced, as he himself admits (450).

A biographical account of the writing of a novel is often considered irrelevant, particularly today, after the 'death of the author'—pronounced by Barthes and certified time and again by his followers—has become a commonplace of the critical jargon. In the case of *The Rescue*, however, one cannot, in my opinion, proceed with a critical analysis without taking note of the tortuous history of the novel and Conrad's relationship with it. Parts I–IV of *The Rescue* were written intermittently between 1896 and 1899, when Conrad decided to give it up. Twenty years later, Conrad took up the unfinished novel again, and finally completed his work in 1920. Conrad's letters to Edward Garnett during the writing of the novel reflect not only the obstinate resistance of his material and the elusiveness of his vision, but also an almost hysterical anxiety and a sense of acute despair produced by the difficulties of writing.

In a letter responding to Garnett's warm approval of the first part of *The Rescuer* (as it was then called) MS, Conrad writes: 'If I don't believe in the book (and I don't somehow) I believe in you . . . Since I sent you the part 1st . . . I have written one page. Just one page. . . . The progressive episodes of the story *will* not emerge from the chaos of my sensations. . . . It's all faded—my very being seems faded and thin like the ghost of a blonde and sentimental woman, haunting romantic ruins pervaded by rats. I am exceedingly miserable. My task appears to me as sensible as lifting the world without a fulcrum which even that conceited ass, Archimedes, admitted to be necessary.'[47]

A month and a half later he writes again: 'I begin to fear that I have not enough imagination—not enough power to make anything out of the situation. . . . I am in desperation and I have practically given up the book. . . . I canot make a step. . . . I am paralyzed by doubt and have just sense enough to feel the agony but am powerless to invent a way out of it. . . . I ask myself whether I am breaking up mentally. I am afraid of it.'[48] Conrad's letters continue in the same vein throughout the period.[49]

I believe that Conrad's desperate struggle with the novel is closely related both to its thematic concerns and to the particular significance that Conrad attached to the vocation of the writer. The nature of Conrad's difficulties with *The Rescue*, the source of his torments, is not clearly specified in his letters to Garnett, but his vague allusions to an acute psychic crisis can be understood in the context of what is happening to his protagonist, a fellow artist, a creator of his world and his identity within it by the power of his word. The failure of the mythical idiom and the protagonist's role as an omnipotent artist is paralleled—as evidenced in the allusions to a loss of power, to a disintegration of the personality, to a paralysis of the creative imagination—by Conrad's fear for his own artistic power and the integrity of his personality which, like that of Lingard in *The Rescue* and Jim in Patusan, seems to have been sustained by his role as an artist. Like his protagonist, Conrad is engaged here in a struggle to sustain the mythical mode of perception, wherein the artist's words are omnipotent, where metaphors create unity, and where one's being is organically interwoven with the life of a community. Like Lingard, Conrad is trying to resist the downwards slide into a romance, the dreaded transformation of the artist into 'a blonde and sentimental woman, haunting romantic ruins' who is probably Edith Travers's prototype.

When Edith asks Lingard about the news in Carter's letter, she says—in a sentence which hangs on a very thin line of contextual plausibility—'It's difficult to imagine that in this wilderness writing can have any significance' (325). This sentence clearly points to the

---

[47] Letter of 19 June 1896, *Collected Letters*, i. 288–9.
[48] Letter of 5 Aug. 1896, *Collected Letters*, i. 296.
[49] See also *Collected Letters*, 301, 338, 360, 392, 394, 411.

abyss on whose brink Conrad had found himself at the loss of the mythical idiom. The failing power of words, the impotence of man-made fictions in a world of stark, meaningless realities, is indeed the 'wilderness' which Conrad had, with heroic desperation, tried again and again to conquer and domesticate through the act of writing.

C. *NOSTROMO*

The most complex instance of what we have called 'the failure of myth' is the case of Nostromo. This problematic protagonist who has given his name to a problematic novel had apparently been a source of bafflement to Conrad himself, whose attitude to his creature wavered between denial and acceptance, long after he had finished the novel. In a letter to Cunninghame Graham, written shortly after the publication of *Nostromo*, Conrad seems to respond to a critique (which may or may not have been expressed by his correspondent) of his protagonist, and refuses to 'defend him as a creation', dismissing him as 'nothing at all,—a fiction, embodied vanity of the sailor kind,—a romantic mouthpiece of the "people" which (I mean "the people") frequently experience the very feeling to which he gives uterance'.[50] Almost two decades later, still haunted by the problematic protagonist, Conrad writes to Ernst Bendtz, 'I will take the liberty to point out that Nostromo has never been intended for the hero of the tale of the Seaboard. Silver is the pivot of the moral and material events affecting the lives of everybody in the tale.'[51] And yet, in his Author's Note to *Nostromo*, written in 1917, Conrad fully endorses Nostromo as 'a man of the People', and 'a power—within the People',

[Nostromo is] a man with the weight of countless generations behind him and no parentage to boast of . . . like the People. In his firm grip of the earth he inherits, in his improvidence and generosity, in his lavishness with his gifts, in his manly vanity, in the obscure sense of his greatness and in his faithful devotion to something despairing as well as desperate in its impulses, he is a Man of the People, their very own unenvious force, disdaining to lead but ruling from within. Years afterwards . . . in the

---

[50] Letter of 31 Oct. 1904, in *Conrad's Letters to Cunninghame Graham*, 157.
[51] Letter to E. Bendtz of 7 Mar. 1923, in *Joseph Conrad: Life and Letters*, ed. Gerard Jean-Aubry (Garden City, N.Y: Doubleday, 1927), ii. 296.

bewildered conviction of having been betrayed, of dying betrayed he hardly knows by what or by whom, he is still of the People, their undoubted Great Man. (xi–xiii)

I would suggest that Conrad's ambivalent attitude to his protagonist reflects the dialogic tension between myth and history—a tension which lies at the very core of the novel and determines its complex dynamics.

The first glimpse of this complexity is offered to the reader in the Author's Note to the novel:

My principal authority for the history of Costaguana is, of course, my venerated friend, the late Don José Avellanos, Minister to the Courts of England and Spain, etc., etc., in his impartial and eloquent 'History of Fifty Years of Misrule'. That work was never published—the reader will discover why—and I am in fact the only person in the world possessed of its contents. I have mastered them in not a few hours of earnest meditation. (Author's Note, x)

This deliberate blurring of the borderlines between fiction and history deserves some elaboration. The 'history' in this context is the author's testimony about the writing of the fiction. The 'fiction' is the ostensibly historical document which, we later learn, was destroyed in the course of the fighting, its sheets 'littering the Plaza, floating in the gutters, fired out as wads for trabucos loaded with handfuls of type, blown on the wind, trampled in the mud' (235).

Conrad's provocative use of the most authorial platform—the Author's Note, which pretends to be external to the novel itself, and which the reader knows to have been written long after the novel was first published—to authenticate a fictional and fictitious source is only the first in a series of similar violations of the borderline between history and fiction. The effect of this introductory passage is compounded by the courteous, elaborate, and flourishing style which, it is tempting to speculate, is probably an echo of the courtly rhetoric of Don José, the fictional protagonist himself.

A similar confusion of history and fiction emerges when Conrad begins by presenting the novel as a work of fiction which grew out of 'a vagrant anecdote' (vii), and the characters as inspired by memories of past acquaintances, and then flatly contradicts himself by intimating that he had been closely and personally involved in that phase of the history of Costaguana: 'I confess that, for me, that time is the time of firm friendship and unforgotten hospital-ities' (xi).

This flagrant disregard for the distinction between history and fiction is particularly marked in the treatment of Antonia Avellanos:

One more figure of those stirring times I would like to mention: and that is Antonia Avellanos—the 'beautiful Antonia.' Whether she is a possible variation of Latin-American girlhood I wouldn't dare to affirm. But, for me, she is. Always a little in the background by the side of her father (my venerated friend) . . . Of all the people who had seen with me the birth of the Occidental Republic, she is the only one who has kept in my memory the aspect of continued life. . . . If anything could induce me to revisit Sulaco (I should hate to see all these changes) it would be Antonia. And the true reason for that—why not be frank about it?—the true reason is that I have modelled her on my first love. (xiii–xiv)

Has Antonia been recalled from living memory or modelled on another figure? Does she belong to the realm of history or to that of fiction? The author seems intent on leaving the question open. I believe that the Author's Note to *Nostromo* is more than a projection of the affable, relaxed, and slightly eccentric public persona that Conrad had tried to project.[52] It is an encapsulation of the dialogic dynamics in the novel, the conflict between two incompatible modes of perception. The deliberate problematization of the relationship between the author's biography and his fiction is closely related to the theme of this extremely difficult novel with its penetrating and painful treatment of the relationship between history and myth.[53]

Myth and history are usually conceived of as contradictory modes of discourse. Paul Ricoeur defines both as 'narratives, that is to say, arrangements of events into unified stories, which can be recounted.' But 'myth is a narrative of origins, taking place in a primordial time, a time other than that of everyday reality', whereas history is 'a narrative of recent events, extending progres-sively to include events that are further in the past but are,

[52] Edward W. Said, *Beginnings: Intention and Method* (Baltimore: Johns Hopkins University Press, 1975), 100–37.

[53] In *Paradise of Snakes* Clare Rosenfield notes the coexistence of a 'traditional' and a 'historical' narrative in *Nostromo*, but does not pursue this distinction in her discussion of Nostromo and Decoud, the respective heroes of these narratives, as she analyses them both in Jungian terms.

nonetheless, situated in human time'. Mythical narratives are 'characterized by being anonymous, and so without any determinant origin. They are received through tradition and accepted as credible by all the members of the group, with no guarantee of authenticity other than the belief of those who transmit them'. History marks 'an "epistemological break" with this mode of transmission and reception', as it entails a rigorous demand for authenticity and verification.[54]

The ostensibly fundamental antagonism between the historical and the mythical modes of perception is presented by Eliade in *Myth and Reality* as symptomatic of different stages in our cultural evolution: 'Just as Modern man believes himself to be constituted by history, the man of archaic societies declares that he is the result of a certain number of mythical events'; 'It is only through the discovery of History—more precisely by the awakening of the historical consciousness . . .—it is only through the radical assimilation of the new mode of being . . . that myth could be left behind'.[55]

Both Eliade and Ricoeur comment on the survival of myth in historiography, which—as we shall see in the testimony of Captain Mitchell and Don José Avellanos in *Nostromo*—is often predicated on teleological assumptions and implicit 'myths'. As we shall see, however, the relationship between these two ostensibly conflicting modes of discourse in *Nostromo* is far too complex to be contained by any set of binary oppositions.

The mythical elements in the novel have been noted by more than one critic. E. M. W. Tillyard notes the 'epic quality' of the novel: the vast scope, geographical, political, and human of the action; Conrad's Homeric treatment of 'the great themes of action and reflection, of material interests and moral idealism'; and the union of the fabulous with the actual. Claire Rosenfield identifies the constituent elements of the 'hero myth' in the figure of Nostromo (his unknown parentage, his kind 'stepparents', his magnificent physical appearance, and his reputation for supernatural exploits), and views his last mission as the ritual adventure

    [54] Paul Ricoeur, 'Myth and History', in *The Encyclopedia of Religion*, ed. Mircea Eliade (New York: Macmillan Publishing Co., 1987), 273.
    [55] Mircea Eliade, *Myth and Reality* (London: George Allen & Unwin, 1964), 12, 113.

of the archetypal mythical hero; and Victor Emmet points to the Vergilian epic elements in the novel. Both Rosenfield and Emmet resort to the formula of ironic displacement or parody to explain the failure of Nostromo as a mythical or epic hero. Rosenfield proposes a Jungian account of the hero's deficiencies, and Emmet defines the novel as an 'anti-epic', a work which undercuts the metaphysic of the imperialist, capitalist age and the very idea of real heroism.[56]

My own view is that the significance of myth in the novel extends beyond parody or ironic displacement. The mythical mode of discourse, as defined in this study, consists of more than epic patterns of plot: it is a distinct frame of reference which produces its own mode of discourse, its own voice, which operates in opposition to the voice of modernity. In order to understand the function of myth in the novel, one ought to examine it against the rival, historical mode of discourse.

Long before the introduction of the political and interpersonal conflicts, which most critics view as the dramatic substance of the novel, the reader is made aware of a tug-of-war between two opposing perceptual modes. The first chapter, which offers a panoramic bird's-eye view of the Sulaco, is riddled with an ambiguity similar to that of the Author's Note: the mythical idiom which seems to predominate in the presentation of the setting is persistently undercut by an ironic narrator who insists on 'correcting' the mythical vision by placing it in a historical context.

The primal-mythical setting is created by the description of an immutable, unpopulated, and isolated geographical enclosure, and the anthropomorphic treatment of nature: 'Sulaco had found an inviolable sanctuary from the temptations of a trading world in the solemn hush of the deep Golfo Placido as if within an enormous semi-circular and unroofed temple open to the ocean, with its walls of lofty mountains hung with the mourning draperies of cloud' (3). 'This is the peninsula of Azuera . . . It lies far out to sea like a rough head of stone stretched from a green-clad coast at the end of a slender neck of sand . . .' (4); 'The wasting edge of the cloud-bank always strives for, but seldom wins, the middle of the gulf.

---

[56] E. M. W. Tillyard, *The Epic Strain in the English Novel* (London: Chatto & Windus, 1967), 166–7; Rosenfield, *Paradise of Snakes*, 43–78; Victor J. Emmet, 'The Aesthetics of Anti-Imperialism: Ironic Distortions of the Vergilian Epic Mode in Conrad's *Nostromo*', *Studies in the Novel*, 4/3 (Autumn, 1972), 459–72.

The sun—as the sailors say—is eating it up' (6); 'Sky, land, and sea disappear together out of the world when the Placido—as the saying is—goes to sleep under its black poncho. The few stars left below the seaward frown of the vault shine feebly as into the mouth of a black cavern' (6). All sense of time is suspended, civilization is kept at bay, and only the elements—the land, the sun, the gulf, the clouds—are there like pagan deities in a primeval world.

But the reader is not allowed to abandon himself or herself to this mythical view: he or she is constantly reminded of the historical perspective by the narrator's qualifying interjections, which 'correct' and relativize the mythical idiom by placing it in inverted commas, as it were, insisting that the anthropomorphic view of nature is a mere fiction of the local inhabitants. The narrator dissociates himself from these fictions, even as he recounts them, by recurrent parenthetical phrases like 'it is said', 'the story goes', 'as the sailors say', as the saying is', 'they add with grim profundity' (3–7).

This strategy of dissociation is most effective in the narrator's account of the legendary accursed treasure buried in the barren peninsula of Azuera.

The poor, associating by an obscure instinct of consolation the ideas of evil and wealth, will tell you that it is deadly because of its forbidden treasures. The common folk of the neighbourhood, peons of the estancias, vaqueroes of the seaboard plains, tame Indians coming miles to market with a bundle of sugar-cane or a basket of maize worth about threepence, are well aware that heaps of shining gold lie in the gloom of the deep precipices . . . Tradition has it that many adventurers of olden time had perished in the search. The story goes also that within man's memory two wandering sailors . . . were never seen again. . . . The two gringos, spectral and alive are believed to be dwelling to this day among the rocks, under the fatal spell of their success. Their souls cannot tear themselves from their bodies mounting guard over the discovered treasure. They are now rich and hungry and thirsty—a strange theory of tenacious gringo ghosts . . . (4–5)

This presentation of the legend as a quaint folk tale, a 'strange theory' of poor, primitive people, is strangely at odds with the factual and detailed rendering of the story. The dissonance is all the more intriguing at a second reading, when one realizes that what is deprecated here as a 'local fiction' is, in fact, real and powerful enough to cast its deadly spell on the protagonists of the story. I will return to this significant dissonance later.

Other, more obvious, means of 'correction' are aimed at a localizing effect: whereas the mythical mode presents a picture of the land as a microcosm, an enclosed totality (cf. 'A semi-circular and unroofed temple') in a timeless space, the historical mode introduces the names of real historical figures (King Charles IV, Bolívar, Garibaldi), and local idioms (*gringos*, *poncho*, *estancias*, *Calle*) which not only create an exotic effect, but supplement the temporal and spatial dimensions by presenting the action as a specific stretch of the history of a specific place. The amazing efficacy of this technique can account for the numerous scholarly articles which attempt to reconstruct the exact chronology of the history of Costaguana or its landscape.[57]

The initial contradiction between myth and history as two widely divergent modes of accounting for the past, becomes even more acute when one realizes that the conceptual framework which opposes the mythical perception in the novel is not merely 'historical' but radically historicist. Historicism is an intellectual movement, 'which recognizes the historical character of all human existence but views history not as an integrated system but as a scene in which a diversity of human wills express themselves'. The historicist outlook 'consists in the recognition that all human ideas and ideals are subject to change' and historically related.[58] The historicist outlook denies the very idea of 'a unified human history', and rejects the idea of progress along with other teleological concepts. The task of the historian, according to this approach, is to reconstruct the concrete reality of the past rather than attempt to contain it in ideological theoretical models.

One does not need to look far for the historicist outlook in *Nostromo*.[59] The painstaking reconstruction of the history of

---

[57] See Hartley S. Spatt, '*Nostromo*'s Chronology: The Shaping of History', *Conradiana*, 8/1 (1976), 37–46; W. R. Martin, 'Charting Conrad's Costaguana', *Conradiana*, 8/2 (1976), 163–7.

[58] Georg G. Iggers, 'Historicism', in *The Dictionary of the History of Ideas* (New York: Charles Scribner's Sons, 1973), 458, 457.

[59] It is not suggested here that Conrad had been directly influenced by the historicist approach or knew of its existence. The relevance of this approach lies not in its contemporaneity with Conrad's work, but in its being symptomatic of the 'age of relativism' which, as suggested in the first chapter, was the realm of Conrad's spiritual exile.

Costaguana by the omniscient narrative voice exposes—even as it pretends to rely on—the essential inadequacy of its two 'historians', Captain Mitchell and Don José Avellanos. The persistent undermining of Captain Mitchell's viewpoint operates through a variety of tactics ranging from disparaging references to his innocent obtuseness, 'portentous gravity' (12), and 'pompous reserve' (13)—a series of comic features which disqualify him as a serious observer and commentator.

Captain Mitchell's pride in his 'profound knowledge of men and things in the country' (11) is undercut by the narrator's sardonic reference to his real position: 'a little disregarded and unconscious of it; utterly in the dark, and imagining himself to be in the thick of things' (112), 'feeling more and more in the thick of history . . . with a strange ignorance of the real forces at work around him' (136). The recurrent allusions of this self-appointed historian to 'epoch-marking' events (112–13) and 'historic occasions', to the 'making of history' (130) and to 'the dawn of a new era' (140), are perpetually deflated by the irony of the real history of Costaguana, which is beyond his access and comprehension. The event which marks the real turning point in the history of the land is precisely that which he excludes from the realm of his version of history and describes as 'a fatality', a 'misfortune pure and simple' (131). It is highly symptomatic of the caustic temperament of the narrative that Captain Mitchell's credentials as a serious historical source are not redeemed by his obvious, though unassuming, courage and integrity, as seen in the rescue of Don Ribiera, which he gallantly recounts as one of Nostromo's prodigious feats (13–14), and in his confrontation with Montero.

If Captain Mitchell is disqualified as a historian by the comic aspects of his character, Don José Avellanos, the 'official' historian of Sulaco, seems to be disqualified for the role, in a rather more subtle manner, by the very opposite attributes. A 'historian who had enough elevation of soul' to treat his cruel persecutor with scrupulous fairness in his work (142), Don Avellanos is rendered unfit for the contaminated politics of his country by his very purity and nobility. He lacks the measure of cynicism and the innate mistrust of human nature which, in terms of the narrative, seem to be the necessary qualification for a historian.

But beyond their respective personal shortcomings—the comic obtuseness of the one and the tragically blind nobility of the other—Captain Mitchell and Don José Avellanos are discredited as historians because their narratives attempt to impose an ideological coherence, a teleology, on the sequence of events which they call history. For Captain Mitchell, the 'Separationist revolution' had saved Sulaco, the 'Treasure House of the World', intact for civilization—for a great future' (481, 483). The 'privileged visitor' on a guided tour of the capital of the Occidental Republic receives a 'stereotyped' official version of its history (473), its respectable Institutions and its eminent Personages. The reader, of course, is well aware of the shady past of Don Juste Lopez, described by Mitchell as the 'actual Chief of the State' and a 'first-rate intellect' (478), the 'famous Hernandez, Minister of War' (480), and of the popular hero of the 'revolution', Nostromo: the first had been all too prepared to surrender Sulaco to the Monterist tyranny in order to keep up the pretence of parliamentary institutions, the second had been a bandit, and the third is a thief.

Don José Avellanos, officially immortalized as a 'Patriot and Statesman . . . [who] died in the woods of Los Hatos worn out with his life-long struggle for Right and Justice at the dawn of a New Era' (477), had, in fact, died defeated and deceived in his 'blind deference to a theory of political purity' (182). His idealistic and naïve vision of a unified Costaguana is doomed to be defeated: the representatives of the 'material interests' which he had unwittingly served will not let their development be jeopardized by the 'mere idea of pity and justice' (509).

What, then, is the 'authorized' version of history in *Nostromo*? The omniscient narrator describes it as 'a brazen-faced scramble for a constantly diminishing quantity of booty' (114–15). Martin Decoud, the spokesman for historicism, views it as *une farce macabre* (152), a series of speculations and an on-going exploitation by European powers and local politicians (174). Piecing together the fragments of narrative which make up the history of the 'Separationist Revolution' without a single thread of unified purpose, the reader must recognize the truth of Decoud's outlook. Decoud is thoroughly sceptical about the ideological presumption which underlies the interpretations of the other 'historians'. His view of man as an essentially egotistical, self-serving creature, makes him suspicious of lofty sentiments and fine words: 'What is a conviction. A particular view of our personal advantage either practical or emotional. No one is a patriot for nothing. The word serves us well' (189).

Rather than the heroic account of the birth of a nation, as presented by Captain Mitchell, the establishment of the Occidental Republic has been a random accumulation and intersection of diverse individual interests: Charles Gould's conception of the success of the silver mine as a source of moral redemption of his father's failure (67), and his subsequent idolization of 'material interests' as the fount of 'law, good faith, order, [and] security' (83–5); Holroyd's grand conception of the link between wealth and religion and his deification of his own role in the affairs of Costaguana (71, 75–81); Emilia Gould's view of her humane mission amidst the people of this land (107, 222); Nostromo's initial view of the events as instrumental to his reputation (226, 246); Pedrito Montero's dreams of the splendour of the Second Empire and his choice of the Duc de Morny as a historical model (387); Sotillo's obsessive rapacity (285–6); Decoud's love for Antonia and Dr Monygham's torments; Father Corbelan's fanatical ambition for the church (194); the engineer's view of the Monterist revolution as a potential threat to his promotion (169); and the dumb obedience of the 'poor peons and Indios, that know nothing either of reason or politics' but make up the 'most forlorn army on earth' in the service of the Republic-to-be (181). This diversity of interests and wills is the raw material for what Captain Mitchell and Don José Avellanos would have described as the history of a nation and the establishment of a state. The parrot's screeching 'Viva Costaguana!' (82) is the most apt comment on this presumption of ideological unity.

Critics have rightly noted that Decoud is, in many ways, a sharer of Conrad's temperament and history.[60] He does, indeed, act as a spokesman for the author—or for a certain aspect of the Conradian temper, as outlined in the second chapter of this study—in his commentary on the universal human need for idealization. Conrad's concept of the 'saving illusion' is finely articulated by his protagonist, who perceives Gould as a 'sentimentalist' endowing his personal desires with 'the shining robe of silk and jewels', and

---

[60] An interesting discussion of the biographical and ideological affinities between Decoud and Conrad is offered by Martin Ray in 'Conrad and Decoud', *The Polish Review*, 29/3 (1984), 53–64.

turning his life into 'a moral romance derived from the tradition of a pretty fairy tale' (218). Decoud, like his author, maintains that men 'live on illusions which somehow or other help them to get a firm hold of the substance' (239).

This recognition of the human need for a 'saving illusion' and the rejection of all idealizations and totalities is the syndrome of historicism. The 'crisis of historicism' immediately before and after the First World War exposed the problematics of this approach: 'the evident irreconcilability of the moral relativism to which [it] seemed to lead ... with the need for something more than mere subjectivism ... the need for common ground between men, a common purpose which, even if not universally accepted, is at any rate valid for many men for long stretches of history, and can provide some approach to objectivity in determining basic values—greatness and littleness, good and evil, progress and retrogression'. Taken to its ultimate conclusion, the historicist outlook threatens to 'run off into a relativism that would no longer recognize anything solid or absolute in history ... [ending up in] "an anarchy of convictions"'.[61]

This, then, is the core of the conflict between the mythical and the historicist modes of perception. Myth is initially that which is truer than history, an attempt to endow man's existence with a totalizing significance, accounting for man's place in creation, his relationship with nature and his social organization. It is a collective attempt to create, in Malinowski's words, 'a pragmatic charter of primitive faith and moral wisdom'. In the modern sense, however, myth is a mere fiction, a construction of ideological coherence. The historicist outlook rejects all generalizations and totalizations as 'myths', i.e. mere fictions, and offers relativistic, particularized accounts in their stead.

The shift in the denotation of 'myth' is not accidental. The secondary—and typically modern—denotation of myth as a fiction is a reflection of a changing social reality. Cassirer's theory of modern political myths illuminates this process and pursues its implications. Cassirer is, of course, concerned with the lethal

---

[61] Sir Isaiah Berlin, Foreword to Friedrich Meineke, *Historicism: The Rise of a New Historical Outlook* (1959), trans. J. E. Anderson (London: Routledge & Kegan Paul, 1972), xi–xii; F. Meineke, 'Ernst Troeltch and the Problem of Historism' (1923), quoted in Carl Hinrich's Introduction to *Historicism*, xviii.

phenomenon of the Nazi myths, but the theory is relevant to the present discussion as well. Man, as Cassirer says, is 'a mythical animal', and his need for myth is the need for some correlation between the realm of the profane and the realm of the sacred. In primitive 'organic' societies, myth is the product of the collective subject, an organic growth of subconscious social activity. In the absence of an organic community which generates organic myths, the need for myth can be exploited as an instrument of manipulation by the wielders of power who fabricate myths for their own ends.[62] Modern political myths are deliberately fabricated, organized, and adjusted to political needs.

Barthes's theory of myths is yet another reflection of the modern debasement of this concept and its decline from the notion of a sacred history to a hollow, manipulative fiction. Barthes defines myth as a 'perpetual alibi', a fictive construct which naturalizes an intentional concept, an instrument used to dehistoricize and depoliticize reality. The task of the 'mythologist', according to Barthes, is to demystify myth, to expose the alibi it provides, and to unmask its distortion of reality.[63]

Nostromo reflects this transition from 'mythicity' to 'historicity', a transition which is enacted in the novel by the changing conception of the silver at various points in Nostromo's development. Initially viewed as an emblem of the protagonist's incorruptibility and magnificence—the silver-grey mare, the silver buttons, the silver whistle (22, 125, 225, 300)—the 'incorruptible' metal seems to be endowed with a magic quality: when given away, it is not diminished. This magic quality, defying the basic economic law of material scarcity, can only operate within the mythical-heroic frame of reference which dissolves the crude materiality of the silver. Nostromo's generosity does not impoverish him but makes him 'rich in glory and reputation' (415). But the magic of the silver is not immune to the corruption of myth. Its emblematic quality for Holroyd and Gould is an embodiment of another myth, the myth of 'material interests' which underlies the ethos of Imperialism and Capitalism. Decoud realizes this when he lays out the

[62] Ernst Cassirer, *Symbol, Myth, and Culture*, ed. Donald Philip Verene (New Haven, Conn.: Yale University Press, 1979), 252–3.
[63] Barthes, 'Myth Today', in *Mythologies* (first published in 1957; London: Jonathan Cape, 1972).

Separation plan, using the language which might appeal to the modern myth makers themselves: 'This stream of silver must be kept flowing north to return in the form of financial backing from the *great house of Holroyd.* . . . The next north-going steamer would carry it off for the *very salvation of the San Tomé mine*' (210, my emphasis).

Gould's initial view of 'material interests' as the means of bringing peace and order to the country degenerates into idolatry when the idea grows into a 'fetish' (221), as his obsession turns the mine to an 'Imperium in Imperio' and the silver to 'the emblem of a common cause, the symbol of the supreme importance of material interests' (148, 260). If Gould is 'El Rey de Sulaco', he rules by the grace of Holroyd who, like God, is 'very far away . . . very high above' (239, 206).

The myth of material interests does its work, as the miners, like the Europeans, turn the mine into a fetish. 'They were proud of, and attached to the mine. It had secured their confidence and belief. They invested it with a protecting and invincible virtue as though it were a fetish made by their own hands, for they were ignorant, and in other respects did not differ appreciably from the rest of mankind which puts infinite trust in its own creations' (239). Their idolatry subjects them to a mechanism which is 'more soulless than any tyrant, more pitiless and autocratic than the worst Government; ready to crush innumerable lives in the expansion of its greatness' (521). This modern myth—fabricated by the powerful and sinister Holroyd and innocently propagated by Gould—vitiates the magic quality of metal as an emblem of the potential mythical hero, as it corrupts the hero himself.

Nostromo is initially defined as 'disinterested and therefore trustworthy' (221). He is, indeed, disinterested because he relates to the silver as a mystical magic emblem rather than a material thing. When enlisted to the service of the modern myth, the myth of material interests, he becomes infected by it. He, too, becomes an 'interested party', and the silver acquires a different meaning for him. Nostromo's gradual conversion to the fabricated myth of material interests begins when he is entrusted with the mission of saving the silver, which introduces him to the idea of 'making a good bargain', and triggers the first intimations of his dissatisfaction with his reward (259, 297–8). His eventual transformation follows the awakening, or rebirth, after the accomplishment of the mission.

Nostromo woke up from a fourteen hours' sleep, and arose full length from his lair in the long grass. He stood knee deep amongst the whispering undulations of the green blades with the lost air of a man just born into the world . . . as natural and free from evil in the moment of waking as a magnificent and unconscious wild beast. Then, in the suddenly steadied glance fixed upon nothing from under a thoughtful frown, appeared the man. (411–12)

The Capataz of the Sulaco Cargadores had lived in splendour and publicity up to the very moment, as it were, when he took charge of the lighter containing the treasure of silver ingots.

The last act he had performed in Sulaco was in complete harmony with his vanity, and as such perfectly genuine. He had given his last dollar to an old woman moaning with grief and fatigue . . . Performed in obsurity and without witnesses it still had the characteristics of splendour and publicity and was in strict keeping with his reputation. But this awakening in solitude, except for the watchful vulture, amongst the ruins of the fort, had no such characteristics. [It] . . . made everything that had gone before for years appear vain and foolish, like a flattering dream come suddenly to an end. . . . He felt the pinch of poverty for the first time in his life. (414–15)

Nostromo's conviction that he had been 'betrayed' and the 'downfall of all the realities that made his power' (418) leave him vulnerable to the myth of material interests: he makes up his mind that 'the treasure should not be betrayed', thus transferring his faith from his native, organic myth to the fabricated myth of 'material interests' (419).

   Nostromo dies twice. The first death is figurative—it is the death of the legend. 'He lay as if dead. . . . The bird stretched his bare neck, craned his bald head, loathsome in the brilliance of varied colouring, with an air of voracious anxiety towards the promising stillness of that prostrate body. . . . He settled himself to wait. The first thing upon which Nostromo's eyes fell on waking was this patient watcher for the signs of death and corruption. . . . [he] muttered, "I am not dead yet." ' (413) But the signs of corruption are already there as Nostromo soon finds out. His decision to appropriate the silver entails a renunciation of his title. 'The Capataz is undone, destroyed. There is no Capataz. Oh, no! You will find the Capataz no more' (436). The transformation of the mythical hero into the 'material man' is thus complete.

Nostromo, 'our man', is a question-begging title not, as is sometimes suggested, because the protagonist turns out to be his own man rather than the faithful and incorruptible retainer his employers believe him to be, but because the reference of the possessive pronoun is a riddle: what is that collective subject to which Nostromo ostensibly belongs? Is it the group of people who work for the advancement of 'material interests' and pay him with praises? Is it the local oligarchy, the Blancos of Costaguana? Or is it the collective consciousness of 'the people'—the proletariat, as some critics maintain—whose uncrowned but uncontested leader he is?[64]

I would suggest that the very absence of an identifiable collective subject or community is the subject of the novel. A. J. Guerard defines Nostromo as 'the lost subject of the book', and thereafter dismisses him altogether.[65] This definition, albeit in an entirely different sense, is the point of departure for the present analysis, for it is precisely the loss of the collective subject that determines the failure of the mythical hero. As we have seen, the heroic ethos depends for its viability on the existence of a community whose survival as a community assigns its individual members their various roles and determines their ethical code. Nostromo fails in his role because he cannot relate, as the epic hero could, to a collective subject, an organic community which would validate the title by which he is known. Without the 'eyes of others', the trust and admiration of the community which had sustained him as a mythical hero, Nostromo dies and is reborn as an individual, a modern man. In this sense he dies of 'subjectivity'.[66]

The vitiation of the mythical idiom by the myth of 'material interests' is paralleled in the destruction of the paradisaical landscape by the invasion of civilization and progress. The most notable instance of this destruction is the dried-up waterfall in the ravine of the San Tomé mountain, a life-giving stream which has been diverted for the mining of the silver leaving 'a big trench filled up

---

[64] Cf. A. Fleishman, *Conrad's Politics* (Baltimore: Johns Hopkins Press, 1967), 161–84.

[65] Guerard, *Conrad the Novelist*, 204.

[66] Berthoud, *Conrad: The Major Phase*, 95–130.

with the refuse of excavations' (106).[67] A similar slide of meaning is evident in the treatment of the religious myth. Conrad does, as critics have noted, treat Emilia Gould iconographically, turning her into a madonna figure who keeps her house open 'for the dispensation of the small graces of existence' (46), who endows the miners' church with an altar-piece representing the Resurrection (103), who ministers, with 'her two lieutenants, the doctor and the priest' to the needs of the poor, the sick, and the old (67, 146, 189, 233). Living as an incarnation of 'the Madonna with blue robes and the Child on her arm' (68, 71, 505), Emilia Gould's only reward is the love of Doctor Monygham (best qualified to appreciate her precisely because he has no illusions about the other characters), a love which is a form of religious 'adoration', a figurative 'kissing [of] the hem of her robe' (513).

But unlike the Madonna in the blue robes, Emilia Gould is childless, 'touched by the withering suspicion of the uselessness of her labours, the powerlessness of her magic' (520). She, too, is defeated by the modern, vitiated myth, or religion, of material interests, as represented in the figure of Holroyd, whom she rightly perceives as an opponent even as her husband enters into an allegiance with him. Holroyd represents 'the religion of silver and iron': he is 'shocked and disgusted at the tawdriness of the dressed-up saints in the cathedral', 'the worship of wood and tinsel'. But his form of religiosity is much closer to idolatry, as Emilia Gould perceives, for he looks upon his own God 'as a sort of influential partner, who gets his share of profit in the endowment of churches' (71). The projection of the imperialist ethos by this 'considerable personage, the millionaire endower of churches' is an obscene blend of the religious with the materialist idiom: 'Time itself has got to wait on the greatest country in the whole of God's universe. We shall be giving the word for everything: industry, trade, law, journalism, art, politics, and religion . . . And then we shall have the leisure to take in hand the outlying islands and continents of the earth. We shall run the world's business whether the world likes it or not' (77).

Can one conclude, then, that the novel is a straightforward refutation of the mythical-epic mode, by the historicist view of myth as a fiction? Had the novel ended with Nostromo's figurative

---

[67] This point has been noted by C. Rosenfield, *Paradise of Snakes*, 51–2.

death and his awakening, or rebirth, as an individual rather than 'Our man', this would, indeed, have been a justifiable conclusion.

But the novel does go on, and Nostromo's figurative death is not his end. The 'real' death, the physical death of the man who had borne the title 'Nostromo', reverses the ostensible triumph of the historicist mode in the novel. If Nostromo's first, figurative death marks his lapse from the mythical conception of his role as 'a man of the people', it is this lapse itself which paradoxically vindicates and activates the mythical curse of the buried treasure. Nostromo becomes possessed by the legendary gringos, 'as if an outcast soul, a quiet, brooding soul, finding that untenanted body in its way, had come in stealthily to take possession' (493). From this moment his relationship with the silver is one of subjection and enslavement:

He could never shake off the treasure. His audacity, greater than that of other men, had welded that vein of silver into his life. And the feeling of fearful and ardent subjection, the feeling of his slavery—so irremediable and profound that often, in his thoughts, he compared himself to the legendary Gringos, neither dead nor alive, bound down to their conquest of unlawful wealth on Azuera—weighed heavily on the independent Captain Fidanza . . . (526)

Nostromo's second death is nothing less than a vindication of myth: he dies, like the legendary gringos, enslaved by the buried treasure, under the primeval curse. The text's inexorable insistence on Nostromo's captivity by the spell of the treasure (529, 531, 533, 539, 540, 542, 544, 545, 546), confirms and reinstates the organic myth which the historicist mode of discourse had attempted to banish into the realm of the 'primitive'. Nostromo's end is, then, a sublime vindication of his life as a mythical hero. It is, in a sense, a triumph of what had sustained him until his lapse into the myth of material interests. It is understandable that Dr Monygham should feel 'defeated by the magnificent Capataz de Cargadores, the man who had lived his own life on the assumption of unbroken fidelity, rectitude and courage' (561), and that our last view of the land is dominated by Nostromo's 'genius' and his 'conquests of treasure and love' (566).

Emilia Gould plays an important role in the ultimate reinstatement of myth. Having recognized the false myth her husband had propagated (at the inspiration of Holroyd, her antagonist) and the

exhaustion of her own magic, it is not surprising that she undertakes the mission of defending the mutilated remains of the first,
organic myth. Her refusal to let Nostromo speak when he wishes
to expose himself and destroy his false heroic reputation is yet
another act of faith. She realizes that the myth of Nostromo, which
might have once been real, must outlive the man for the sake of the
community. The legend of Nostromo, his 'genius', as Conrad
finally calls it, is preserved as the last word.

Conrad's reinstatement of myth is probably at the source of the
profound dissatisfaction with which most modern readers have
viewed the ending of the novel. Guerard regards it as a 'great but
radically defective' work which is 'at least two hundred pages too
long'; C. B. Cox, following Alan Friedman, views the last two
chapters as a false conclusion, a 'trap' which Conrad had fallen
into; Jenkins and Parry, whose readings of the novel are related to
the Marxist approach, disapprove of what they regard as Conrad's
eventual withdrawal from a historical critique of imperialism; and
Keith Carabine, argues that the 'melodramatic' and 'florid' treatment of Nostromo's end is an ironic exposure of his 'primitive
temperament' and of the impossibility of his dream.[68] One may
well say, using Kermode's terms in *The Sense of an Ending*, that
Conrad's return to myth is found unacceptable by the modern
reader because it entails a withdrawal from the 'clerical scepticism'
he has practised through the figure of Decoud. The modern reader
is probably far closer to Decoud and to Dr Monygham than to the
mythical hero, and the consolations of myth are no longer easily
accessible to him or to her.

But bearing in mind the end of Decoud, and the profound
affinities between this character and his author, one may also
perceive this ending as Conrad's withdrawal from the brink of the
abyss of which his character had had a fatal glimpse. Decoud, too,
dies of 'subjectivity'. Having surrendered to the sceptical relativistic
outlook, he ends up by being stranded, both literally and figuratively, without a foothold in an indifferent, senseless universe.
Conrad is well aware, as evidenced in Decoud's suicide, of man's

---

[68] Guerard, *Conrad the Novelist*, 203; C. B. Cox, *Conrad: The Modern
Imagination*, 62; Parry, *Conrad and Imperialism*, 99–127; Gareth Jenkins, 'Con-
rad's *Nostromo* and History', *Literature and History*, 6 (Autumn 1977), 138–78;
Keith Carabine, ed. and intr., *Nostromo*, The World's Classics (Oxford: Oxford
University Press, 1984), Introduction, xxiv.

need for a stable frame of reference, for a belief in some Absolute. He cannot afford to loosen his hold on all 'saving illusions' as his character had done. But his reinstatement of myth at the end of the novel is already tainted with scepticism: the mythical idiom no longer relates to the living product of a collective subject, a community seeking to endow its existence with meaning, but to a mere relic of what may have once been a living truth. Emilia Gould, who realizes the need to preserve 'simple and picturesque things' (120), can do no more than keep their memory alive. She can present the villagers with an altar-cloth with a painting of the Resurrection, she can draw the picture of the waterfall before its destruction, and she can preserve the legend of Nostromo by her silence. As an artist *manquée* in a thoroughly modern world, she can no longer infuse these preserved relics with life.

3

The Failure of Metaphysics

> The search for the ultimate foundation is as much an unre-
> movable part of human culture as is the denial of the
> legitimacy of this search. (L. Kolakowski, *Metaphysical
> Horror*)

IN the previous section we have discussed the tentative regression
into an archaic heroic-epic model, where morality is identical with
the survival needs of a close-knit community. The ultimate failure
of this regression is related, as we have seen, to the modern concept
of the individual as prior to the community, and the loss of the
communal ethos underlying the heroic myth. But the failure of
myth does not signify the end of the search for the 'ultimate
foundation', the centripetal drive which lies at the heart of Conrad's work. The need to find confirmation for the 'realm of the
profane' in the 'realm of the sacred', to view existence as inherently
endowed with meaning, is still there.[1] It is most acutely felt in the
sphere of ethics, which, as Prof. Kolakowski rightly argues, is
entirely predicated on an acceptance of myths. Reality as such does
not contain any ethical criteria or guidelines: it is amoral and
indifferent. Morality is founded on the tension between what *is*
and what *ought to be*. But any conception of 'what ought to be'
refers to values which are, by definition, transcendent and non-
empirical. Our criteria for ethical judgement are thus derived from
a priori concepts (e.g. our view of 'human nature', 'justice', and
other non-empirical entities), concepts which have little to do with

[1] Mirceda Eliade, *Myth and Reality*, World Perspectives (London: George Allen
& Unwin, 1964.

the world as we find it. All value systems are, then, mythical or metaphysical.[2]

If myth is predicated on metaphor, an embodiment of the symbolic within the real, as a trope of consciousness, the master-trope of medieval metaphysics is synecdoche, a relationship of containment rather than embodiment, of representation rather than presence.

The noblest synecdoche, the perfect paradigm or prototype for all lesser usages, is found in metaphysical doctrines proclaiming the identity of 'microcosm' and 'macrocosm'. In such doctrines, where the individual is treated as a replica of the universe, and vice versa, we have the real synecdoche, since microcosm is related to macrocosm as part to the whole, and either the whole can represent the part or the part can represent the whole.[3]

The ethics of medieval Christianity are informed by the analogy between the sacred and the profane as projected in the imperative of *Imitatio Dei*, the enactment of the analogy between the human (microcosm) and the divine (macrocosm). The soverign power, the word of authority is located in the other-worldly ideal, in a 'world structured according to pure verticality'.[4]

This 'vertical axis' of medieval metaphysics has gradually been invalidated by the syndrome of modernity, the secularization of Western civilization, and the increasing denial of the transcendental source of moral authority. The gradual displacement of metaphysics by Reason has led to the institution of two separate areas of philosophical investigation where there had formerly been one: 'metaphysics' and 'ethics' emerged as two distinct sets of philosophical issues, and a new conceptual framework was sought to serve as a modern, rational foundation for morality.

The history of the word 'moral' cannot be told adequately apart from an account of the attempts to provide a rational justification for morality in that historical period—from say 1630 to 1850—when . . . 'morality' became the name for that particular sphere in which rules of conduct which are neither theological nor legal or aesthetic are allowed a cultural

    [2] Kolakowski, *The Presence of Myth*, chap. 3.
    [3] Kenneth Burke, *A Grammar of Motives* (Englewood Cliffs, NJ: Prentice-Hall, 1954), 508.
    [4] Bakhtin on Dante's work, 'Forms of Time and Chronotope in the Novel', in *The Dialogic Imagination*, 157–8.

space of their own. It was only in the late seventeenth century and the eighteenth century, when this distinguishing of the moral from the theological, the legal and the aesthetic had become a received doctrine, that the project of an independent rational justification of morality becomes not merely the concern of individual thinkers, but central to Northern European culture ... *the breakdown of this project provided the historical background against which the predicaments of our own culture can become intelligible.*[5]

By the mid-nineteenth century, this 'project' of the englightenment, the attempt to substitute Reason for Metaphysics as the foundation of morality, was recognized to have failed. In his essay on 'Religion and Ethics' in *The Eclipse of God*, Martin Buber focuses on the historical process of the divergence of the ethical from the Absolute. Where 'there is no primordial function of assent and dissent, inherent in Being itself', where man is the measure of all things, 'the good is not ... one and consistent, it is "variegated and manifold" '.[6] Ethics in a secular world are no longer conceived as the imperatives of 'a sovereign power'; they are mere human constructs, variable, partial, and relative.

The crisis of ethics reached its peak at the turn of the century, when Nietzsche's relentless pursuit of the ethical implications of the death of God had finally been grasped. Conrad's temperamental affinity with and ideological rejection of Nietzsche has already been noted. Like Nietzsche, he was fully aware of the ethical vacuum left by the demise of God. But he could not bring himself to celebrate, as Nietzsche did, the liberation of ethics from the metaphysical bondage. He did not have any faith in man's ability to sustain and act on any ethical code which is not situated outside and beyond the individual self, and could not divorce the ethical/ didactic from the aesthetic function of art. He was impelled, by his 'fidelity to a lost cause', to formulate an alternative code of ethics.

The three works discussed under the title 'The Failure of Metaphysics' are *Heart of Darkness*, *Under Western Eyes*, and *The Shadow-Line*. I believe that the protagonists in these works are initially viewed as pilgrims, people who are motivated, both literally and figuratively, by a quest for a metaphysical object, or— as Marlow has initially put it in *Lord Jim*—a 'sovereign power'.

[5] MacIntyre, *After Virtue*, 39, my emphasis.
[6] Martin Buber, *The Eclipse of God* (London: Victor Gollancz, 1953), 148.

The quest for the sacred is expressed as a mysterious driving 'notion' in Marlow's case, as a search for parental and ideological authority in Razumov's case, and as an inexplicable urge to find out some 'truth' in the case of the narrator of *The Shadow-Line*. As we shall see, the language used to describe the protagonists' states of mind before their respective journeys is heavily loaded with religious overtones and allusions.

Their respective quests are interpretable both on a psychological level, i.e. as a projection of their need to be authored and given identity by a sovereign Word, and on a spiritual level, as the expression of the need for a transcendentally fixed standard of conduct. This initial pilgrimage is thwarted, in all three works, by the protagonist's recognition of the fictitious nature of the meta-physical framework, by a constant undercutting of the religious diction, and an eventual exposure of a glaring vacuum where the metaphysical object was believed to be found. The would-be pilgrimage ends with a sense of utter moral and physical disorientation.

But the quest for the Absolute does not end there. To understand the ultimate affirmation of the three works one must return to the biblical paradigm of Cain and Abel which seems to have preoccu-pied Conrad throughout his work. I believe that the curse of Cain, which has so often served the Romantics and their descendents as a paradigm of modernity, should be viewed as a threefold process: the separation from the transcendental (i.e. God's unexplained rejection of Cain's offering), the slaying of the still-innocent brother, and the subsequent verdict of eternal exile. The Romantic homesickness, the longing for a primal unity which humanity had lost on becoming conscious of itself, is closely related to the loss of the Absolute, the authorial and authorizing Word.

The biblical paradigm emerges with particular clarity and force in 'The Secret Sharer', written during an intermission in Conrad's work on *Under Western Eyes*. Leggatt, the murderer, refers to his state as 'the "Brand of Cain" business', and accepts the curse as he declares himself ready to be, like his biblical prototype, 'driven off the face of the earth' ('*Twixt Land and Sea*, 107). In an interesting study of 'echo structures' in the story, Louis H. Leiter argues that the archetypal relationship is symbolically paralleled by Leggatt's relationship with the captain of the *Sephora* on the one hand and by his relationship with the narrator on the other, and concludes that 'the echo structure, by identifying various members of the ship's crew now as Cain and now as Abel', suggests that all men in the ship-world are both Cain and Abel, that 'the Cain–Abel personality dwells in every man'.[7] I believe that this conclusion is far too sweeping to be helpful: the narrator's acceptance of the other as his secret sharer (his 'double', or his 'twin'), and his unconditional affirmation of his role as his 'brother's keeper', reverse the curse of Cain and evoke the powerful sense of redemption to which readers invariably respond.[8]

Conrad's concern with the biblical paradigm is less overt, but no less powerful, in the three works under discussion. The subversion of the initial metaphysical (i.e. 'vertical') framework, leaves the three protagonists utterly disorientated and homeless. They all try to regain their spiritual home by reversing the primal curse of Cain. In the absence of the metaphysical vertical analogy, they set up a horizontal, lateral analogy of brotherhood. In terms of the master-tropes of consciousness we have posited for Conrad's modes of response to modernity, the movement here is from synecdoche to metonymy, from a perception of sameness through containment to a perception of sameness through contiguity.

What we seem to have here is close to Bakhtin's concept of 'lateral transgradience', applicable both on the psychological and the ethical level, i.e. the need of the self to be authored and the need for one's acts to be authorized. The perception of the self is constituted by the perception of the other.[9]

The most important acts, constitutive of self-consciousness, are determined by their relation to another consciousness (a 'thou'). Cutting oneself off, isolating oneself, closing oneself off, those are the basic reasons for the loss of self. . . . To be means to communicate. . . . To be means to be for the other, and through him, for oneself. Man has no internal sovereign territory; he is all and always on the boundary; looking within himself he looks in the eyes of the other or through the other; I cannot become myself

---

[7] 'Echo Structures: Conrad's *The Secret Sharer*', *Twentieth Century Literature*, 5/4 (Jan. 1960).

[8] The inversion of the role of Cain has also been noted by Cedric Watts in 'The Mirror-tale: An Ethico-structural Analysis of Conrad's "The Secret Sharer"', *Critical Quarterly*, 19/3 (1977), 25–37.

[9] An illuminating account of 'lateral transgradience' is offered in Tzvetan Todorov's 'Human and Interhuman: Mikhail Bakhtin', in *Literature and Its Theorists* (London: Routledge & Kegan Paul, 1988), 70–88.

without the other; I must find myself in the other, finding the other in me (in mutual reflection and perception). Justification cannot be justification of oneself, confession cannot be confession of myself. I receive my name from the other.[10]

The quest for the word of authority, the pilgrimage undertaken by Conrad's protagonists, ends in silence. But in the absence of a transcendental, sovereign Word, there emerges the word of the other, and the concept of answerability and responsibility. The response to the other, the perception of the other as a self-other, entails an acceptance of responsibility for him or her as well as for one's own other-created self.[11]

Assuming full and unconditional responsibility for a rejected 'other' who becomes a 'twin', a 'secret sharer' or a 'double'—Kurtz for Marlow, Haldin for Razumov, and the dead mad captain for the narrator of *The Shadow-Line*—Conrad's protagonists deny the modern predicament, the essential alienation of man from man, man from nature, and word from world. Cain, the forefather who sentenced his progeny to exile, had denied the metaphysical-ethical imperative in asking, 'Am I my brother's keeper?' The archetypal denial turns into an affirmation as Conrad's protagonists implicitly declare: 'I am'.

A. HEART OF DARKNESS

The failure of metaphysics is nowhere more evident than in *Heart of Darkness*, a novella which hinges on the tension between the strong religious overtones in Marlow's narration and the explicit denial of the metaphysical which his story carries. Marlow himself refuses to explore the question of his initial motive for the journey, dismissing it as a 'notion', an inexplicable urge to get to the heart

---

[10] Bakhtin, 'Towards a Reworking of the Dostoevsky Book' (1961), in *Problems of Dostoevsky's Poetics*, appendix II, ed. and trans. Caryl Emerson (Minneapolis: University of Minnesota Press, 1984), 311–12.

[11] In the absence of primary sources in English on Bakhtin's concept of 'answerability' at the time of writing, this brief comment is indebted to the discussion of the 'Architectonics of Answerability', in *Mikhail Bakhtin* by Katerina Klark and Michael Holquist (Cambridge, Mass.: Harvard University Press, 1984), 63–94. Todorov rightly notes that Bakhtin's concept of answerability is close to Buber's formulation of the 'I-thou' relationship (*The Dialogic Principle*, 117 n. 1). Bakhtin, however, extends the concept of dialogicity from the ethical into the aesthetic realm, perceiving it as the structuring principle of authorial creation.

of Africa. This notion is clearly not an idealized conception of the appointed task which sets Marlow going, for there can be no doubt that he sees through the rhetoric of imperialism even before his discovery of the actual atrocities committed in the name of progress and enlightenment. When the 'excellent aunt' talks of his role as 'an emissary of light, a lower sort of apostle' or of 'weaning those ignorant millions from their horrid ways' he becomes acutely 'uncomfortable' and reminds her 'that the Company was run for profit', dissociating himself from all that 'rot' and 'humbug' of good intentions which the other so readily accepts (59). Marlow, then, is clearly not an emissary for the 'cause of Progress' even at the outset of his journey, and the theory of his idealistic 'benign' form of imperialism should clearly be ruled out.

However whimsically he chooses to present his venture into the heart of darkness, Marlow's description of his state of mind before setting out on his journey points to a vague but pressing state of *ennui*, a spiritual coma: the city is 'a whited sepulchre', shrouded in 'a dead silence' with 'grass sprouting between the stones' (55), the coast is 'featureless . . . with an aspect of monotonous grimness' (60), and Marlow himself is submerged, even at the beginning of his journey, in a state of numb despair: 'the idleness of a passenger, my isolation among all these men with whom I had no point of contact, the oily and languid sea, the uniform sombreness of the coast, seemed to keep me away from the truth of things, within the toil of a mournful and senseless delusion' (61).

This state of *ennui* and the need to break away from a debilitating stasis and to get at 'the truth of things' are, I believe, fundamentally related to the intellectual unease of the *fin de siècle*, and the cultural pessimism that generated the notion of the decline of the West. Marlow sets out on a journey in search of that lost vitality, the essential wholeness man has lost in the course of his material progress, the distinctly human godlike stature the late Victorians were not certain about any more. Defined in the terms of the present discussion, Marlow's quest is an attempt to reintegrate the 'symbolic' and the 'real,' the sacred and the profane.

Marlow himself may not be fully aware of his motives, but for all his self-deprecating bluffness, he does seem to attach a definite personal significance to his voyage. There is a strong sense of urgency and intense anticipation in his account: 'I . . . could not shake off the idea. . . . The snake had charmed me. . . . I felt somehow I must get there by hook or by crook. . . . Well, you see, the notion drove me' (53). 'I felt as though, instead of going to the centre of a continent, I were about to set off for the centre of the earth' (60).

Marlow's description of his destination is couched in religious terminology which suggests the spiritual nature of his quest. The 'biggest, most blank' space on the map which had so fascinated him when he was 'a little chap', had 'ceased to be a blank space of delightful mystery—a white patch for a boy to dream gloriously over. It had become a place of darkness' (52). The literal meaning of the change is, of course, the on-going European exploration and appropriation of the dark continent, but the very same words might as well have related to the loss of the child's innate and ready faith in a transcendental *locus*, and the onset of the adult's inability to 'see' anything in that space. All that remains of the Eden of childhood is the serpent, 'an immense snake uncoiled, with its head in the sea . . .' (52). Marlow's quest is an attempt to reinstate the 'blank space' as the explorer's destination.

Conrad's use of religious terminology and biblical allusions in *Heart of Darkness* has been noted by critics and effectively summarized by Joan E. Steiner.[12] The allusions to the 'whited sepulchre', the 'apostles', the 'pilgrims' who carry their staves, and the indictment of blindness, hypocrisy, and greed, are used against the colonizing Europeans in an obvious ironic sense. As we shall see, however, Marlow, too, is implicated in the conception of the journey as a pilgrimage, and the irony which is initially directed against the 'false apostles' and the 'faithless pilgrims', ultimately recoils on him.

Marlow's journey is initially presented as a pilgrimage, an escape from the mundane into another dimension of existence. It is a quest which entails the assumption that there exists a metaphysical object, a *locus* of worship to which the pilgrim directs himself. One cannot, however, appreciate the full significance of the journey without taking account of the persistent dissonance between its initial religious context and the unravelling of the metaphysical fabric throughout the text. The dark overtones of religiosity that characterize Marlow's initial account are persistently subverted by

[12] 'Modern Pharisees and False Apostles: Ironic New Testament Parallels in Conrad's "Heart of Darkness"', *Nineteenth-Century Fiction*, 37/1 (1982), 75–96.

a rival discourse, a note of scepticism and despair, and an explicit rejection of the very concept of the pilgrimage. Marlow's pejorative use of the term 'pilgrims' by which he designates the other passengers and the colonialists living in the Congo invalidates his own underlying motivation. One might argue that he refers to the others who idolize the ivory as 'faithless pilgrims' (76), thus implying that he is the only true (i.e. faithful) pilgrim on board. But the incongruous blend of the 'notion' which drives him on a metaphysical quest and the awareness of the cruel farce which is the reality of the journey, the 'merry dance of death and trade' (62) in which he takes part, will remain with Marlow throughout his quest.[13]

In defining Marlow's journey as a pilgrimage, I have so far related only to his state of mind, which is similar to that of a pilgrim, a man in quest of spiritual salvation. But a pilgrimage should rightly be defined by its destination or object as well, and it is at this point that the reader comes up against the elusive, troubling quality of this work, as the object of Marlow's pilgrimage is systematically veiled under a mist of adjectives. The glitter of the sea is 'blurred by a creeping mist' (60), Marlow feels cut off from 'the world of straightforward facts' (61), as he travels through 'places with farcical names' along a 'formless coast', in a 'weary pilgrimage amongst hints for nightmares' (62). The reader who expects this 'mistiness' to clear as Marlow progresses towards the heart of darkness, and towards the 'revelation' implicitly promised in the concept of the pilgrimage, is faced with a thickening fog in which concrete noun-objects seem to be swallowed by vague and portentous qualifications. The 'merry dance of death and trade' goes on and gathers further momentum, the people become more grotesque and even less comprehensible, and the natural surroundings present a hostile, inscrutable front, in a crescendo of adjectives which culminates in the notorious 'implacable force brooding over an inscrutable intention' (92–3).

This apparent failure of language, here and elsewhere in the novella, had elicited some exasperated comments, such as E. M.

---

[13] This process of subversion, the constant undercutting of the initial message of the text, can be accounted for as a process of 'deconstruction'. I have avoided the use of this term, or put it in inverted commas, to indicate the 'anti-deconstructionist' thrust of Conrad's work, more fully discussed in the introduction and in Chapter 4.

Forster's note that Conrad 'is misty in the middle as well as in the edges,. . . the secret casket of his genius contains a vapour rather than a jewel',[14] and F. R. Leavis's disapproval of Conrad's 'adjectival insistence', and of his attempt "to impose on his readers and on himself . . . a "significance" that is merely an emotional insistence on the presence of what he can't produce'. Leavis concludes that 'the insistence betrays the absence, the willed "intensity", the nullity. He [Conrad] is intent on making a virtue out of not knowing what he means'.[15]

A more recent critical response to that adjectival insistence and mistiness of the narrative regards it as a problematization of the relationship between language and reality, the awareness of language as a factor which constructs—rather than refers to—reality.[16] Ian Watt relates the persistent use of mist or haze imagery to an 'impressionistic' quality in Conrad's work, 'the tendency to focus attention on individual sensation as the only reliable source of ascertainable truth'. This 'epistemological solipsism', which is predominant in the cultural atmosphere of the nineties, is evident in *Heart of Darkness* in its acceptance, as asserted by its very form, of the 'bounded and ambiguous nature of individual understanding' and 'the basis of its narrative method as subjective moral impressionism'. Watt concludes that 'Marlow's emphasis on the difficulty of understanding and communicating his own individual experience aligns *Heart of Darkness* with the subjective relativism of the impressionist attitude'.[17]

My own feeling is that, while the epistemological issues are undoubtedly present in *Heart of Darkness* and form an integral part of its modernist outlook, they too—like the political and ethical issues of imperialism—are only another dimension of the larger, metaphysical theme. I believe that the dialogic dynamics of the novella, the tension between a metaphysical discourse and a hostile, sceptical, anti-metaphysical discourse, operate on the stylistic level as well. Leavis, then, was essentially right in his diagnosis, if not in his diapproval: the promise of an ultimate significance, of

[14] 'Joseph Conrad: A Note', in *Abinger Harvest* (1936; Harmondsworth: Penguin, 1967), 134–5.

[15] *The Great Tradition* (1948; repr. London: Chatto & Windus, 1979), 180.

[16] The 'epistemological quest' serves as a point of departure for various readings of the novella which are to be dealt with later in this chapter.

[17] Watt, *Conrad in the Nineteenth Century*, 169, 171, 172–4, 179.

illumination at the heart of darkness (implicit in the metaphysical discourse which sets Marlow's voyage in the context of a pilgrimage), is voided by the conspicuous absence of the object which would carry the meaning. It is belied and subverted by the impressionistic quality which reflects the utterly subjective, incommunicable, and ultimately undecipherable nature of reality. Marlow's language—the adjectives which blur rather than define, the scarcity of concrete noun-objects, and his frequent avowals of the inadequacy of words—is symptomatic of his predicament. His journey is a metaphysical quest which has no object to project itself onto: the spiritual drive, the 'notion', is there, but the once-blank space on the map, the ultimate destination and object, has now dissolved into the heart of darkness.

The powerful anti-metaphysical discourse in *Heart of Darkness*, which seems to submerge the initial metaphysical terms of Marlow's quest, has been construed in recent readings of the novella as its main message, or rather its anti-message. A precursor of this line is undoubtedly James Guetti who, as early as 1967, argued in *The Limits of Metaphor* that 'The Heart of Darkness may be seen to deny . . . the relevance of such a moral framework [within which Kurtz's degeneration may be placed, and of which Marlow's journey is a process of discovery], and to question, generally, the possibilities of meaning for the journey itself. . . . as the narrative develops it is redefined so as to deny the basic assumptions upon which it appears to be constructed.'[18] The novella, according to Guetti, points to a 'disparity between . . . moral fictions and an amoral reality', defining both meaning and morality as 'matters of the surface'. Marlow's inability to illuminate and penetrate the heart of darkness points, according to Guetti, to the 'collapse of a reality behind language. . . . [and] of the expectations of ultimate significance'.[19] This interpretation, extremely radical in its philosophical implications at the time, has had a large following in more recent readings.[20]

[18] *The Limits of Metaphor: A Study of Melville, Conrad and Faulkner* (Ithaca, NY: Cornell University Press, 1967), 46.

[19] Ibid. 53, 57, 120.

[20] Some of the most interesting readings along this line are those offered by Bruce Johnson in *Conrad's Models of Mind*; J. Hillis Miller, *Poets of Reality: Six Twentieth Century Writers* (Cambridge, Mass.: Harvard University Press, 1965), chap. 2; J. Hillis Miller, 'Heart of Darkness Revisited', in Ross. C. Murfin, ed.,

My own view is that, while these readings of *Heart of Darkness* are finely attuned to its anti-metaphysical thrust, they do not, by any means, exhaust its significance. I would argue that the power of the novella and its enduring position as a twentieth-century classic are derived from its defiance of, rather than concession to eternal negativity or 'éternullité', from the affirmation which does eventually emerge, after a painful and desperate struggle, from under the rubble of the metaphysical edifice.[21] The key to this final affirmation is Marlow's attitude to Kurtz.

One prefatory comment is needed before one turns to the examination of this relationship. Kurtz has often featured in critical discussions as the protagonist, whose moral decline or atavistic regression is the thematic core of the novella. I would argue that he should be treated as a figure, or an aspect of Marlow's consciousness rather than a fully realized character. At no point in the tale is the reader presented with any direct evidence which would corroborate the theory of Kurtz's 'fall', suggested by Marlow and embraced by critics: in fact, there is some evidence (such as the posthumous testimony of the journalist, who had known Kurtz in Europe) to show that he had never occupied a higher moral plane, that his elevated rhetoric and devotion to the 'idea' might have been as hollow at the outset as they appear to be in the end. With this reservation in mind one can now examine Marlow's involvement with Kurtz independently of any objective truth about the latter, purely as evidence of what is happening to Marlow in the context of the 'metaphysical paradox'.

Marlow's pilgrimage, his need to get at the 'ultimate foundation', is perceived as a return to a primary state of wholeness:

Going up the river was like travelling back to the earliest beginnings of the world, when vegetation rioted on the earth. . . . An empty stream, a great silence, an impenetrable forest. . . . There were moments when one's past

---

Conrad Revisited: Essays for the Eighties; Allon White, *The Uses of Obscurity: The Fiction of Early Modernism* (London: Routledge & Kegan Paul, 1981); Royal Roussel, *The Metaphysics of Darkness: A Study in the Unity and Development of Conrad's Fiction* (Baltimore: Johns Hopkins University Press, 1971); Vincent Pecora, '*Heart of Darkness* and the Phenomenology of Voice', *ELH*, 52 (1985), 993–1011. See esp. 1006–7.

[21] The term 'éternullité' is an elegant formulation of the 'infinite negativity' which lies at the heart of darkness. This term has been borrowed from the symbolist poet Jules Laforgue and aptly used by Allon White, *The Uses of Obscurity*, 120.

came back to one . . . but it came in the shape of an unrestful and noisy
dream, remembered with wonder amongst the overwhelming realities of
this strange world of plants, and water, and silence . . . It was the stillness
of an implacable force brooding over an inscrutable intention. (92–3)

This description, so blatantly and insistently 'adjectival', harks
back to a primordial scene, a Genesis state of undifferentiated
vitality, in which Marlow hopes to find his Adam.

I have earlier related the 'mistiness' of Marlow's language to the
essential objectlessness of his pilgrimage. Bruce Johnson, who views
the novella as a proto-existentialist text, suggests that Marlow's
awareness of the futility of language in the face of experience, the
meaninglessness of names and the hollowing out of definitions, is
related to the question of authority:

Where is the authority that will allow him to give to experience names
that have some substance [?] He is Adam in the Garden watching the
parade of nameless experience, but without the complete sense of authority
that Adam feels delegated from God. Ultimately, Marlow looks forward
to meeting Kurtz—that marvelous 'voice'—as a possible source of authority . . . [and expects him to] offer correct and substantial names—names
that have some connection with reality. He expects from Kurtz that most
primitive sense of names: that they will have something intrinsic to do
with the thing named, even that they possess in some way its magic.[22]

I would suggest that the 'Adamic' quality which Johnson perceives
in Marlow is more appropriately related to Kurtz, who is not only
perceived as the ultimate giver of names as Johnson rightly
suggests, but as the very prototype of humanity produced by
European civilization (see 79, 117). Marlow's need for an object, a
destination towards which he can direct his pilgrimage, is increasingly projected onto the figure of Kurtz. The reverent hostility with
which his name is mentioned by the representatives of the Company (69, 75), and the identification of Marlow with this 'universal
genius' (83), the 'emissary of pity, and science, and progress' (79),
insidiously orientate Marlow's pilgrimage towards Kurtz, in whom
he hopes to find the object of his quest. In the course of his three-
month stay at the Central Station Marlow becomes an unconscious
disciple to a deity of his own making.[23]

---

[22] Johnson, *Conrad's Models of Mind*, 76.
[23] In 'The Value of Facts in the *Heart of Darkness*' one of the best recent studies
of the novella, Michael Levenson relates Marlow's choice of nightmares to the

Marlow's conversion is accompanied by a process of assimilation into the group of the 'faithless pilgrims'. He consciously takes up their conception of Kurtz and manipulates them by pretending to be in league with him, in order to advance his ends. He realizes that by doing so he has become 'as much of a pretence as the rest of the bewitched pilgrims' (82), but defends himself with the wish to help that unseen being on whom he had pinned his quest. His description of his peculiar allegiance with Kurtz takes on an uninhibited overtone of religiosity:

The smell of mud, of primeval mud, by Jove! was in my nostrils, the high stillness of primeval forest was in my eyes. . . . All this was great, expectant, mute. . . . I felt how big, how confoundedly big, was that thing that couldn't talk, and perhaps was deaf as well. What was in there? I could see a little ivory coming out from there, and I had heard Mr. Kurtz was in there. . . . Somehow it didn't bring any image with it—no more than if I had been told an angel or a fiend was in there. I believed in it in the same way one may believe there are inhabitants in the planet Mars. . . . He was just a word for me. I did not see the man in the name any more than you do. (81–2).

The adjectival mistiness of Marlow's account transcends the literal context of the tale. Kurtz is no longer perceived in human terms: he has been turned into a numinous being, a 'thing' to be 'believed in', a 'word' emerging from the primeval forest.

But any anticipation of spiritual comfort—which might be created by the obvious metaphysical overtones in Marlow's account of his attitude to Kurtz, and by the analogies between his journey and other literary models of metaphysical quests[24]—is brutally dispelled as Marlow realizes, on the very threshold of his encounter with Kurtz, that he, too, had been a pilgrim in the

choice between Weber's concepts of bureaucracy and charisma—the former represented by the 'flabby devils' of institutionalized colonialism, and the latter represented by Kurtz—as two fundamental types of social authority. Levenson rightly shows that both these alternatives are rejected, but the notion of 'moral sensation' produced by individual sensibility, which he posits as the third alternative, seems unconvincing to me. I believe that Conrad would have found individual 'sensations' far too subjective to serve as criteria for ethical judgement. The article appeared in *Nineteenth-Century Fiction*, 40/3 (1985), 261–80.

[24] See Lillian Feder, 'Marlow's Descent into Hell', *Nineteenth-Century Fiction*, 9 (Mar. 1955), 280–92; Robert O. Evans, 'Conrad's Underworld', *Modern Fiction Studies* 2 (1956), 56–62.

worship of a false deity, that the Adam he had hoped to find is, in fact, a Cain.

We were *wanderers on prehistoric earth*, on an earth that wore the aspect of an unknown planet. We should have fancied ourselves the first of men taking possession of *an accursed inheritance*, to be subdued at the cost of profound anguish and of excessive toil. (95, my emphases)

Marlow realizes that Kurtz is, in fact, a paragon of the blind omnivorous greed which motivates the others, that the plenitude he had hoped to encounter is merely the culmination of the hollowness which is their essence: the manager with 'nothing within him' (74), the 'papier-mâché Mephistopheles' who seems to have 'nothing inside him but a little loose dirt' (81), lead up to Kurtz, the superior agent of the company who is 'hollow at the core' (131). His only distinction is in the intensity and energy with which he had conducted his business, his 'efficiency', indeed.[25]

Marlow's eventual and explicit condemnation of Kurtz is not only a moral condemnation of a fellow human being whose lapse into savagery is a hard blow to Marlow's preconceptions. It is also the dethroning of a sham idol. Kurtz has attained a deific stature in the course of Marlow's journey, and his initial exposure carries a reverberating metaphysical significance: 'many powers of darkness claimed him for their own . . . He had taken a high seat amongst the devils of the land' (116); 'He had the power to charm or frighten rudimentary souls into an aggravated witch-dance in his honour' (119).

But the grandeur which seems to be conferred on Kurtz by the sheer magnitude of his moral degeneration is later deflated as the metaphysical aura is stripped off, and the Satanic fascination wears thin. Having met the pathetic, shabby disciple of this sham Satan, Marlow protests that 'Mr Kurtz was no idol of mine' (142); he now sees Kurtz as 'an atrocious phantom' (133), a 'pitiful Jupiter' (134); he realizes that Kurtz's exalted discourse, the voice towards which he had made his pilgrimage, is 'an immense jabber, silly, atrocious, sordid, savage, or simply mean, without any kind of sense' (115). Marlow's admission that he 'had been robbed of belief' (114), is not only a verdict on the civilization of which Kurtz

---

[25] This point is rightly noted by D. Hewitt in *Joseph Conrad: A Reassessment* (1952; 3rd edn., London: Bowes & Bowes, 1975), 24.

has been the paragon and the torch-carrier, but also a renunciation of the quest for a metaphysical source of epistemological and ethical authority.

Marlow's ultimate and explicit condemnation of Kurtz presents the reader with three unresolved questions. Why does Marlow remain loyal to Kurtz even after having exposed him as the monstrous product (rather than a mutation) of Western civilization at its worst? Why does Marlow choose the implausible interpretation of Kurtz's last cry as a 'victory'? What is the significance of Marlow's lie to the Intended?

In a comprehensive study of doubles in literature, Karl Miller notes the fact that both Marlow and Kurtz (and, of course, Conrad himself) 'make people see' by the power of their voices, and argues that Kurtz is Marlow's 'secret sharer' and 'adversary self' who represents the possibility of surrender to the romantic impulse (about which Conrad was acutely ambiguous) to get away, to go 'too far', against the socially orientated, duty-bound self.[26] My own view is that while Miller is right about Kurtz's being Marlow's double, there are two points which should relate this doubleness to a different line of interpretation. First, as has been suggested above, there is no indication of Kurtz's initial motives, and rather than a romantic escapist, a drifter, as portrayed by Miller, he seems to be a 'superior agent' of Europeanism, its purposeful emissary rather than a renegade. His obsession with power is not confined to his deific status among the natives; it is an extension of his European dreams of fame and glory. In fact, the only grounds for disapproval of his career as far as the representatives of the Company are concerned are quantitative and tactical; his 'unsound methods' have 'ruined the district' (131), but there seems to be no doubt that he was fundamentally loyal to his employers. Kurtz, then, is not a romantic deserter of duty, but a 'superior agent' of civilization, an agent who discharges his duties all too well.

The second point is that this 'doubleness' is not an a priori state, but a condition which grows on Marlow as the story unfolds. The identification with Kurtz, which is initially based on Marlow's projected need for an idol, and his belief that Kurtz is 'a man who had come out with noble ideals' (87), is paradoxically intensified

---

[26] Karl Miller, *Doubles: Studies in Literary History* (Oxford: Oxford University Press, 1985), 261–5.

after Kurtz's exposure. At the moment one would have expected Marlow to sever his bond with the sham idol, he perversely asserts his affinity with Kurtz; 'I did not betray Mr Kurtz—it was written I should be loyal to the nightmare of my choice' (141). His repeated allusions to the man as his 'choice of nightmares' (138), and his 'shadow' (141, 143), are oddly coupled with the utmost moral condemnation of the other. 'He had kicked himself loose of the earth. . . . He had kicked the very earth to pieces. He was alone, and I before him did not know whether I stood on the ground or floated in the air. . . . If anybody had ever struggled with a soul, I am the man. . . . his soul as mad. . . . I had—for my sins, I suppose—to go through the ordeal of looking into it myself' (144–5). The ambiguity of the personal pronouns is hardly accidental, for the only soul one can attempt to look into is, of course, one's own.

Marlow's acceptance of doubleness is complete when he follows in Kurtz's footsteps almost unto death: 'The pilgrims looked upon me with disfavour, I was, so to speak, numbered with the dead. It is strange how I accepted this unforeseen partnership, this choice of nightmare forced upon me' (147). He disposes of Kurtz's burial in a flat, laconic account: 'next day the pilgrims buried something in a muddy hole', which is immediately followed by, 'and then they very nearly buried me' (150). But Marlow eventually recovers to finish his self-appointed task, 'to dream the nightmare out to the end, and to show my loyalty to Kurtz once more' (150).

To understand the full significance of Marlow's gradual acceptance of this doubleness one needs to digress for a while and examine a process that I would call 'the denial of otherness' which, I believe, accounts both for the structure of the novella and for the ultimate resolution of its theme. The essence of this process is a deliberate eradication of boundary lines between the self and the other.

The invasion of Marlow's story into the frame narrative is one of the ways in which the denial of otherness operates in the novella: the ostensibly clear-cut distinction between the two narratives is consistently probed into the questioned, not only in the explicit extrapolation of Marlow's reflections on the human condition (94), or the analogy between Britain and Africa as the 'dark place of the earth' (49), but also in the narrator's use of the anonymous functional titles to designate his companions—The Director of

Companies, the Accountant, the Lawyer—echoed by Marlow's references to the hollow characters who feature in his story: the chief accountant (68), the manager (73), and the brickmaker (77–9). Marlow's listeners, who are initially perceived as an intimate group of the pillars of society in a traditional setting of male camaraderie and well-being, are implicitly indicted, by this labelling procedure, as passive accomplices in the atrocities at the heart of darkness. They are implicated by the very fact of their respectability and status as representatives of the European community.[27]

The 'denial of otherness' operates most clearly within Marlow's narrative, and pre-empts the convenient polarization of its themes into binary opposites (such as civilization vs. savagery, work vs. word) which will inevitably fail to account for its unique complexity and depth. The ready-made distinction between civilization and savagery, for example, is gradually whittled down until these concepts become virtually identical. We have already noted the deadness and unreality of the European city, but if Marlow goes out into the wilderness in search of reality and vitality as he seems to imply on his first contact with the natives (61), he soon finds out that the civilized touch of death has contaminated the very heart of the savage continent. Far from the source of vitality and harmony with nature that the narrative has led us to expect, we discover with Marlow a 'grove of death' (66–7). The peculiar static, nightmarish quality of the journey is produced by the fact that the scenery of death and decay is hardly affected by the travellers' physical progress (60–7).

A similar process takes place in the human categories delineated in the narrative. Marlow's explicit dissociation of himself from the other 'pilgrims' and his manifest contempt for their flabbiness, greed, and stupidity, are belied by his own use of religious terminology, his realization that he, too, is 'part of the great cause' whose 'high and just proceedings' (65) he witnesses, and his adoption of the strategy of lies for survival which turns him into 'as much of a pretence as the rest of the bewitched pilgrims' (82). His very contempt for the others inspires in him a strain of

---

[27] As Cedric Watts rightly points out in his perceptive analysis of the echoes of 'bones' in the frame-narrative and in Marlow's story. *Conrad's 'Heart of Darkness'* (Milan: Mursia International, 1977), 38.

callousness not unlike theirs, when he comments on his dead predecessor as the 'supernatural being' with 'the grass growing through his ribs' (54), or on the fate of the Eldorado Expedition: 'Long afterwards the news came that all the donkeys were dead. I know nothing as to the fate of the less valuable animals. They, no doubt, like the rest of us, found what they deserved' (92). The 'less valuable animals' are, of course, the men.

Marlow's unconscious identification with the other Europeans is counter-balanced by his overt recognition of the fundamental affinity between him and the 'savages': 'I looked at them as you would at any other human being, with a curiosity of their impulses, motives, capacities, weaknesses, when brought to the test of an inexorable physical necessity'. Realizing the extent of their hunger, he marvels at their capacity for restraint: 'Restraint! What possible restraint? Was it superstition, disgust, patience, fear—or some kind of primitive honour? No fear can stand up to hunger, no patience can wear it out, disgust simply does not exist where hunger is; and as to superstition, beliefs, and what you may call principles, they are less than chaff in a breeze. Don't you know the devilry of lingering starvation . . .? Well, I do' (105). The extent of Marlow's knowledge of hunger and of the capacity for restraint is presented as a mock echo of that of the savages: 'being hungry, you know, and kept on my feet, too, I was getting savage' (75).

Savagery, then, is a matter of circumstances rather than a peculiar essence of a certain group; the primitive cannibals are ultimately perceived as more civilized in their capacity for restraint than Kurtz, who has completely reverted to savagery in the name of progress and enlightenment. Marlow's realization of the erased borderline between Europe and Africa, the 'civilized' and the 'savage', disorientates and shocks him: 'that was the worst of it— this suspicion of their not being inhuman' (96). It is, however, a useful introduction to the ultimate discovery of Kurtz, that paragon of Europeanism, whose 'humanity' is so seriously questioned.

By the time Marlow realizes the full extent of Kurtz's moral degradation, he can no longer dissociate himself from him: he realizes that he is Kurtz's 'double' just as the 'pilgrims' on the one side and cannibals on the other, are *his*. Marlow's perception of doubleness, of a fundamental affinity between human beings, however culturally or ethically distant, is the first step in a process of disillusionment. The realization that 'there, but for the grace of

God, go I', the recognition of one's potential self in the other, is paradoxically coupled with a sense of orphanhood, of the conspicuous absence of 'the grace of God'. The metaphysical-ethical paradox engenders a tragic awareness, an irreconcilable tension between the need to believe in an ultimate sovereign source of moral authority and the impossibility of any naïve reinstatement of the metaphysical dimension in a Godless universe.

In a letter he wrote to Cunninghame Graham while working on *Heart of Darkness*, Conrad voices his scepticism about the notion of universal brotherhood of which Graham was a fervent proponent:

International fraternity may be an object to strive for . . . but that illusion imposes by its size alone. Franchement what would you think of an attempt to promote fraternity amongst people living in the same street. I don't even mention two neighbouring streets. Two ends of the same street. There is already as much fraternity as there can be—and thats very little and that very little is no good. What does fraternity mean. Abnegation—self sacrifice means something. Fraternity means nothing unless the Cain–Abel business. That's your true fraternity. Assez.[28]

Marlow seems to defy his author's jaded scepticism. He realizes that the Adamic unity he has been looking for is irrevocably lost, that—by the mere fact of his humanity—he is a descendant of Cain. But his commitment to Kurtz in spite of his explicit abhorrence of the man's career is a *reversal* of the role of Cain. He becomes his brother's keeper when he realizes that human beings are fundamentally each other's doubles, and this responsibility for the other, even in his extreme otherness, is perhaps the only valid ethical code left to a society which has lost its belief in the 'vertical', metaphysical order.

Marlow's resolution to 'dream the nightmare through' involves him in a series of misconstructions, misrepresentation, and lies. He invests Kurtz's last cry with deep moral implications, interpreting it—against all the evidence to the contrary—as 'a victory' (151); he gives the journalist the Report on 'The Suppression of Savage Customs' with the incriminating postscript torn off (153–4); and he compounds these deliberate misconstructions by lying to the Intended. How are we to interpret these lies and half-lies of a

[28] In Joseph Conrad's *Letters to Cunninghame Graham*, 116–17.

protagonist who professes to associate the act of lying with a 'taint of death, a flavour of mortality' at an earlier point in the story (82)? Are they no more than 'sustaining illusions' deliberately fostered by a disillusioned man?

I would suggest that Marlow's lies are deliberate and willed attempts to redeem Kurtz by retrospectively investing his life and death with an ethical significance. But these misconstructions are not merely 'pretty fictions' or 'saving Illusions', for Marlow has earned the right to impose his own meaning upon Kurtz's life by having accepted the role of the double. He can act and speak *for* the dead man and not only *of* him.

The much-debated lie to the Intended is also embedded in the context of redemption. Just before he enters the house, Marlow is subjected to an acute sense of doubleness, of his commitment of brotherhood to the man he so utterly condemns.

I remembered his abject pleading, his abject threats, the colossal scale of his vile desires, the meanness, the torment, the tempestuous anguish of his soul. . . . I rang the bell before a mahogany door on the first floor, and while I waited he seemed to stare at me out of the glassy panel—stare with that wide and immense stare embracing, condemning, loathing all the universe. I seemed to hear the whispered cry, 'the horror! The horror!' (156)

The face which Marlow sees reflected in the glassy panel is, of course, his own, just as the horror is, but he has by now fully assimilated the dead man's burden, and has become his double and his keeper.

Marlow's lie to the Intended may be all too casually dismissed as a white lie, and attributed to his pity of the deluded woman, or to his newly gained awareness that civilization cannot exist without its sustaining illusions of idealism and purity. I would suggest that when Marlow chooses to lie to the Intended, he consciously performs a gesture of laying down his life for the redemption of his loathsome double, not only because he himself associates the act of lying with death, but because he is presented at this point with the opportunity to enter the story, as it were, to exorcize the memory of Kurtz by exposing him, and perhaps to succeed him in the affections of the Intended, for whom he has obviously conceived deep feelings.[29] Marlow realizes that his lie has sealed the bond

[29] 'I was left with a slim packet of letters and the girl's portrait. She struck me

between Kurtz and his Intended. He knows that by renouncing the opportunity to disown his double, he has sentenced himself to a 'narrative existence': he will never become a full character in his own story, he will always remain on the borderline as a witness.

The self-referential quality of the novella—Marlow's preoccupation with the efficacy of his words, with story-telling and with 'voices'—points to another level of 'doubleness', an identification of Marlow and his author, which transgresses the boundaries of the text itself.

The critical response to this aspect of *Heart of Darkness* has naturally gathered momentum—as noted by Owen Knowles in a recent survey of the year's work in Conrad studies—with the post-modernist shift of focus 'from mimesis to the self-referential or culturally produced, from the "Conradian" to the "Con-radical", from the notion of character to the phenomenology of voice and voiced fiction, from the stability of the author-centered *œuvre* to text as encoding epistemological space, absent causes, and the free play of signification'.[30] The obvious voguishness of this trend would seem to justify Knowles's concern about 'the changing face of Charlie Marlow', but there can be little doubt that the novella is indeed an artistic *manifesto*, perhaps not less so than the famous Preface to *The Nigger of the Narcissus*. *Heart of Darkness* marks a significant shift in Conrad's perception of the role of the artist, and a transition (thematic rather than chronological) from the mythical protagonist, who is an artist because he creates his world by the power of his word, to the teller of the tale.

Both Kurtz, a quasi-mythical protagonist, and Marlow, the narrator, are perceived as 'voices'. Marlow's anticipation of his meeting with Kurtz is auditory rather than visual:

I had never imagined him as doing, you know, but as discoursing. . . . The man presented himself as a voice. . . . The point was in his being a gifted creature, that of all his gifts the one that stood out preeminently, that carried with it the seal of real presence, was his ability to talk, his words—

as beautiful—I mean she had a beautiful expression . . . I concluded I would go and give her back her portrait and those letters myself. Curiosity? Yes; and also some other feeling perhaps' (155).

[30] Owen Knowles, 'The Year's Work in Conrad Studies, 1985: A Survey of Periodical Literature', *The Conradian*, 2/1 (1986), 57.

the gift of expression, the bewildering, the illuminating, the most exalted and the most contemptible, the pulsating stream of light, or the deceitful flow from the heart of an impenetrable darkness. (113–14, see also 115)

But Marlow, too, is perceived as 'a voice' by the frame narrator: 'For a long time already [Marlow], sitting apart, had been no more than a voice. . . . I listened, I listened on the watch for the sentence, for the word, that would give me the clue . . .' (83).

The difference between these voices is significant: whereas the Kurtzian voice initially holds the promise of illumination and enlightenment, Marlow professes: 'there was nothing behind me' (83). He subverts the illusion of authority which is associated with the teller's voice, and pre-empts the notion of 'a clue' which the frame narrator anticipates of him, just as he had anticipated the darkness to be illuminated by Kurtz's voice. The metaphysical vacuum, the denial of a transcendental authority or 'voice', sets the scene for a modified view of the artist: no longer a mythical being, an omnipotent creator of a world, he is now seen in the Orphic role, as a hero who descends into hell, armed with a voice to enchant the furies for a while, and returns empty-handed to tell his tale.

Marlow's affirmation, 'mine is the voice that can never be silenced' (97), is a pledge of commitment both to the role of the narrator and to the essential sameness which turns the other into a 'twin', or a 'double'. He has, in fact, assimilated Kurtz's Voice and Word, but this assimilation is radically different from that of a pilgrim: for Kurtz's voice is no longer the voice of authority, impregnable and immutable, and Marlow is not a ventriloquist. He has taken on the voice of the other to redeem it through his own.

B. *UNDER WESTERN EYES*

Conrad's epigraph to *Under Western Eyes*—a quotation of Nathalie Haldin's defiant farewell to the narrator, 'I would take liberty from any hand as a hungry man would snatch a piece of bread'—is a less than subtle directive to read this work as a novel 'about' liberty. But readers who respond to the author's masterful invitation are bound to find out that the concept of liberty in the novel is problematic in the extreme, for if one takes the ostensible political meaning of the word as a thematic indication, anticipating a sympathetic treatment of the revolutionaries (those who fight for liberty), one is bound to be disappointed. Some of the revolutionaries, like Haldin and Sophia Antonovna, are indeed treated with compassion and respect, but others, like Peter Ivanovitch and Madame de S—, are grossly caricatured and derided, whereas a man like Mikulin, a representative of the autocratic regime, is presented as complex and worthy of respect in his downfall, as he sacrifices himself for the system which 'devours' him (305–6). This unexpected treatment of characters on the 'right' and 'wrong' sides of the cause of liberty should, I believe, constitute sufficient warning against a narrow political interpretation of the novel, as Conrad's sympathies are obviously not enlisted either in the cause of conservative autocracy or in that of the revolution. The thematic significance of 'liberty', highlighted by the epigraph, should, then, be sought for elsewhere.

In his now classical essay, 'The Two Concepts of Liberty', Sir Isaiah Berlin presents two radically different concepts of political liberty.[31] The notion of 'negative' freedom postulates that a man is free 'to the degree in which no human being interferes with [his or her] activity'. This concept of liberty lies at the origin of all theories of Western political liberalism. The 'positive' notion of liberty, according to Berlin, begins with the desire for self-realization. But the self which is to be realized is often perceived as a 'higher', 'ideal' self who should be the 'transcendental, dominant controller' over and above the 'lower' self, an 'empirical bundle of desires and passions to be disciplined and brought to heel'.[32] This division of the self is often employed for the justification of tyranny, as the 'positive' concept of liberty entails an acceptance of authority in so far as it strives to realize what is claimed to be the higher, truer self. People may be prepared to 'barter their own and others' liberty of individual action' in order to assert this 'higher', collective and socialized self.[33] Berlin concludes his essay with a note of warning against this mutation of the 'positive' concept of liberty, which all too often turns upon itself, as it ends in a justification of totalitarian autocracy.

[31] Sir Isaiah Berlin, 'Two Concepts of Liberty', Inaugural Lecture as Chichele Professor of Social and Political Theory (Oxford: Clarendon Press, 1958); repr. in *Four Essays on Liberty* (Oxford, Oxford University Press, 1969), 118–72.
[32] Ibid. 134.   [33] Ibid. 159.

It seems to me that Berlin's essay touches upon a basic and universal human dilemma, but what he defines as the 'positive concept of liberty' might, perhaps, be more aptly described as the need to serve, to belong to a totality larger than one's self. As Berlin observes, this 'deep and incurable metaphysical need' most often finds expression within a religious or a quasi-religious framework. Service, in this context, is conceived as a liberation of a higher, truer self from the bonds of the earthly and the mundane.[34] This view of liberty transcends the political context: I believe it is closely related to what Prof. Kolakowski has called the 'hunger for myth': the need to define the self within a given value system which is felt to be charismatic; the desire to transcend the self and view it as part of a larger whole.[35] The need for 'negative' liberty (i.e. Non-interference, complete individual autonomy, self-sufficiency) and the need to relativize the self within a larger whole are not only the foundations of opposite political ideologies: they are equally powerful and universal human needs, eternally at war with each other. I believe that the dialogic dynamics of *Under Western Eyes* can be understood in terms of this opposition.

The mainspring of the action is, as the narrator indicates at the very outset, the orphanhood of the protagonist, which marks him as an ideal accomplice after the fact, as his involvement would implicate no one but himself. The narrator notes that Razumov's isolation and namelessness also render him morally and psychologically susceptible to the role of the double agent which has been thrust on him (10, 26), and this observation is later validated by Razumov himself (60, 61). There is, another, more problematic dimension to Razumov's orphanhood, an aspect which has hitherto been largely overlooked in critical readings of the novel and of Conrad's work in general. Razumov's orphanhood is, first and foremost, metaphysical. The psychological quest for a father-figure is only a reflection of the need for a sovereign source of authority, a point of reference beyond the protagonist's fragile and isolated self.

Razumov is introduced by the narrator as 'the man who called himself, after the Russian custom, Cyril son of Isidor—Kirylo Sidorovitch—Razumov' (3). His namelessness is, then, the essential condition of his life: 'the word Razumov was the mere label of a

---

[34] Ibid. 80.   [35] *The Presence of Myth*, chap. 3.

solitary individuality. There were no Razumovs belonging to him anywhere. His closest parentage was defined in the statement that he was a Russian' (10–11); 'Distinction would convert the label Razumov into an honoured name' (13–14). The absence of a father, who would have entitled Razumov to a patronymic, assumes a significance beyond its obvious social and psychological implications when one learns that Razumov is in the habit of mentally designating his natural father, Prince K., by the capitalized 'He' (13). This is where the metaphysical dimension comes in, for the search for a father, the need to be authored and authorized, will eventually determine the course chosen by this emotionally and socially starving orphan.

I have argued that the concept of liberty in the novel is psychological and metaphysical rather than political. However, a straightforward religious outlet for the 'incurable metaphysical need' is not an available option for the protagonist who, as we shall presently see, prides himself on his Western (i.e. secular, rational, and materialistic) outlook. The religious concept of freedom-in-service is therefore projected from the metaphysical onto human institutions. The religious tonality which pervades the political discourse is unmistakable: the initial equation of autocracy with enslavement and revolution with liberty, an equation which is ostensibly called for by the epigraph, crumbles under the weight of religious allusion which is equally applied to both parties. The autocrats appropriate a religious mode of discourse to sanction oppression and tyranny: Mr de P—, the Minister of State, is 'invested with extraordinary powers', and is known by his 'mystic acceptance of the principle of autocracy' which he articulates in his famous 'State paper':

the thought of liberty has never existed in the Act of the Creator. From the multitude of men's counsel nothing could come but revolt and disorder; and revolt and disorder in a world created for obedience and stability is sin. It was not Reason but Authority which expressed the Divine intention. God was the Autocrat of the Universe. (7–8)

The same ideas are echoed later with varying degrees of crudity by General T. and Councillor Mikulin, other representatives of authority.

Victor Haldin acts in the name of liberty, but he, too, encodes his political conceptions in religious terminology:

You have enough heart to have heard the sound of weeping and gnashing of teeth this man raised in the land . . . He was uprooting the tender plant. (16)

Men like me leave no posterity, but their souls are not lost. No man's soul is ever lost. It works for itself—or else where would be the sense of self-sacrifice, of martyrdom of conviction, of faith . . . a new revelation shall come out of Russia . . . There is a divine soul in things . . . you forget what's divine in the Russian soul—and that's resignation. . . . I was resigned. I thought 'God's will be done'. (23)

Razumov's betrayal of Haldin is undoubtedly motivated by the interest of self-preservation and ambition, but the ideological transformation he undergoes is more than a cynical rationalization of his baser motives. The decision is, in a sense, made for him when the full extent of his orphanhood dawns on him, when his emotional need for a parent-figure coalesces with a spiritual need for a source of moral authority.

Other men had somewhere a corner of the earth . . . a material refuge. He had nothing. He had not even a moral refuge—the refuge of confidence. To whom should he go with this tale—in all this great, great land? Razumov stamped his foot and under the carpet of snow felt the hard ground of Russia, inanimate, cold, inert, like a sullen and tragic mother hiding her face under a winding sheet. (33)

And then, 'as if by a miracle' he responds to this cold immensity:

It was a sort of sacred inertia. . . . It was a guarantee of duration, of safety . . . of peace. What it needed was not the conflicting aspirations of a people, but a will strong and one: it wanted not the babble of many voices, but a man—strong and one! Razumov stood on the point of conversion. (33)

At that moment, on the point of conversion, Razumov catches a 'glimpse of a passing grey whisker' which evokes 'the complete image of Prince K—', his father. This momentary vision, triggered, no doubt, by the need for 'some other mind's sanction', is perceived as the sign he has been looking for (38–9). The quest for moral sanction is no longer separable from the need for social affiliation and for parental love, the need for the numinous and the need to be named, become one, and Razumov's decision is made. He joins the ranks of those who 'turned to autocracy for the peace of their patriotic conscience as a weary unbeliever, touched by grace, turns

to the faith of his fathers for the blessing of spiritual rest ...
Razumov, in conflict with himself, felt the touch of grace upon his
forehead' (34). But Razumov's conversion to the faith of his father,
the autocrat, is as spurious as the subsequent reunion with Prince
K. turns out to be. After the encounter with General T., whose
autocratic babble sounds like a crude parody of Razumov's newly
acquired faith, it dawns on Razumov that he has enlisted to the
service of demonic powers.

The introduction of the demonic element and its subsequent
ubiquity in the narrative have been viewed by critics as a transgression which needs to be explained away in a novel which so
ostensibly subscribes to the norms and proprieties of the realistic
mode.[36] My own view is that the evident critical discomfort at the
presence of the demonic is probably due to the general avoidance
of the metaphysical aspect of the drama, and it is in these terms
that the demonic should be grappled with. When confronted with
the moral horror of his act, Razumov's need for the numinous, for
a metaphysical frame of reference, is not eradicated but inverted.
The conflict is still perceived in quasi-religious terms, but Haldin
now becomes a Christ-figure, and Razumov, with the touch of
grace or the mark of Cain upon his forehead, takes on the demonic
role to which he believes he has committed himself.

Even at the very moment of betrayal, Razumov's 'diabolical
impulse' to tell Haldin of his betrayal (55), and the 'insane
temptation to grip that exposed throat and squeeze the breath out
of that body' (57), are foregrounded against the thickening cluster
of religious allusions relating to the betrayed man. Haldin talks of
'the guests for the feast of freedom' (56); he tells Razumov that he
has often slept in the stable of the house which is earlier described
as 'a hive of human vermin, a monumental abode of misery
towering on the verge of starvation and despair' (28); he proclaims,
in phrases which reverberate with echoes of the Passion of Christ,
his belief in the immortality of his soul and his readiness to forgive
the destroyers of his body: 'They can kill my body, but they cannot
exile my soul from this world. . . . That is perhaps the reason I am

---

[36] Guerard, *Conrad the Novelist*, 240–1; Claire Rosenfield, *Paradise of Snakes*,
145, 149; H. Gilliam, 'The Daemonic in *Under Western Eyes*', *Conradiana*, 9/2
(1977), 219–36; J. E. Saveson, 'The Moral Discovery of *Under Western Eyes*',
Criticism, 14/1 (1972), 37; Avrom Fleishman, *Conrad's Politics*, 225–6.

ready to die. . . . As to the destroyers of my mere body, I have forgiven them beforehand' (58).[37]

From this point onwards there is an increasingly widening split in Razumov's personality between the thin coating of detached rationality which he tries to maintain along with his claim for individual autonomy and his view of himself as a demonic figure engaged in a transcendental struggle, which gradually takes over and colours his entire outlook. The dialogic quality of the novel can, I think, be traced to an irreconcilable split between the two modes of perception: the Russian mode of perception, which recognizes and accepts the metaphysical, and the 'Western' outlook, which is secular, rational, and materialistic.

Razumov believes that he can rationalize away the metaphysical viewpoint which is essentially Russian—typical of the autocrats and the revolutionaries alike. He tries to opt out of the Russian mode of perception by denying the mysticism of his compatriots and asserting himself as a thinking man, independent and rational. Having had no right to a patronymic, a father's name, he has named himself Razumov, the man of reason. But his on-going search for the father and his essential 'Russianness' compel him to grapple with the metaphysical which he so vehemently denies.

A significant correlative of this attitude is the broken watch which seems to be the touchstone of the protagonist's mode of perception. When Haldin talks to Razumov of his belief in eternity and the immortality of a man's soul, the latter answers sceptically: 'Eternity, of course. I, too, can very well represent it to myself . . . I imagine it, however, as something quiet and dull. There would be nothing unexpected—don't you see? The element of time would be wanting.' And then: 'He pulled out his watch and gazed at it. Haldin turned over on his side and looked at it intently' (59). This silent duel over the conception of time is brought to a conclusion when Haldin leaves the room to meet his executioners, and

---

[37] These and many other instances of biblical allusion in *Under Western Eyes* have been carefully recorded and traced by D. Purdy in 'Peace that Passeth Understanding': The Professor's English bible in *Under Western Eyes*', *Conradiana*, 13/1 (1981), 83–93, but Purdy views these instances as parodic devices which 'lay bare Haldin's messianic delusion, a metaphysical disease that affects Razumov, too' (86), and later—somewhat paradoxically, to my mind—as a reflection of the 'severely limited point of view' of the narrator who uses the English Bible as 'his Baedecker' to find his way in the incomprehensible territory of the Russian mind (88).

Razumov's cherished watch fails him and breaks down (64). In his anxiety over the stopped watch, and his need to know that his act of betrayal has been accomplished, Razumov looks 'wildly about him as if for some means of seizing upon time which seemed to have escaped him altogether. He has never, as far as he could remember, heard the striking of that town clock in his room before this night. And he was not even sure now whether he had heard it really on this night. . . . The faint deep boom of the distant clock seemed to explode in his head—he heard it so clearly' (65). Razumov is clutching at the Western conception of ordered, linear, and irrevocable time, to anchor himself in what he believes is the only existence worthy of a man of reason, but his betrayal of Haldin forcefully initiates him into the timeless realm of the metaphysical.

Having betrayed Haldin in the name of his own individual free will and autonomy, Razumov paradoxically finds that his freedom and individuality begin to dissolve under the new role he has undertaken. He feels trapped, unable to pursue his former life or to start a new one with—like his biblical prototype—nowhere to go to, as Councillor Mikulin acutely perceives (Part IV, chapter 1). His gradual loss of autonomy is, then, not simply an awareness that he is serving as a pawn in a political game, but a reflection of the creeping invasion of the metaphysical, in its demonic dimension, into his self-professed Western (i.e. rational, materialistic, and free) outlook.

The most significant aspect of this process is, of course, Haldin's ubiquitous phantom which pursues Razumov throughout the story. Its first appearances occur even before the act of betrayal.

Suddenly on the snow, stretched on his back right across his path, he saw Haldin, solid, distinct, real, with his inverted hands over his eyes, clad in a brown close-fitting coat and long boots. He was lying out of the way a little as though he had selected that place on purpose. The snow round him was untrodden. The hallucination had such a solidity of aspect that the first movement of Razumov was to reach for his pocket to assure himself that the key of his rooms was there. But he checked the impulse with a disdainful curve of his lips. He understood. His thoughts, concentrated intently on the figure left lying on his bed, had culminated in this extraordinary illusion of the sight. Razumov tackled the phenomenon calmly. With a stern face, without a check and gazing far beyond the vision, he walked on, experiencing nothing but a slight tightening of the chest. After passing he turned his head for a glance, and saw only the unbroken track of his footsteps over the place where the breast of the phantom had been lying. (36–7)

The act of exorcism by trampling on the phantom's breast is also, paradoxically, an admission of its existence by the ritualistic sacrilege.[38] From this point on, Haldin's living body seems to have 'less substance than its own phantom walked over by Razumov in the street white with snow' (55). The apparition of the phantom recurs throughout the story until it becomes one of the fixed characters in the cast of the novel, a constant shadow-figure for Razumov (59, 99, 246, 300, 302).

Various critics have responded to the phantom—as Razumov himself initially does—by attempting to exorcize it, by treating it as a clinical symptom of a diseased, guilt-ridden psyche.[39] I would suggest that this recurrent apparition cannot by exorcized by the power of psychology alone, and that its overt defiance of the realistic convention calls for a different approach. Some of the points made by Paul Coates in The Realist Fantasy are worth noting at this point. Coates follows the distinction between latent and overt doubles suggested by Robert Rogers in his psychoanalytic study of doubles in literature, but observes that

whether 'concealed' doubles appear in traditionally 'realist' works, 'manifest' ones are characteristic of stories in which the writer is conscious that to write a story at all is to decompose the self, and that changes occurring in external reality are altering the very nature of perception, exteriorizing that which seemed condemned to remain locked within the self as an aspiration or dream. Lines between realism and fantasy, selfhood and otherness, begin to dissolve.

Coates further points to 'the double's ironic critique of individuality, the dialectical reversal whereby isolation employs the imagination to generate company out of itself even as it remains real solitude'.[40] Coates's brief discussion of Conrad within this modernist tradition of the overt double does not touch upon Under

---

[38] Berthoud, Joseph Conrad: The Major Phase 175.

[39] Cf. Tanner, 'Nightmare and Complacency: Razumov and the Western Eye', Critical Quarterly, 4/3 (1962), 173–85, Rosenfield, Paradise of Snakes, 139–51, Gilliam, 'The Daemonic in Under Western Eyes', 225.

[40] Paul Coates, The Realist Fantasy: Fiction and Reality since 'Clarissa' (London: Macmillan, 1983), 114–15.

Western Eyes at all, but it seems to me that Haldin's phantom is clearly a case of an overt shadow, and in approaching him one should put aside the urge to defend the conventions of the realistic novel, and attend to its function from a broader viewpoint.

Razumov's betrayal of Haldin has cost him his treasured sense of individual autonomy and freedom. In his refusal to accept the bond of brotherhood, he has condemned himself to live with 'the corpse around his neck' (32). Only by accepting the rejected other, by overtly identifying with him, can he regain his former individuality. The metaphysical oxymoron—which he has had to accept in his need for a father and a name—postulates that he can become himself only when he becomes that other he has denied, that he can attain a measure of freedom only if he should submit to the bond of brotherhood. The concept of doubleness is, in this sense, a reintegration rather than a split of personality.

This process of reintegration by the acceptance of doubleness is at first unconscious and involuntary. Haldin's sudden departure leaves Razumov 'on the borders of delirium. He heard himself suddenly saying, "I confess," as a person might do on the rack. "I am on the rack," he thought' (65). His involuntary identification with the victim is brought out in the long waiting for the culmination of his betrayal. Razumov remains shut up in his rooms as in a prison cell, and the word 'arrested' reverberates in the narrative as it probably does for the man who has been imprisoned in fact:

when he looked at his watch he saw both hands *arrested* at twelve o'clock. . . . He glanced down at the bed on which he had not slept that night. The hollow in the pillow made by the weight of Haldin's head was very noticeable. . . . The idea of going out never occurred to him . . . He spent some time drumming on the window with his finger-tips quietly. In his listless wanderings round he caught sight of his own face in the looking-glass and that *arrested* him. (68–9, my emphases)

The unconscious re-enactment of Haldin's ordeal in prison continues during his interview with Mikulin, when he suddenly conjures up a picture of 'his own brain suffering on the rack—a long pale figure drawn asunder horizontally with terrible force . . . whose face he failed to see . . . the solitude of the racked victim was particularly odious to behold. The mysterious impossibility to see the face . . . inspired a sort of terror' (88). On hearing the definite announcement of Haldin's death, Razumov compulsively acts as the other's mouthpiece, and says: 'He had a belief in a future existence' (94). He will later realize just what the meaning of Haldin's future existence is.

When Razumov appears in Geneva he is wearing a 'brown coat' (178), which he seems to have borrowed from the dead man whose brown coat was the only identifying feature the police could obtain (14, 45). The identification with Haldin is at first forced on him by the need to become one of the revolutionaries, and the incipient pressure of the others' view of him. But the identification seems to go far beyond what is required of him in his role as a double agent, and is entirely out of line with his personality as formerly perceived. In fact, it is the voice of Haldin, the discourse of the betrayed other, which we hear in Razumov's anger at the complacency of the West (189, 191), in his contempt of theories (212), and in his passionate talk of hunger and starvation (221, 227).

Even as he gloats over the 'wrong-headedness', the self-deception, and the false assumptions of Peter Ivanovitch and Sophia Antonovna, the revolutionists who cannot see through his mask (258), and takes 'triumphant pleasure' in deceiving them 'out of [their] own mouth' (261), Razumov does not appear to be in the superior position that one might have expected in view of his superior knowledge of the truth. The irony of his insinuations and *double entendres* recoils on him, as the innocent utterances of those who 'do not know' take on an oracular meaning for him. Peter Ivanovitch defines him as 'a marked personality' (206), a man 'quite above the common—h'm—susceptibilities' (210); the sinister Madam de S— seems to look through him at 'some sort of phantom' in his image (224); and Sophia Antonovna tells him of the need 'to trample down every particle of your own feelings' (245) in echo of the first appearance of the phantom which Razumov had ritualistically trampled on. Razumov's own knowledge of his crime and his position as Cain—a branded man, with nowhere to go to, who is yet mysteriously immune to revenge by the very mark which sets him apart from the fellow men—turns the irony of the situation against him.

The boomerang action of the irony, which Razumov is well aware of, brings about a gradual change in his conscious perception, and forces him to acknowledge the metaphysical, irrational mode he had hitherto claimed to reject. He no longer sees himself as a free agent (249, 297), as he realizes that his superior knowledge and his subsequent ability to deceive and manipulate the other characters are only part of a larger irony of which he himself is the butt. The 'piece of sinister luck' (258) which befalls him as the circumstances surrounding Haldin's betrayal seem to conspire in his favour (the letter from Petersburg, and the suicide of Ziemian-itch which clears him from all suspicion), reinforces the metaphys-ical mode of perception, the 'absurdity' which his intelligence has so vehemently rejected as the opposite of reason and individual freedom (198). He is beginning to suspect—notwithstanding his angry protest that he is not 'a young man in a novel' (186)—that he may, in fact, be part of a larger, transcendental plan: 'This was a comedy of errors. It was as if the devil himself were playing a game with all of them in turn. . . . He interrupted his earnest mental soliloquy with a jocular thought at his own expense. "Hallo! I am falling into mysticism too" ' (284); ' "I have the greatest difficulty in saving myself from the superstition of an active Providence. It's irresistible. . . . The alternative, of course would be the personal Devil of our simple ancestors. But, if so, he had overdone it altogether—the old Father of Lies" ' (350).

Along with this growing—albeit reluctant—acceptance of the metaphysical framework, the 'Russian Curse' (194), Razumov begins to accept his phantom, who now becomes a 'sharer of his mind' (230), a 'shape extremely familiar, yet utterly inexpressive, except for its air of discreet waiting in the dusk. It was not alarming' (246). His acceptance of his identity with the phantom is reflected in his account of the assassination which derives directly from Haldin's viewpoint: 'The snow was coming down very thick, you know. . . . I turned into a narrow side street. . . . I felt inclined to lie down and go to sleep there. . . . I went up *like a shadow.* . . . the stairs were dark. I glided *like a phantom*' (256-7). Only when he is entirely cleared of suspicion, when the phantom seems to have finally been 'walked over' and exorcized, does Razumov discover that it is himself which he had 'given up to destruction' (341). The fear of retribution is superseded by the need for atonement and reintegration. In his private and public confession and in his re-enactment of Haldin's last hours (365), Razumov eventually accepts the 'doubleness' which has bound him to the other.

The acceptance of this bond is marked by the almost voluntary submission to the piercing of his ear-drums, in its distinct biblical echo:

If thou buy an Hebrew servant, six years he shall serve: and in the seventh he shall go out free for nothing. If he came in by himself, he shall go out by himself . . . If his master have given him a wife, and she have born him sons and daughters; the wife and her children shall be her master's, and he shall go out by himself. And if the servant shall plainly say, I love my master, my wife and my children; I will not go out free: Then his master shall bring him unto the judges; he shall also bring him to the door, or unto the door post; and his master shall bore his ear through with an aul; and he shall serve him forever.[41]

The symbolic piercing of the slave's ears, which marks him as a man who had willed his own bondage, takes on a different significance in *Under Western Eyes*. Razumov has, in a sense, renounced his autonomy and freedom in his recognition of the bond and in his need to confess and be punished according to a moral code which his 'superior reason' had earlier rejected. He renounces the Western notion of liberty as the individual's freedom from interference (the 'negative' concept of freedom, in Berlin's terms), for the need to serve.

The 'Western Eyes' through which the story is filtered and rendered are those of the old teacher of languages who—while acting from the vantage point of a virtually omniscient narrator—persistently disclaims his knowledge and draws attention to the limitations of his Western outlook and his inability to understand the characters. This disturbing duality in the position of the narrator—the incompatibility of his pose as 'a dense occidental' (112) with his virtual omniscience—has led some critics to dismiss him as an awkward and not wholly successful technical device,[42] while others have chosen to accept his self-derogatory attitude at face value, and treat him as an obtuse, complacent, and unwitting foil to the passionate drama of the other characters.[43] I would attempt to relate the Western eyes of the narrator to the developement of the protagonist's story.

Like Razumov, the old teacher of languages predicates his story

[41] Exodus 21: 2–6, see also Deuteronomy 15: 17.
[42] Cox, *The Modern Imagination*, 104.
[43] Cf. Tony Tanner, 'Nightmare and Complacency'; Robert Secor, 'The Function of the Narrator in *Under Western Eyes*', *Conradiana*, 3/1 (1970–1), 27–38. Daniel Schwarz takes up the case for the narrator in *Conrad: 'Almayer's Folly' to 'Under Western Eyes'*, 195–211.

from the very outset on the fact of his 'otherness'. What he claims to offer is a Western viewpoint, radically different from and hostile to Russian mysticism, lawlessness, and cynicism:

This is not a story of the West of Europe. . . . It is unthinkable that any young Englishman should find himself in Razumov's situation. This being so it would be a vain enterprise to imagine what he would think. The only safe surmise to make is that he would not think as Mr Razumov thought at this crisis of his fate. . . . This is but a crude and obvious example of the different conditions of Western thought. (25)

My mind, the decent mind of an old teacher of languages feels more and more the difficulty of the task. . . . the rendering of the moral conditions ruling over a large portion of this earth's surface; conditions not easily to be understood, much less discovered in the limits of a story until some key-word is found. (67)

The key word which the narrator finds to render the Russian state of mind is 'cynicism':

In its pride of numbers, in its strange pretensions of sanctity, and in the secret readiness to abase itself in suffering, the spirit of Russia is the spirit of cynicism. It informs the declarations of statesmen, the theories of her revolutionists, and the mystic vaticinations of prophets to the point of *making freedom sound like a form of debauch*, and the Christian virtues themselves appear actually indecent. (67, my emphasis)

The teacher goes on to condemn 'the propensity of lifting every problem from the plane of the understandable by means of some sort of mystic expression' which is 'very Russian' (104), and repeatedly asserts the irreconcilable gap between the Western and the Russian frame of mind (141, 163, 169, 202, 287, 293, 377), which, he claims, makes it almost impossible for him to understand the protagonists or to communicate their story to the Western reader.

But the narrator protests too much. The ostensible 'otherness' of Razumov and of the other Russians, which he so often reiterates, gradually wears down as the reader realizes that the old teacher of languages has, in fact, much in common with the apparently incomprehensible protagonist of his story: both of them are lonely and reticent and yet have the gift of inspiring confidence in others, both were born in Russia and claim an affinity with the West and particularly with England, both are initially the exponents of rationality, and both are, of course, in love with Nathalie Haldin.

The parallels between Razumov and the narrator have been pointed out by several critics, and interpreted as symptoms of a psychological 'doubling', similar to that which links Razumov and Haldin, a reflection of a suppressed part of one's personality in another's. The old teacher of languages is, according to this view, a potential version of Razumov himself, had his career not been cut short by the betrayal.[44]

But this 'doubling' can also be viewed as a reflection of an ideological-cultural relationship. The narrator who introduces himself as a sample of the Western mind, who is—as Berthoud points out—'on guard against metaphysics'[45]—represents the alternative to the 'Russian' state of mind. He lives, in Berlin's terms, by the 'negative' concept of liberty. Razumov, who, as we have already seen, is initially trying to opt out of the passionate transcendentalism of his compatriots and glorifies (Western) rationality, eventually discovers that he cannot break free of the metaphysical, and submits to it. The narrator cannot will himself into Razumov's submission, but as the story unfolds he gradually learns to perceive his inability to do so as a lack, an absence in himself and in what he represents. Far from being a superior vantage point of reason, individual autonomy, and freedom, the West becomes a wasteland of sterile proprieties and impotent grief.

The first intimations of the narrator's inadequacy concern his relationship with Nathalie Haldin. The teacher is obviously in love with the girl, but persistently disqualifies himself as a lover: 'I became aware, notwithstanding my years, of how attractive physically her personality would be to a man capable of appreciating in a woman something else than the mere grace of femininity. . . . She was—to look at her was enough—very capable of being roused by an idea or simply by a person. At least so I judged with I believe an unbiased mind; for clearly my person could not be the person— and as to my ideas! . . .' (102); 'I am not ashamed of the warmth of my regard for Miss Haldin. It was, it must be admitted, an unselfish sentiment, being its own reward' (164, see also 143, 179–80, 184, 318–19). This emotional withdrawal from the role

    [44] Rosenfield, *Paradise of Snakes*, 161–6; Gilliam, 'The Daemonic in *Under Western Eyes*', 227–32.
    [45] Berthoud, *Joseph Conrad: The Major Phase*, 163.

of a lover can only be understood against the background of the narrator's withdrawal from life itself.

Another symptom of this withdrawal is the narrator's insistence on his position as an outsider, a non-participant in the drama he narrates: 'Removed by the difference of age and nationality as if into the sphere of another existence, I produced, even upon myself, the effect of a dumb helpless ghost, of an anxious immaterial thing that could only hover about without the power to protect or guide by as much as a whisper' (126); '. . . and once more I had the sense of being out of it . . . altogether out of it, on another plane whence I could only watch her from afar' (170). He repeatedly refers to himself as 'a mere attendant' (327), a 'disregarded Westerner' (329), 'a helpless spectator' (336, see also 339, 345, 346, 347, 376–7).

As we can see, the narrator's denial of his own part in the action intensifies and builds up towards the end of his story. It seems that the greater his emotional involvement is, the more intent he becomes on repressing it. The withdrawal from the world of desire and will culminates in a virtual death, when the narrator realizes that he has ceased to exist for the other protagonists: 'I observed them. There was nothing else to do. My existence seemed so utterly forgotten by these two that I dared not now make a movement . . . I knew that the next time they met I would not be there, either remembered or forgotten. I would have virtually ceased to exist for both these young people' (346–7).

And yet, if the narrator is not a full protagonist, by his own admission, he is not an authorial figure either. His somewhat pedantic apologies for his omniscience (25, 66, 100, 162, 183, 357, 379) and his need to explain away the complete access he has to Razumov's whereabouts and 'movements d'âme' (105), are as persistent as his professions of non-involvement in the protagonists' tale. This non-authorial pose—ostensibly affected for the sake of authenticity (as Conrad claims in his Author's Note)—places the narrator in a peculiar borderline position, a position which has been responded to in the recent extensive commentary on the metafictional aspect of *Under Western Eyes*.[46] My own view is that

---

[46] Avrom Fleishman, 'Speech and Writing in *Under Western Eyes*', in N. Sherry, ed, *Joseph Conrad: A Commemoration*, 119–28; F. Kermode, 'Secrets and Narrative Sequence', *Critical Inquiry* 7 (1980), 83–101, repr. in *Essays on Fiction*

the non-authorial pose is related to the absence of a metaphysical dimension in the world represented by the narrator, an absence which is often construed as freedom. What the narrator views, with his Western eyes, as Russian 'cynicism' (67), a tendency to clothe sordid realities in the metaphysical discourse, reflects—for Razumov at least—the need to serve, or the 'positive' concept of freedom.

For the old teacher of languages, a true representative of the secular, rational West, the reconciliation of service with freedom is no longer acceptable and he retains his autonomy and independence to the end. But the price of freedom is dearly paid: his non-participation corrodes his very existence until he virtually ceases to be. The terms of Razumov's initial dilemma 'whether he should continue to live' when deprived of his free will and autonomy by the bond with Haldin which has been thrust on him (77–8), are reversed on the narrator. His own exile is the culmination of a self-imposed process of withdrawal and repression, in comparison to which Razumov's eventual choice of 'enslavement' seems to be the happier alternative. This concept of freedom as non-interference may lead to what Berlin calls 'the retreat to the inner citadel', an attempt to avoid the frustration of one's desires by curbing them, by choosing not to desire what is unattainable. It is the 'traditional self-emancipation of ascetics and quietists' which enables them to retain their independence of the world by remaining isolated 'on its edges'.[47]

The old teacher of languages is not an obtuse narrator. His tragedy lies precisely in the fact that he is perceptive and intelligent enough to recognize his captivity in the desert of freedom. He tells Nathalie to go back to Russia (133), and when she finally does, he allows himself a note of bitterness, entirely self-directed and impotent: 'It was all to be as I had wished it. And it was to be for life. We should never see each other again. Never! I gathered this success to my breast' (373). His muted grief and bitterness are far more eloquent than his former verbosity. He becomes, in a sense, an ageing Orpheus: the silences on which he had prided himself

(London: Routledge & Kegan Paul, 1983), 133–54; Ron Schleifer, 'Public and Private Narrative in *Under Western Eyes*', *Conradiana*, 9/3 (1977), 232–54; Penn R. Szittya, 'Metafiction: The Double Narration in *Under Western Eyes*', *ELH*, 48 (1981), 817–40.

    [47] Berlin, 'Two Concepts of Liberty; 122, 135.

(118) have failed him. His Euridice has chosen to go back to the Hell of Russia, to 'burn rather than rot' in Geneva with him.

In the course of the story the narrator is offered, more than once, an opportunity to step into his story, as it were, to become a full participant rather than a 'helpless spectator' by asserting his feelings for Nathalie or his affinity with Razumov. But the Westerner in him can never attain the ultimate submission to this 'doubleness' as Razumov eventually does. And yet, there are moments when the old teacher of languages unconsciously approaches his 'double' to an extent which belies his protestations of 'otherness'. His unacknowledged rivalry with Razumov, who is in so many ways his younger 'double', asserts itself in an unconscious imitation of the protagonists' actions, as when they both stand at night outside Nathalie's lighted windows (200–1), or in further suppression and self-abnegation, when the teacher chooses to avoid the girl in her meetings with Razumov (201), and offers 'to withdraw' when they meet (174).

This unconscious doubling process which underlies the narrator's relationship with the protagonist can account for two major problem areas in the novel which have not, to my mind, been satisfactorily incorporated either in the 'political' or in the 'psychological' interpretations of this work. The first difficulty is the narrator's view of Geneva and of the Swiss. Geneva, stronghold of democracy and liberalism, is described by the narrator as 'comely without grace, and hospitable without sympathy' (141), and the Swiss as obtuse and complacent: 'I observed a solitary Swiss couple, whose fate was made secure from the cradle to the grave by the perfected mechanism of democratic institutions in a republic that could almost be held in the palm of one's hand. The man, colourlessly uncouth,. . . The woman, rustic and placid . . .' (175). These recurrent expressions of contempt for the paragon of Western political virtues are not quite in keeping with the ostensible attitude of a man who regards himself as the 'Western eye'. The explanation for this puzzling viewpoint, and its contradiction of the narrator's self-professed Westernism seems to lie in the fact that a similar attitude to Geneva and to the Swiss recur in the private thoughts of Razumov himself.

Razumov turned his back on it [i.e. the view of the city] with contempt. He thought it odious—oppressively odious—in its unsuggestive finish; the very perfection of mediocrity attained at last after centuries of toil and culture . . . 'Democratic virtue. There are no thieves here, apparently,' he muttered to himself . . . He looked back sourly at an idle working man lounging on a bench . . . 'Elector! Eligible! Enlightened!' Razumov muttered to himself. 'A brute, all the same'. (203–4)

Despite his 'Western' mind, the narrator's view of Geneva seems like a reflection of that of his protagonist. The old teacher of languages reaches out of his isolation for an instant, borrowing his antagonist's voice and discourse, and bridges over the 'otherness' which, he insists, separates them.

On the structural level, too, there seems to be an unresolved oddity in the relationship between the narrator and his protagonist. The pedantic citation of documents and sources and the careful demarcation of the story and the narrator's comments on it are suddenly loosened in Part III, in which the narrator often 'walks into' his own story, and the frequent shifts from Razumov's viewpoint to his own are veiled and baffling (see 198, 200, 289, 291). The very nature of this particular flaw in a novel which is so overtly concerned with point of view should suggest that it is not merely a technical flaw on the writer's part. I believe that this sudden dissolution of the structural border-lines between the narrator and his protagonist ought to be accounted for as an extension of the doubling process. When the teacher enters his own story he acknowledges his involvement in it. When he sees the action virtually through his protagonist's eyes and forgets for a while his own Western outlook, he acknowledges the 'doubleness' which is offered to him.

The teacher of languages persistently apologizes for and explains away his virtual omniscience by elaborate references to the sources and documents he had patched together in the making of the story. This uncomfortable attitude to authorial omniscience, the non-authorial pose of the narrator, is highly symptomatic of a world which has lost its view of an *auctor mundi* and denies the relatedness of the ethical to the Absolute. The old teacher of languages, thoroughly modern and Westernized in his renunciation of knowledge and authority, appropriately concludes his story on a note of confusion and loss, with a shrug, as it were. The reader's own sense of lack and frustration in the face of this epilogue may be a testimony not only to the usual preference for neat, well-rounded endings, but to a more profound and significant longing for an authorial voice in the wilderness of our Western freedom.

C. *THE SHADOW-LINE*

The Author's Note to *The Shadow-Line* is almost entirely devoted to a denial of the supernatural elements which early reviewers have noted in the story: 'This story . . . was not intended to touch on the supernatural. . . . I believe that if I attempted to put the strain of the Supernatural on it, it would fail deplorably and exhibit an unlovely gap. But I could never have attempted such a thing . . .' (ix)

The author's explicit directive that the novella should be read as a *Bildungsroman*, an account of 'the change from youth, care-free and fervent, to the more self conscious and more poignant period of maturer life (x), and his adamant disavowals of the supernatural elements have been obediently attended to by critics. *The Shadow-Line* has been hailed as a story of moral initiation whose main ideas are 'stated with such unusual explicitness that it hardly seems to call for analysis'; as a presentation of simple, straightforward, and clear-cut moral distinctions, 'less complex in design and markedly free from all the flow of lush rhetoric and moralizing' that 'disfigure' Conrad's other works; as a 'public gesture' which affirms the individual's dependence on the community; and as a celebration of the 'moral question of responsibility and work as a technique of survival'.[48] This common-sensical approach to *The Shadow-Line* not only enjoys the author's explicit approval, but has the obvious advantage of compatibility with the secular, materialistic, and rational mode of perception practised by our Western eyes. It seems to me, however, that a certain measure of scepticism is called for when one is directed to overlook one of the most conspicuous parameters of this work, which so often and so blatantly violates the proprieties of realism.

Conrad's indulgence in a more than casual flirting with the

---

[48] Ian Watt, 'Story and Idea in Conrad's *The Shadow-Line*,' *Critical Quarterly*, 2/2 (1960), 133–48; D. Hewitt, *Joseph Conrad*, 112–17; B. Johnson, *Conrad's Models of Mind*, pp. 136–9; Gary Geddes, *Conrad's Later Novels*, 81–113. As one can see in this sampling of critical views which ranges from the 1960s to the 1980s, the reception of *The Shadow-Line* has not been affected by the more recent, suspicious attitude to the author's authority.

supernatural—which, I hope, will become apparent in the course of this discussion—is not the only difficulty in the story.

There are other problem areas which are not resolved by the straightforward reading of this work: what is the point of the long episode on shore which precedes the 'real story' of the narrator's trial at sea? What is the function of the conflict with Hamilton, the narrator's would-be rival for the command? How do the obvious echoes of *The Ancient Mariner* serve the theme?

It seems to me that this novella which so successfully pretends to be a straightforward *Bildungsroman* is yet another testimony of the need for the reinstatement of metaphysics. *The Shadow-Line*, no less than *Heart of Darkness* and *Under Western Eyes*, traces the quest of the protagonist for that 'sovereign power' which would author and authorize him.

The story begins with the narrator's inexplicable resignation from his comfortable position as mate of a steamship. His recurrent emphasis on the irrationality of his motives and his description of the state of mind which had driven him to this act are not unlike Marlow's account of his outlook just before his journey into the heart of darkness:

I left . . . as though all unknowing I had heard a whisper or seen something. Well—perhaps! One day I was perfectly right and the next everything was gone—glamour, flavour, interest, contentment—everything. (5).

I was more discontented, disgusted, and dogged than ever. The past eighteen months, so full of new and varied experience, appeared a dreary, prosaic waste of days. I felt—how shall I put it?—that *there was no truth to be got out of them*. (7, my emphasis)

That obscure feeling of life being a waste of days . . . had driven me out of a comfortable berth, away from men I liked, to flee from *the menace of emptiness* . . . A great discouragement fell on me. *A spiritual drowsiness.* . . . There was nothing original, nothing new, startling, informing to expect from the world. (23, my emphasis)

This state of *ennui*, a need to break away from the mundane in search of some enlightenment or 'truth', and the view of the voyage as a pilgrimage, a journey of spiritual redemption, lay the ground for the religious overtones of the narrative which follows.

The narrator's younger self assumes a pose of world-weary scepticism in his dealings with Captain Giles, but his account of their peculiar relationship is embedded in a quasi-religious discourse which seems to belie the ostensible tone of the narrative. The cynical, casual posture is deflated by the persistent recurrence of metaphysical allusions in the account, even as the narrator tries to undercut and suppress them with sarcastic asides. Of his first encounter with Captain Giles he says: 'To me (I know how absurd it is) he looked like a church warden' (12). The young man's resistance to what he regards as an unwelcome interference in his life gives way before 'the influence of Captain Giles' mysterious earnestness' (25), as he admits that his own 'will [has] nothing to do with it' (25). The narrator's ultimate, albeit reluctant, concession to the old man's mysterious wisdom turns the latter into an archetypal mentor-figure and guide: 'I . . . perceived Captain Giles . . . surveying quietly the scene, *his own handiwork*, if I may express it in this way. His smouldering black pipe was very noticeable in his big, *paternal* fist . . . He exhaled an atmosphere of virtuous sagacity thick enough for any innocent soul to fly to confidently. *I flew to him*' (26–7, my emphasis).

These suggestions of the paternal aspect of Captain Giles, the architect of the story, as it were, are further reinforced by the recurrent allusions to his role as a guardian figure, not only for the young narrator but for the other characters as well. His compassion for the wretched stranger in the officers' home (16), and his defence of the pathetic steward (39) as well as his apparent omniscience which enables him to 'see the inside' of things (38), and his active intervention in the narrator's fate, established him as a semi-divine moral authority in this part of the world which he seems to be 'looking after' (39).[49]

The narrator's acceptance of the summons for the command of the ship is also coloured by a quasi-religious attitude, which is again only imperfectly overlaid with deprecatory sarcasm:

The emphatic He [i.e. Captain Ellis] was the supreme authority, the Marine superintendent, the Harbour-Master,—a very great person in the eyes of every quill-driver in the room. But that was nothing to the opinion he held of his own greatness. Captain Ellis looked upon himself as a sort

[49] The allusion to the parable of the Unjust Steward (Luke 16: 1–13)—the steward's inability to collect the money from Hamilton, and his attempt to set the accounts right by a dishonest act—also establish Captain Giles as the figure of 'the lord' who 'commended the unjust steward' (Luke 16: 8). The allusion to the parable is later reinforced in the figure of Ransome, who is clearly designated as the 'faithful and wise steward' (Luke 12: 42).

of divine (pagan) emanation, the deputy-Neptune of the circumambient
seas. If he did not actually rule the waves, he pretended to rule the fate of
the mortals whose lives were cast upon the waters. (29–30)

But this heavy-handed sarcasm seems to recoil on the young man
when it appears that the superhuman powers he mockingly ascribes
to the Harbour-Master are, in fact, more real to him than he would
be willing to admit:

He gave [the agreement] to me to read, and when I handed it back to him
with the remark that I accepted its terms, the deputy-Neptune signed it,
stamped it with his own exalted hand, folded it in four . . ., and presented
it to me—a gift of extraordinary power for, as I put it in my pocket, my
head swam a little. (32)

The narrator's acceptance of the command marks the first stage in
the subtle undermining of naturalistic narrative conventions. His
allusions to the fantastic become less inhibited and more frequent.
His use of the terminology of the supernatural is no longer qualified
by scepticism: 'It was only another miraculous manifestation of
that day of miracles' (35); 'I had been specially destined for that
ship I did not know, by some power higher than the prosaic
agencies of the commercial world' (36); 'I was very much like
people in fairy tales. Nothing ever astonishes them' (40). What we
have here, in Conrad's words, is 'the conception of life as an
enchanted state' (ix).

One should note, however, that the narrator's emphasis at this
first innocent phase is on the exclusion of ethics from the fairy-tale
context of his account:

I perceived that my imagination had been running on conventional
channels and that my hope had always been drab stuff. I had envisaged a
command as . . . the result of faithful service . . . There is something
distasteful in the notion of a reward . . . And now I had my command,
absolutely in my pocket. (36)

Here I was, invested with a command in the twinkling of an eye, not in
the common course of human affairs, but more as if by enchantment. (39)

The narrator's younger self acknowledges the fantastic, but relates
it to a realm which is entirely divorced from the ethical. Being
elected has nothing to do with merit:

In that community I stood, like a king in his country, in a class all by
myself. I mean an hereditary king, not a mere elected head of state. I was

brought here to rule by an agency as remote from the people and as inscrutable to them as the Grace of God. (62)

At this stage the narrator's attitude is not unlike that of Hamilton, his would-be rival for the command. Hamilton is a man who 'won't settle his bills' at the officer's home (10), who has a tremendous sense of his own importance (11), and regards both the narrator and Captain Giles as 'rank outsiders' (11, 12). The narrator's initial view of his own 'election' for the command as a miracle which does not have to be deserved or justified by merit, as well as his recurrent expressions of contempt for all the others— Captain Ellis, Captain Giles, and especially the pathetic steward who does not seem to him 'very fit to live' (39)—are all indicative of a potential affinity with Hamilton, who is 'full of dignity for the station in life Providence had been pleased to place him in' (11).

Captain Giles, the mentor-figure, realizes that the young officer will have to undergo a painful initiation ordeal—a *rite de passage*—which will inevitably exact a heavy toll, if he is not to turn into another Hamilton. His apparently innocent and technical question regarding the narrator's arrangements for the homeward journey—"paid your passage money yet?" (18)—takes on a larger significance on a second reading: the passage of the young man will indeed have to be paid for.

From the moment of his boarding the ship, the narrator's account assumes a different shade as it plunges deeper and deeper into a supernatural context. The undeserved blessing seems to turn into a curse; the enchantment becomes an evil spell. The nightmarish context is formed by the narrator's use of adjectival tags suggesting a sense of unreality and absurdity: Burns's physiognomy is 'pugnacious in (strange to say) a ghastly sort of way' (53), he looks at the narrator 'with that strange air as if all this were make-believe', and there is 'an odd stress in the situation' (54) long before anything happens to warrant these allusions to the unnatural.

These signals of the uncanny multiply and thicken as the story unfolds: Burns turns out to be a 'man of enigmatic moods' whose statements are 'obscurely suggestive' (56), the narrator's predecessor is visualized as 'a remarkably peculiar old man' (58), and his mistress is portrayed as a diabolic parody of the siren who lures the sailors to madness and death with her sweet songs: 'an awful, mature, white female with rapacious nostrils and a cheaply ill-omened stare in her enormous eye' resembling a 'low-class medium' or a fortune teller. The 'secret of her sortilege' is, as the narrator sardonically conjectures, the musical instrument she is holding (59).

The suggestions of the supernatural through the relatively simple device of repeated adjectival tags are augmented by more sophisticated devices, the most interesting of which is the 'delayed decoding' effect, in which the immediate sensory effect of an event precedes and subordinates its 'real' significance of function.[50] Some instances of this effect occur in *The Shadow-Line*, enhancing the weird resistance of experience to human understanding and control. The first instance occurs when the narrator boards the ship: 'the first thing I saw down there was the upper part of a man's body projecting backwards, as it were, from one of the doors at the foot of the stairs' (52). The grotesque sight turns out, of course, to be a whole man, who later dies of the tropical fever. This description is also an instance of what Watts termed 'reductive reification', a 'presentation of the animate as though it were inanimate, the human being as though he were a mere thing',[51] which increases the sense of absurdity and disconnectedness. The second instance of the 'delayed decoding' effect occurs when the narrator goes down to Mr Burns's cabin to tell him of the missing quinine: 'He was sitting up in his bunk, his body looking immensely long, his head drooping a little sideways, with affected complacency. He flourished, in his trembling hand, on the end of a forearm no thicker than a stout walking-stick, a shining pair of scissors which he tried before my very eyes to jab at his throat.' The horror of the narrator, and the reader, at this sight, lingers on even after the narrator's explanation that, 'in reality, he was simply overtaxing his returning strength in a shaky attempt to clip off the thick growth of his red beard' (89–90). The third instance occurs on the night of the storm when the narrator trips over 'a thing' as he paces the deck: 'It was something big and alive. Not a dog—more like a ship, rather . . . It was an added and fantastic horror which I could not resist . . . I could see It—that Thing!' (115). The 'thing'

---

[50] The term 'delayed decoding' has been suggested by Ian Watt. Cedric Watts's illuminating study, 'Conrad's Absurdist Techniques: A Terminology', deals with this and other alienating devices in Conrad's work. *Conradiana*, 9/2 (1977), 141–8.

[51] Ibid. 142.

turns out to be Mr Burns, who has left his sick-bed and climbed up on deck.

Throughout the ordeal the narrator still insists on his ability to uphold the distinction between the fantastic and the real, which he maintains as a proof of his 'sanity' against the mounting hysteria of Mr Burns, who is entangled in his 'fancies' and superstitions. But the question of sanity is more complex than that. One should remember the retrospective commentary of the older self which cautions the reader at the very beginning not to accept the younger self's judgement at face value or to overrate the Western virtue of sanity on which he places such a high premium: 'It never occurred to me then that I didn't know in what soundness of mind exactly consisted and what a delicate and, upon the whole, unimportant matter it was' (21). This qualification, as well as the opinion voiced by Captain Giles that 'everybody in the world is a little mad' (42), undercuts the narrator's—and probably the reader's—neat conception of the bounds of normality.

If sanity consists in the exclusion of all but material, natural interpretations of the world, than the narrator is, indeed, close to losing it in the course of his ordeal, and his occasional lapses into Burns's mode of perception seem to justify his mounting fears for his 'soundness of mind': 'It's like being bewitched upon my word' (84): 'I believed in it [i.e. the quinine]. I pinned my faith to it. It would save the men, the ship, break the spell ... like a magic powder working against mysterious malefices' (88). The young Captain's 'sane' view of the natural world is assailed and undermined by the elements themselves: the comforting regularity of nature is disrupted by what seems to be a purposeful conspiracy of unseen forces against the ship. There are some notable instances of what C. Watts calls the 'antipathetic fallacy', a presentation of nature as actively and deliberately hostile to man.[52] The climate attacks Mr Burns with 'the swiftness of an invisible monster ambushed in the air, in the water, in the mud of the river bank' (67). The darkness rises around the ship 'like a mysterious emanation from the dumb and lonely waters' (73–4), The stars seem 'weary of waiting for daybreak' (77), and the rising sun turns the land into a 'mere dark vapour, a doubtful, massive shadow trembling in the hot glare' (77). The fever seems to have 'stretched

---

[52] Ibid. 141.

its claw' after the crew over the sea (79), the cape is 'an ominous retreating shadow in the last gleams of twilight' (81), and the ship drifts with 'mysterious currents' whose 'stealthy power' matches the action of 'fitful and deceitful' winds (83–4, see also 104–5).

The mariner's meteorological knowledge and navigational skills, those scientific, objective tools by which man can (or so he believes) set a destination for himself and control his course, are entirely invalidated, as it seems that invisible powers have 'put out of joint the meteorology of this part of the world' which has gone 'utterly wrong' (84). The conclusion of the young captain in the face of this meteorological wreckage, is that 'only purposeful malevolence could account for it' (87). 'The impenetrable darkness beset the ship so close that it seemed that by thrusting one's hand over the side one could touch some unearthly substance. There was in it an effect of inconceivable terror and of inexpressible mystery' (108).

Other 'absurdist techniques', as defined by Watts, contribute to this overwhelming sense of alienation and hostility of nature to man. The 'frustrating context', a context which 'appears to render unattainable the goal of an activity', predominates throughout the efforts of the narrator and his crew to set the ship in motion, and blends with a 'dwarfing perspective'[53] of the ship and its men in the grip of hostile cosmic forces: the sea is 'gorgeous and barren, monotonous and without hope under the empty curve of the sky' (91); 'They are there: stars, sun, sea, light, darkness, space, great waters; the formidable Work of the Seven Days, into which mankind seems to have blundered unbidden. Or else decoyed' (97);

This nightmarish experience which the young Captain goes through completes the diametric reversal of the initial fairy-tale context: the 'enchanted state' has turned into a horrifying evil spell, the king has turned into a scape-goat. But the difference between the two states is not yet a qualitative one: both the fairy-tale and the nightmare are conceived as arbitrary, random states. Both are undeserved and inexplicable. It is at this point that one should examine the relationship of the novella with its apparent literary model.

The obvious thematic and verbal echoes of Coleridge's *Rime of the Ancient Mariner* which resonate throughout the story have been noted by Cedric Watts:

---

[53] *Conradiana*, 9/2 (1977), 143.

In each case the vessel seems accursed: it becomes becalmed and seems doomed to drift the seas for ever. In 'The Ancyent Marinere,' the men of the crew die but their ghosts man the ship. In *The Shadow-Line*, the men undergo such severe illness that they are described as ghosts. . . . In the poem, the curse comes from a subaqueous spirit, nine fathoms deep. . . . And in the novel, the curse comes from the subaqueous spirit of a captain buried at sea.

Watts also notes some remarkable verbal echoes in the descriptions of the becalmed ship in both works, of the narrator's feeling that the crew regard him with reproach, and of the drenching rain that marks the lifting of the curse.[54]

I would suggest that the significance of this literary relationship lies not in the resemblance of *The Shadow-Line* to its poetic model, but in its marked divergence from it. Whereas the evil spell is cast on the Mariner's ship as a result of an evident breach of ethics, the curse which seems to be laid upon the narrator's ship has not been incurred by any ethical transgression on his part. It is as unmerited as his former 'election' had been. There can be little doubt that the young Captain is, indeed, worthy of his command, and that none of the misfortunes of the ship is due to negligence on his part. His failure to discover the substitution of the quinine is largely extenuated by the reassurances of the doctor that he had made the inspection himself, that 'everything was completed and in order' (71), and the Captain could 'put his trust' in his provision of quinine (80). Apart from this problem, it is obvious that the young Captain looks after the health of the ailing crew from the very start: 'Care was taken to expose them as little as possible to the sun. They were employed on light work under the awnings. And the humane doctor commended me' (66). He spends the entire seventeen days and nights on deck, on his own, with very little food or sleep: 'No doubt I must have been snatching short dozes when leaning against the rail for a moment in sheer exhaustion . . .' (98); 'I suppose at that period I did exist on food in the usual way; but the memory is now that in those days life was sustained on invisible anguish . . .' (105); he takes part in the physical work, toiling with his exhausted crew as one of them: 'Of course, I took the lead in the work myself . . . I stood amongst them like a tower

[54] C. Watts, *The Deceptive Text: An Introduction to Covert Plots* (Sussex: Harvester Press, 1984), 94–6.

of strength, impervious to disease and feeling only the sickness of my soul' (109). The narrator's compassion for his men, his entire devotion to his task, and his love for the ship prove him to be worthy of his place in the dynasty to which he believed he had been rather randomly elected.

And yet, in spite of his own testimony, the Captain believes himself to be entirely responsible for the misfortunes of the ship. 'The person I should never forgive was myself ... The seed of everlasting remorse was sown in my breast' (95); 'No confessed criminal had ever been so oppressed by his sense of guilt' (96); 'I feel as if all my sins have found me out' (106); 'I waited for some time, fighting against the weight of my sins, against my sense of unworthiness ...' (109, see also 111, 117, 121, 126). What, then, is the trigger of this heavy sense of guilt and shame to which the young Captain all but abandons himself? What is the source of the overpowering *mea culpa* with which he responds to his ill luck? Why does he use the heavily loaded term 'sin' for what is, at worst, an understandable omission? The answer to these questions which are, to my mind, the thematic nexus of this puzzle-ridden novella, may be suggested by the parameters of the metaphysical mode.

The narrator's need for a coherent frame of reference, for a 'truth' to be got out of life, invests the apparently inexplicable chain of misfortunes with an ethical significance. This need for meaning—however arbitrarily constructed or imposed on an essentially meaningless existence—is what bridges the 'unlovely gap' to which Conrad refers in his Author's Note, for the story is not concerned with the work of supernatural powers but with man's need for a metaphysical frame of reference, a continuum between the material and the ethical spheres. If the young captain could formerly, in his state of bliss, believe his luck to be as arbitrary and undeserved as that of the characters in fairy-tales, he cannot treat his present misfortunes in the same way. The notion of reward and punishment, though hardly supported by experience, is as primal and deep-rooted as the need to find order in the world.

The narrator's need to comprehend the objective world within an ethical conception, to draw a moral from his own story, as it were, brings the ethical dimension into the account. Paradoxically, it is the young Captain's perverse sense of guilt and shame (for sins which he had not committed), and his view of the inexplicable and apparently random conspiracy of nature against the ship as a punishment, which help him impose some order on the surrounding madness. Here, again, redemption is brought about by the reversal of the archetypal transgression. The narrator, who had initially felt himself to be part of an elect dynasty, a 'composite soul, the soul of command' (53), has now come to discover the other face of his continuity, and the extent of his own responsibility to it. Even at the very beginning of his voyage, when he is still elated with the sense of enchantment and the unmerited grace of the mysterious powers which had brought him to rule the ship (62), he already has a premonition of the presence of the other: 'It struck me that this quietly staring man whom I was watching [in the mirror], both as if he were myself and somebody else, was not exactly a lonely figure. He had his place in a line of men . . .' (53). The young Captain cannot disown the other, the dead predecessor who had betrayed the composite soul of command. His own tortuous voyage is a realization of the other's deranged wishes, his guilt is that of the other man's sins. It is not a coincidence that neither the narrator nor his predecessor are named: they are both designated as 'Captains', sharers of the same role.

The narrator has been initiated in the course of his *rite de passage* into the role of his brother's keeper. The 'sins' which have 'found him out' and for which he is racked with guilt and shame are those of his dead predecessor. It was, in fact, the dead Captain who had sold the quinine; who had refused to face the responsibilities of his command and his crew; who "used to keep the ship loafing at sea for inscrutable reasons" (58); who held the ship at anchor for three weeks in a 'pestilential hot harbour without air' (59), which had probably caused the onslaught of the fever; who wanted to set out 'against a fierce monsoon, with a ship not sufficiently ballasted and with her supply of water not completed' (59–60); and who had literally and explicitly wished for the destruction of both the ship and her crew: ' "If I had my wish, neither the ship nor any of you would ever reach a port. I hope you won't" ' (61). It is only by accepting his sameness with the other, by acknowledging the twin or the double, that the young captain can liberate his men and his ship.

This, then, is the fundamental distinction between the 'supernatural' which Conrad had so vehemently denied and the 'metaphysical' as defined in this study. The 'supernatural' which appears to predominate the first part of the narrator's account is entirely divorced from the ethical sphere, from notions of reward and punishment, merit and guilt. The 'metaphysical' implies a continuum between ethics and physics, an assumption of a transcendental ordering principle. The distinction between these two modes of perception is as wide, or as narrow, as that between magic and religion. The narrator's quest for revelation, for a truth to be got out of life, ends up in a circular course. After twenty-one days of trial by water he returns to the very same port from which he had departed. He has attained a truth which, though less exhilarating than the revelation he had expected, makes it possible for him and for us to conclude the ordeal on a note of redemption.

But Conrad's dalliance with the supernatural seems to have a deconstructive, boomerang effect: the narrator's final truth is still framed within inverted commas, and the apparently affirmative resolution is tainted with the shadow of doubt. The aftermath of the conflict between the supernatural and the metaphysical constructions, as represented by Mr Burns and the narrator respectively, is not conclusive. The actual breaking of the spell seems to be effected in a final nightmarish scene, when Mr Burns pits himself against the 'old dodging Devil' with a burst of mad, mocking laughter (119). One is left with an uneasy suspicion that it may have been the 'exorcising virtue' of this laughter (125), rather than the heroic devotion of the narrator and his crew, which has lifted the curse and saved the ship.

The Shadow-Line is not a naïvely affirmative work. It is not 'about' the reinstatement of metaphysics. The novella is concerned with the all too human need to read experience within a significant ethical framework, with the 'saving illusion' of order and meaning, which is all we have to live by. It is also concerned with the act of reading and the still-incurable need—if the present reader be allowed a personal note—to find a good moral in a good story.

4

The Failure of Textuality

> All the nobler aspects of our life are based upon fictions. . . .
> It is an error to suppose that an absolute truth, an absolute
> criterion of knowledge and behaviour, can be discovered.
> The higher aspects of life are based upon noble delusions.
> (H. Vaihinger, *The Philosophy of As If*, 84)

> Though, strictly speaking, life is but a web of illusion and a
> dream within a dream, it is a dream that needs to be managed
> with the utmost discretion, if it is not to turn into a nightmare.
> In other words, however much life may mock the metaphysi-
> cian, the problem of conduct remains. (Irving Babbitt, *Rous-
> seau and Romanticism*, xiv)

THE problem underlying this last section of the discussion is,
once again, the concept of 'life as a text'. Conrad is still concerned
with, to use Stein's words, the question of 'how to be', and with
the role of art in providing the answer to this question. But the
relation between art and life is almost entirely reversed now:
whereas in the early phase of Conrad's work, the prototext is
myth, which signifies an alternative mode of perception and
conduct, the prototext in the late phase is, appropriately enough,
the romance, signifying a sense of unreality, fictionality, and
illusion. In order to mark the distinction between these two
opposite conceptions of life as a text, which represent, in fact, the
two opposite meanings of myth, I have used the term 'textuality'
for the latter phase. The notion of 'textuality' is, of course, a
fashionable post-modernist construct, but its philosophical source
is, not surprisingly, the radical scepticism of Nietzsche, and the
concept of 'the will of illusion'.

A systematic formulation of the Nietzschean outlook was

offered as early as 1911 by Hans Vaihinger in *The Philosophy of As If.*[1]

It must be remembered that the object of the world of ideas as a whole is not a portrayal of reality—this would be an utterly impossible task—but rather to provide us with an *instrument for finding our way about more easily in this world.*[2]

Many thought-processes and thought-constructs appear to be *consciously false assumptions*, which either contradict reality or are even contradictory in themselves, but which are intentionally thus formed in order to overcome difficulties of thought by this artificial deviation and reach the goal of thought [i.e. To serve 'the Will to Live and dominate'] by roundabout ways and by-paths. These artificial thought-constructs are called Scientific Fictions, and distinguished as conscious creations by their 'As If' character.

The 'As If' world, which is formed in this manner, the world of the 'unreal', is just as important as the world of the so-called real or actual (in the ordinary sense of the word); indeed *it is far more important for ethics and aesthetics. This aesthetic and ethical world of 'As If', the world of the unreal, becomes finally for us a world of values* which, particularly in the form of religion, must be sharply distinguished in our mind from the world of becoming.[3]

We encounter at the very threshold of these fictions one of the most important concepts ever formed by man, the idea of *freedom*; human actions are regarded as free, and therefore as 'responsible' . . . In the course of their development men have formed this important construct from immanent necessity, because only on this basis is a high degree of culture and morality possible. . . . There is nothing in the real world corresponding to the idea of liberty, though in practice it is an exceedingly necessary fiction.[4]

In the category of practical fictions a number of other moral concepts and postulates are also to be enumerated, such as the concept of duty, immortality, etc. . . . Here belong all the so-called 'ideals' of ordinary life. From a logical standpoint they are really fictions, but in practice they possess tremendous value in history. The ideal is an ideational construct

---

[1] Hans Vaihinger, *The Philosophy of 'As If: A System of the Theoretical, Practical and Religious Fictions of Mankind*. First published in Berlin, 1911, trans. C. K. Ogden (1924; London: Routledge & Kegan Paul, 1952), xlvii–xlviii. In 1919 Vaihinger founded, together with Dr Raymund Schmidt, the journal *Annalen der Philosophie* ('with particular reference to the problems of the "As If" approach').

[2] Ibid. 15.   [3] Ibid. xlvi–xlvii, my emphasis.   [4] Ibid. 43.

contradictory in itself and in contradiction with reality, but it has an irresistible power. *The ideal is a practical fiction.*[5]

True morality must always rest on a *fictional* basis. . . . We must act with the same seriousness and the same scruples *as if* the duty were imposed by God, *as if* we would be judged therefore, *as if* we would be punished for immorality.[6]

In a long section entitled 'Historical Confirmations', Vaihinger acknowledges his indebtedness to Nietzsche and to other sceptics. His exposition of Nietzsche's radical scepticism is of particular relevance to the present discussion.

[Nietzsche] holds that over against the world of shifting, evanescent becoming, there is set up, in the interests of understanding and of the aesthetic satisfaction of the fantasy, as world of 'being' in which everything appears rounded off and complete . . . This invented world is a justified and indispensable myth; from which it finally follows that false and true are relative concepts.

'Lying, in the extra-moral sense', is what Nietzsche . . . calls the conscious deviation from reality to be found in myth, art, metaphor, etc. The intentional adherence to illusion, in spite of the realization of its nature, is a kind of 'lie in an extra-moral sense'; and 'lying' is simply the conscious, intentional encouragement of illusion.[7]

Other Nietzschean concepts are taken up by Vaihinger in the same spirit: the reference to 'all customary articles of belief and even the convictions of science' as mere 'regulative fictions',[8] the exposure of a 'philosophical mythology [which] lies hidden in language [and which] breaks through at every moment, no matter how careful we may be';[9] and the designation of the ideas of freedom and responsibility, cause and effect, means and ends, as 'fictions', i.e. non-referential and arbitrary constructions. 'When we read this sign-world into things as something really existing and mix it up with them, we are merely doing what we have always done, namely mythologizing'.[10] From Nietzsche's concept of 'mythologizing' to current structuralist and post-structuralist poetics, it is but a short distance, easily traversed by Derrida's invocation of 'the joyful Nietzschean affirmation of the play of the world and the innocence of becoming, the affirmation of a world of signs which has no

---

[5] Ibid. 48.   [6] Ibid. 49.   [7] Quoted Ibid. 342.
[8] Ibid. 346.   [9] Ibid. 349.   [10] Ibid. 354.

truth, no origin, no nostalgic guilt, and is proffered for active interpretation'.[11]

I would suggest that the 'textual' phase in Conrad's work is marked by a Nietzschean sensibility, by a renunciation of the ideological quest for authority. The tropological mode underlying this phase is the *aporia*, a self-engendered paradox, a logical impasse. It is no accident that this trope has gained such currency with deconstruction: the radical epistemological scepticism of deconstruction, its substitution of discourse for essence, its refusal to accept the consolations of authority, and its suspicion of rhetoric, have turned the *aporia* into a pervasive mode of authorial and critical consciousness.

Sooner or later there is the encounter with an 'aporia' or impasse. The bottom drops out . . . The center of the work of the uncanny critics is in one way or another a formulation of this experience which momentarily and not wholly successfully rationalizes it, puts it in an image, a figure, a narrative or a myth. Here, however, the distinction between story, concept, and image breaks down, at the vanishing point where each turns into something other than itself, concept into the alogical figure into catachresis, narrative into ironical allegory. . . . The aporia, like the chasm it opens, cannot, in fact, be mastered.

The deconstructive critic seeks to find, by this process of retracing, the element in the system studied which is alogical, the thread in the text which will unravel it all, or the loose stone which will pull down the whole building. The deconstruction, rather, annihilates the ground on which the building stands by showing that the text has already annihilated that ground, knowingly or unknowingly. Deconstruction is not a dismantling of the structure of a text but a demonstration that it has already dismantled itself. Its apparently solid ground is not rock but thin air.[12]

This shibboleth of deconstruction is, of course, directly related to the scepticism of Nietzsche and Vaihinger: no rhetorical device could be more aporetic than the innocent 'as if' construction, an analogy that proclaims its own invalidity even as it is made. The 'textual' phase on Conrad's work is dominated by an aporetic consciousness closely related to that of Nietzsche and Vaihinger:

[11] Jonathan Culler, *Structuralist Poetics* (London: Routledge & Kegan Paul, 1975), 247.

[12] J. Hillis Miller, 'Stevens' Rock and Criticism as Cure', *Georgia Review*, 30 (1976), 338, 341.

his characters seem to be aware of their literariness, conscious of their own fictionality, even as they act out their self-assigned roles as knights in romances of their own making.

Conrad's affinity with the Nietzschean temperament has already been demonstrated in the first chapter of this study. But unlike Nietzsche, the prophet of modernity, or Vaihinger, his own contemporary, Conrad was already able to recognize the devastating moral implications of the philosophy of 'As If'. His letter to the *New York Times*, pubished on 2 August 1901, reads like a passage of Vaihinger's:

Science . . ., whatever authority it may claim, is not concerned with truth at all, but with the exact order of such phenomena as fall under the perception of the senses. Its conclusions are quite true enough if they can be made useful to the furtherance of our little schemes to make our earth a little more habitable. The laws it discovers remain certain and immovable for the time of several generations . . . The only indisputable truth of life is our ignorance. Besides this there is nothing evident, nothing absolute, nothing uncontradicted; there is no principle, no instinct, no impulse that can stand alone at the beginning of things and look confidently to the end.[13]

Theory is a cold and lying tombstone of departed truth. (For truth is no more immortal than any other delusion).[14]

The ultimate implication of this old-new philosophical outlook, as pointed out by Gerald Graff, is that if 'the artifice is the only reality available', and if 'reality does not exist, or rather exists only in a fictionalized version', then 'everything is swallowed up in an infinite regress of textuality', and literature, like other sense-making procedures, should renounce any truth-claims that it may have once possessed.[15]

Knowing and naming itself as fiction, literature becomes a vehicle for a nihilistic metaphysics, an anti-didactic form of preaching. In a world in which nobody can look outside the walls of the prison house of language, literature, with its built-in confession of its self-imprisonment, becomes once again the great orcale of truth, but now the truth is that there is no

---

[13] Quoted in *Collected Letters*, ii. 348.
[14] Letter to Garnett on 15 Mar. 1895, in *Collected Letters*, i. 205.
[15] Gerald Graff, *Literature against Itself: Literary Ideas in Modern Society* (Chicago: University of Chicago Press, 1979), 60–1.

truth . . . Where reality has become unreal, literature qualifies as our guide to reality by de-realizing itself.[16]

Graff's poignant analysis follows the idea of 'textuality' to its ultimate and inevitable conclusion. If we accept the view that reality is ultimately unknowable or non-existent apart from our mythical (i.e. fictional) constructions of it, we will lose all power of action. The fallacy of the theories of 'As If' is only too clear: 'Somehow we are supposed to "order" our attitude to the world by making use of fictions whose lack of truth we recognize but decide to regard as irrelevant. . . . The very admission that our beliefs are founded on myths undermines their ability to generate credence.'[17]

In terms of the present analysis, the view of reality as a text reverses the concept of myth as used in the first section: in the mythical mode, as experienced by Jim, Karain, Lingard, and Nostromo, the word is endowed with the power to create a world. In the textual mode, as we shall see, the 'world' has been *reduced* to a 'mere word'. If myth, as used in the first section of this study, implies a metaphysics of presence, textuality implies a metaphysics of absence, a void covered by a thin network of interpretations. This metaphysics of absence, the radical epistemological scepticism, the conception of life as a mere text are undoubtedly familiar to the reader at the close of the twentieth century, but they are as old as modernity itself, and closely related to the Romantic legacy and its current prophets.

Critical periodizations of Conrad's writings often relegate the works written after 1912 to the writer's 'decline', with *The Shadow-Line* as an exception to an otherwise inferior range of works. D. Hewitt, T. Moser, and A. J. Guerard are the first and most notable exponents of this view, which has by now gained such currency amongst Conrad scholars that one need hardly recapitulate it here.[18] The apparent depletion of creative energy in this last phase has been attributed to various psychological causes, such as the separation from Ford and a subsequent 'Infection-Exhaustion Psychosis', ill-health and the mental lassitude of old

---

[16] Gerald Graff, *Literature against Itself: Literary Ideas in Modern Society* (Chicago: University of Chicago Press, 1979), 179.   [17] Ibid. 184.
[18] Hewitt, *Joseph Conrad*, 103–11; Moser, *Achievement and Decline*, 116–19, 155–6, 158–9 and *passim*; Guerard, *Conrad the Novelist*, 255–61, 272–8.

age, or a 'postdepressive reaction' which activated a movement to a more 'affirmative' mood as a self-defensive mechanism.[19]

I believe that the last phase of Conrad's work does reflect a considerable decline in artistic quality and seriousness, but it seems to me that to accuse Conrad of having turned from his former scepticism to glib moralizing is a misconstruction of the dynamics of his work.[20] I would argue that the opposite is true, that Conrad's decline works his surrender to the radical scepticism of the Nietzschean outlook which he had managed to keep at bay throughout the best part of this creative career. This Nietzschean outlook, which has so far broken through only in Conrad's letters and in the peculiar thematic and structural tensions already pointed to, now emerges in full force, when both the author and his characters seem to be afflicted with an acute sense of the unreality of their world.

In a later section of this chapter, I will, of course, have to account for this question-begging last point and establish the legitimacy of the analogy between the writer and his protagonists, and the extrapolation from the moral or practical failure of the characters within a given literary work to the artistic failure of the work. I would argue that this last phase of Conrad's work is not merely *about* the failure of textuality: it is, in fact, a *symptom* of this failure.

The first two novels discussed in this section, *Chance* and *Victory*, cannot be summarily relegated to Conrad's phase of decline, in spite of the considerable diversity of critical evaluations of their artistic quality. I believe, however, that these two controversial novels already share the syndrome of textuality and should be considered as border-line cases. There is little doubt that the third novel, *The Arrow of Gold*, is, indeed, an artistic failure, but it is an extremely interesting failure for the purpose of this study, if only because its dynamics are so inextricably linked with this

---

[19] B. C. Meyer, *Joseph Conrad: A Psychoanalytic Biography.* (Princeton: Princeton University Press, 1967), 221–43; F. Karl, *Joseph Conrad: The Three Lives* (London: Faber & Faber, 1979), 749, 764, 770–2, 797–800; Z. Najder, *Joseph Conrad: A Chronicle*, trans. Carroll-Najder (Cambridge: Cambridge University Press, 1983).

[20] This view is shared by most critics who accept the theory of the later decline and view Conrad's later works as informed by a 'sentimental ethic' (Guerard's term), an easy affirmation of values which had been questioned before, an exteriorization of the source of evil, etc.

failure of vision which is to be demonstrated. All three works proclaim themselves as romances by a profusion of generic signals: the protagonists are a 'damsel in distress' and a knightly male figure, and the plot revolves around the rescue of the damsel from a sinister rival figure. The stories of Lena and Heyst, Flora and Captain Anthony, Rita and M. George can be, and indeed have been, read as traditional stories of Love and Adventure. As we have already seen, the story of Edith Travers and Captain Lingard in *The Rescue*, which was completed at this late stage after an interval of twenty-three years, has also been construed—by readers as well as by some of the characters themselves—in this light.[21]

But these strong generic statements, or 'signals', are systematically questioned and eventually pre-empted in the three novels: the male protagonists, the 'knightly' figures, are all presented as essentially powerless, bewildered, and uncertain of their roles. The plot, too, does not entirely conform to the generic conventions: in *Victory* it ends with a failure; in *Chance* and in *The Arrow*, where the 'rescue' does seem to conclude with the traditional happy ending, it goes beyond the union of the lovers and ends with their eventual separation. And finally, there is a corrosive undercurrent of narrative irony and sarcasm, which exposes and challenges the naïve conventions characteristic of this genre.

The subversion or 'deconstruction' of the generic statement which the novels initially seem to make is closely related to the problem of textuality. The protagonists seem to be strangely aware of their own fictionality. They are all apparently aware that 'such a thing as character has no real existence. It is only a helpful abstraction' and that 'the subject, the *ego* is only a fiction'.[22] It is this awareness which renders them impotent, weak, and unfit for their roles.

Marlow, who, I would argue, is the real protagonist of *Chance*, is persistently calling attention to the interpretative nature of his enterprise. He never pretends to have at his disposal anything but

---

[21] *The Rescue* is, in many ways, similar to the novels discussed in this section, in that it reflects the tension between myth and textuality, which, as we shall see, are the two poles of the romantic outlook. This novel, begun in 1896 and finished in 1919, belongs in fact, to both these phases in Conrad's work, thematically as well as chronologically. My reasons for placing it in the 'mythical' phase are largely methodological.

[22] Quoted by Vaihinger, *The Philosophy of 'As If'*, 350, 357.

'bits of disconnected statements' which he is trying to 'piece together' (222), and fills the gaps between these fragments with his own conjectures and constructions. His constant allusions to literature and his explicit search for the generic model of his story enhance the sense of unreality of which so many readers of the novel have complained. Heyst, the chivalrous protagonist of *Victory* views life as ' a delusion and a snare' (212), and has lost 'all belief in realities' (350). Having inherited the profound philosophical scepticism of his father (whom, as we shall see, is an extremely Nietzschean figure), he can only relate to Lena as to a text, which remains undecipherable to the very end. M. George, the young protagonist of *The Arrow of Gold* is also presented as a fictional entity, a 'young Ulysses'. Both he and Rita, acting under assumed names in a ludicrous game of conspiracy with remarkably little conviction or zeal, are, as we shall see, uncomfortably conscious of their own fictionality.

This view of life as a text or a spectacle yields in all three protagonists a detached aestheticist attitude, which inhibits and undermines their performance. They all seem to obey the Nietzschean dictum 'not to measure the world by our personal feelings but as if it were a play and we were part of a play',[23] 'to regard our manner of living and acting as parts in a play, including therein our maxims and principles'.[24] The peculiar emotional aridity of Marlow, the failure of Heyst, and the eventual disillusionment of M. George are, as we shall see, directly related to their view of life as a text and of all convictions as mere illusions or precarious interpretations. The fallacy of the philosophy of 'As If' is embodied in these literary characters who are so fatally aware of their own fictionality, and of the 'textual' quality of life, that they lose all powers of action. The only protagonist who eventually renounces this outlook, and thereby redeems both himself and the novel, is Marlow. The other two remain hopelessly locked within their respective fictions, detached spectators of their own plays, unable to act out their knightly roles with full conviction.

It is not surprising that Conrad who, as we have seen, was afflicted with the same sense of 'textuality', has chosen a literary genre with a non-realistic orientation. The derivative romance,

---

[23] Ibid. 297.   [24] Ibid. 282.

which is the ostensible generic model of these novels, does not try to tell us anything about reality; it leads us away from it; it makes no truth-claims, and does not aspire to transcend the boundaries of fiction.[25] Conrad himself seems to have held a low opinion of the genre to which so much of his work pretends to belong. In a letter to Edward Noble, a seaman with literary aspirations who must have reminded him of his younger self he wrote:

My dear Noble, do not throw yourself away in fables ... You have a remarkable gift of expression, the outcome of an artistic feeling for the world around You, and You must not waste the gift in (if I may say so) illegitimate sensation.[26]

Conrad's dismissal of *Romance* (written in collaboration with Ford Madox Ford between 1898 and 1902 and published in 1903) is also indicative of his attitude to the genre which seeks to produce an 'illegitimate sensation':

There are certain things that are difficult to explain, especially after they have happened. I consider *Romance* as *something of no importance*; I collaborated on it at a time when it was impossible for me to do anything else. It was easy to relate a few events without being otherwise involved in the subject. *The idea was purely aesthetic*: to depict in an appropriate way certain scenes and certain situations. Also it did not displease us to be able to show that we could do *something which was very much in vogue with the public at that moment*. The heroic gospel of St Henry, dear Sir, rules the entire world and, as you know, there is more than one way of laughing at it. There were moments when both Hueffer and I were very gay while working on this *construction*. Nevertheless we took pains with the technical side of the work.[27]

Why, then, did Conrad go back, time and again, to a genre for which he seemed to have so little repsect? How are we to understand the 'romantic feeling of reality' which he believed to be

---

[25] I am, of course, familiar with recent re-evaluations of the genre, and the feminist claim that it is subversive in its ostensible escapism. But I believe that, in view of the letters quoted below, and the poorer quality of Conrad's romances (with the exception of *Lord Jim*, which is not so much a romance as a study of the romantic temperament), one may legitimately argue that as far as Conrad is concerned, the view of romance as a 'less serious' genre is true.

[26] A letter to Noble on 25th Oct. 1895, in *Collected Letters*, i. 251–2.

[27] A letter to Kazimierz Waliszewski, 8 Nov. 1903. First published in *Lettres françaises*, 54–5. Repr. in Z. Najder, *Conrad's Polish Background*, 236, my emphasis.

his 'inborn faculty' and which his biographers view as a vital part of his cultural heritage?[28]

This last point has been dealt with by Elsa Nettels, who views Conrad's departures from the patterns of romance as an implied rejection of its norms. 'Conrad in his fiction retains much more of the paraphernalia of romance than James does . . . [but] if James internalizes the romance plot, Conrad inverts it, leading his characters not to inward victory but to failure and degeneration'; 'In most of Conrad's novels . . . romantic adventure culminates either in the inward defeat of the protagonist or in an act of self-destruction by which the protagonist attempts to expiate past failure or to vindicate an ideal of conduct, the value of which is never conclusively affirmed.'[29] Nettels also concedes, however, that a novel like *Chance* is 'a strange mixture' in that it 'contains Conrad's sharpest criticism of the conventions and sentiments of romantic chivalry' but 'it is also the novel . . . which goes farthest in making the kind of idealizations it seems to reject'.[30]

I believe that the clue to the generic ambiguity of Conrad's work may be found, not incidentally, in recent critical accounts of the relationship between romance and Romanticism. For Geoffrey Hartman Romanticism entails an acceptance of the 'plenitude that belongs to the Romance imagination', but it is a 'purification of Romance' a distillation and aesthetization of its mode of enchantment, a movement from the knight to the poet, from a primitive to a sophisticated kind of 'visionariness'.[31] Harold Bloom goes further than that: for him Romanticism is an internalization of the quest romance, a 'journey toward home . . . [or] a journey toward a supreme trial after which home is possible, or else homelessness will suffice'. Romanticism is a revival, however radically displaced,

---

[28] The Author's Note to *Within the Tides*, vii; Z. Najder, *Conrad's Polish Background*, 1–31; and 'Conrad in his Historical Perspective', *English Literature in Transition* 14/3 (1971), 157–66.

[29] Elsa Nettels, *James and Conrad* (Athens, Ga: University of Georgia Press, 1977), 131, 133.

[30] Ibid. 124. David Thorborn discusses Conrad's relationship with the genre from a different position, focusing on Conrad's 'redemptive role' in the rescue of romance from its debased, popular form in *Conrad's Romanticism* (New Haven: Yale University Press, 1974).

[31] Hartman, 'False Themes and Gentle Minds', in *Beyond Formalism* (New Haven: Yale University Press, 1970), 283–97.

of the romance, where 'the poet takes the patterns of quest romance and transposes them into his own imaginative life'.[32]

The aporetic character of Conrad's last works seems to be closely related to an ambivalence inherent in the 'romantic feeling of reality' itself, and its potential affinity with nihilism. This affinity had already been recognized in Conrad's time by intellectuals of widely divergent cutural positions.[33] A recent exposition of this ambivalence has been proposed by Gerald Graff who tracks the roots of the 'post-modernist' outlook back to the Romantics and the Modernists. The 'religion of art', the 'romantic glorification of the creative imagination', is inevitably undermined by the idea of the autonomy of the creative imagination: it implicitly 'concedes that artistic meaning is a fiction, without any corresponding object in the extra-artistic world'. This is an 'ambivalence [which] pervades romantic writing'. 'The view of literature as the sovereign orderer of reality and our most valuable means of making sense of the world is strangely licensed by our view that reality is not susceptible to comprehension and management.'[34].

According to the 'visionary view', characteristic of Romantic theories of art, 'literature does not withdraw from objective reality but appropriates it, calling into question the entire opposition between the imaginative and the real, the world of the work and the world of reality'. 'The extreme instance of this view is that all our "ideas of order" are essentially fictions projected on a world that, in itself, is without order.[35]' Graff agrees, therefore, with recent critics, like Hartman and Bloom, who view the implications (though not the intentions) of Romanticism as nihilistic. 'The Romantic belief in the power of the autonomous imagination was chastened by the recognition that the order and truth generated by this imagination are no more than arbitrary and subjective constructions.' The notion of aesthetic autonomy is simply a positive construction of 'literature's dispossession of an objective world view'.[36]

---

[32] Harold Bloom, *The Ringers in the Tower: Studies in Romantic Tradition* (Chicago: University of Chicago Press, 1971), chaps. 1–2.

[33] Cf. Irving Babbitt in *Rousseau and Romanticism*; Carl Schmitt in *Political Romanticism* (Berlin, 1919) trans. and intr. by Guy Oakes (Cambridge, Mass.: The MIT Press, 1986).

[34] Graff, *Literature against Itself*, 35–6, 7.

[35] Ibid. 13–14.   [36] Ibid. 39, 36, 45.

For an alternative formulation of the ambivalence inherent in the Romantic vision, one can go back to the distinction between 'myth' and 'textuality' as suggested earlier. If myth represents the power of the imagination to create and order a world (a power with which Jim, Lingard, and Nostromo are all endowed, and later surrender), i.e. the 'positive' concept of Romanticism, textuality exposes this world as a mere fabrication or illusion, and undermines the redeeming power of the word. The transition from 'Deification to Demystification' from 'autotelic to anti-teleological art' is thus attained.[37]

I believe that 'the romantic feeling of reality', which Conrad professed to be his 'inborn faculty' is neither an idealized concept of Love and Adventure, nor a leaning towards the exotic and the fabulous. It is a quality which is closer to a feeling of *unreality*, an awareness of the absence of an a priori essence in oneself and in the world, and a sense of constant 'becoming'. *Lord Jim* is subtitled 'A Romance' because the protagonist shares this inborn faculty of perceiving himself in a literary role, and creating both himself and his microcosm in Patusan—like a true romantic artist—with the power of his imagination and his word. The oracular pronouncements of Stein can, therefore, be construed as a qualified endorsement of the romantic spirit. His acute diagnosis of Jim as a 'romantic', is ambivalent precisely because the romantic spirit can be 'very bad' and 'very good, too' (216). Stein, the arch-romantic magician-figure decides to give Jim 'a totally new set of conditions for his imaginative faculty to work upon' (218). It, is, indeed, his imagination which eventually makes his heroic dream come true, just as it is the fulfilment of the dream which eventually brings about his suicide. The regression to the mythical mode, as seen in *Lord Jim*, *The Rescue*, and *Nostromo*, is doomed to failure when invaded by the modern temper. But it still serves, however temporarily and precariously, as a real alternative realm of action for Conrad's protagonists, and an affirmation of the power of the word. Jim's life in Patusan is a realization of a mythical frame of reference. Jim's 'fiction' (i.e. the heroic role he has set up for himself in following his literary models) thus becomes a powerful reality

[37] Michael P. Jones, *Conrad's Heroism: A Paradise Lost* (Ann Arbor: Mich.: UMI Research Press, 1985), 41.

when he is prepared to act it out. Life may, indeed, be only a dream, but it has to be dreamt through with integrity and faith.

The protagonists of *Chance, Victory,* and *The Arrow of Gold* belong to a different conception, which is the opposite pole of the romantic vision. Myth in this late phase of Conrad's work assumes the meaning of a lie, a fiction of order and meaning consciously imposed on an essentially meaningless and chaotic reality. But this fiction, once acknowledged as such, can no longer be followed 'as if' it were true. Conrad's later protagonists are all suffering from a sense of unreality', from a debilitating consciousness of their own fictionality and the fictitiousness of the values on which their roles are predicated.

We find Conrad's characters divided between those who have accepted illusion as the cost (or reward) of action and those who can recognize— not without pathos—the fragility of man's illusion. To the extents that we are idiots, we take the illusion as truth and act unquestioningly in its name, tyrants and slaves at once of the idea. To the extent that we are convicts we recognize the illusion for what it is and see beyond it to the ironic indifference of the 'sublime spectacle'. We may live by our traditional moral beliefs without needing to claim some illusory authority for them; but the very reflection which makes us recognize these beliefs as the 'illusions' they are may disqualify us in turn for action.[38]

Martin Price refers, of course, to Conrad's famous letter to Marguerite Poradowska.[39] If the heroic characters of the mythical phase can afford to be heroic because they are, in this very particular sense, idiots, because they are not afflicted with a disabling self-consciousness, the protagonists of the textual phase are already 'convicts'. There is no doubt in my mind that Conrad, too, identified himself as one of the latter.

Having argued that Conrad was afflicted with the same syndrome of unreality which paralyses his protagonists, we must now justify this dangerous analogy. The close relationship between Conrad's psychological problems and his artistic difficulties has been explored in depth in the biographies and in semi-biographical

---

[38] Martin Price, *Forms of Life: Character and Moral Imagination in the Novel* (New Haven: Yale University Press, 1983), 243.

[39] The letter was probably written on 20 July 1894. See *Collected Letters,* i. 162–3.

studies of his work.[40] The recurrent 'identity crises' to which he was prone, the difficulties he had encountered in his attempt to create 'a coherent identity', were clearly the result of his early orphanhood, his political and cultural exile, and his physical rootlessness. His inability 'to establish a consistent point of view that would enable him to impose some order upon the multitude of imagined facts' is a concomitant of the same psychological and artistic constitution.

The use of Marlow, the surrogate narrator, gave Conrad 'an integrating point of view', although 'it did not permanently resolve his search for a consistant consciousness of self-identity'.

Marlow, a model English gentleman, ex-officer of the merchant marine, was the embodiment of all that Conrad would wish to be if he were to become completely anglicized. And since that was not the case, and since he did not quite share his hero's point of view, there was no need to identify himself with Marlow either emotionally or intellectually. Thanks to Marlow's duality, Conrad could feel solidarity with, and a sense of belonging to, England by proxy, at the same time maintaining a distance such as one has toward a creation of one's own imagination.[41]

Conrad's obvious need to dissociate himself from his fiction has naturally led critics to scan his work for autobiographical materials, and visible traces of the author's past and personality have, in fact, been found in figures like Jim, Decoud, and Razumov.[42] But Conrad's involuntary self-exposure seems to be particularly intense and significant during this phase of his career. The discussion of these last three novels will therefore touch upon some biographical aspects which can only be briefly indicated here.

Conrad's letters of this period reflect not only a state of depression and lassitude, but an awareness of having changed. 'And so you've kept my letters! Have you! Ah my dear you'll never meet the man who wrote them again. I feel as if I had somehow smashed myself'; 'my days of fine things are done I fear; still one must go on'; 'Life—an awful grind. The feeling that the game is no longer

[40] Said, *Joseph Conrad and Fiction of Autobiography* (Cambridge, Mass.: Harvard University Press, 1966).

[41] Najder, *Conrad: A Chronicle*, 231.

[42] See Martin Ray on 'Conrad and Decoud', Gustav Morf, *Polish Heritage*. In the 1987 Conference of the Joseph Conrad Society (UK), Joseph Dobrinsky offered an impressive biographical interpretation of Razumov. To the best of my knowledge, this paper has not yet been published.

worth the candle . . . and yet [I] must go on spinning out of myself like a disillusioned spider his web in a gale'.[43] This 'identity crisis' was not a new phenomenon in Conrad's life. He had undergone similar crises, depressions, and breakdowns several times before. The only element which is significantly new about this particular identity crisis is Conrad's inability to contain it within his letters and dissociate it from his fiction.

The Marlow of *Chance* is radically different from the honest, bluff, and essentially trustworthy Marlow of 'Youth', *Lord Jim*, and *Heart of Darkness*: whatever complexity he had in the previous works had not been psychological. It derived from an avowed sense of confusion, an occasional state of physical, emotional, and ethical disorientation, caused by the complexity of the situations he had to cope with. It had nothing to do with the character of this man who, throughout his ordeals, had remained a model seaman and a perfect English gentleman, almost stolid in his invariable steadfastness and sanity. In *Chance* we meet a different man: Marlow, who has now retired, is a cynical, often callous narrator, wavering between complacent pomposity and sardonic gloating at his protagonist's predicaments, even as he is drawn into the plot. His obsessive misogyny and his idiosyncratic behaviour endow him with a new type of complexity: he is no longer the reliable narrator who offers the reader a fixed viewpoint; he has become a character in his own right, a complex personality to be deciphered and related to. Conrad had apparently felt that this Marlow, who is so much more representative of his author now than he had formerly been, will not do for an intermediary consciousness, or a public persona, and interposed yet another narrator, the anonymous frame narrator, between himself and the reader. Unlike the frame narrators of 'Youth' and *Heart of Darkness*, this frame narrator, who is identified as a writer of fiction in the serial version of the novel, is also a sharer in his author's incurable Romanticism.

Heyst, too, has been rightly described by critics as a sharer in his author's temperamental scepticism. The protagonist himself seems to point to this resemblance when he talks of 'the man with the quill pen in his hand' who is 'responsible for my existence' (195). The double allusion to his father (at whose portrait he points) and

---

[43] Letters to Garnett on 12 Jan. 1911; to Arthur Symons on 7 Feb. 1911; to Ford on 29 Mar. 1911. Quoted in Najder, *Joseph Conrad: A Chronicle*, 368.

to the author is significant: the nihilistic scepticism of Heyst Sr., which has turned the son into a spectator of rather than a participant in life, is closely related to the inverted Romanticism of the author.

The intrusion of autobiography into *The Arrow of Gold* is the most interesting of all, not least because the ostensible factual autobiographical elements in the novel are obviously fictitious. I would argue that Conrad's apparent loss of artistic control in this work loosened the tight grip on the persona he had previously held up for the public's view, and exposed the tensions inherent in his incurable Romanticism and his eventual surrender to textuality.

A proper deconstructionist analysis of these three novels would probably challenge some of the assumptions underlying this section. I believe, however, that the question-begging title of this chapter is justified: Conrad was a thoroughly didactic writer. He was primarily concerned with the problem of 'how to be'. The view of reality as a text could not be a joyful celebration of an endless play of indeterminate meanings. It was an admission of ethical and aesthetic bankruptcy. If reality is ultimately unknowable or non-existent apart from our fictional constructions, there is no reason to prefer any one code of ethics over any other; there is no lesson to be learned of art which is itself only a conscious fiction; and the power of the imagination is no more significant than that of the 'disillusioned spider' endlessly spinning 'his web in a gale'. The problem of 'how to be' cannot be resolved in the absence of a 'sovereign power enthroned in a fixed standard of conduct'.

Once the truth is grasped that one's own personality is only a ridiculous and aimless masquerade of something hopelessly unknown the attainment of serenity is not far off . . . If we are 'ever becoming—never being' then I would be a fool if I tried to become this thing rather than that; for I know well that I will never be anything.[44]

Conrad's last two novels are already the works of a bankrupt artist, a writer who has lost his faith in the power of the word and become 'the ideal singer of an empty day'. *The Rover* and the unfinished *Suspense* are entirely trivialized and diluted of all traces of the tension which makes the other novels significant in their

---

[44] A letter to Edward Garnett on 29 Sept. 1898, in *Collected Letters*, 267–8.

very failure, and I would not deal with them beyond the following brief comment. I believe that those works, so vastly inferior to Conrad's earlier writings, are not only the products of mental fatigue and old age. They are sad cases of 'literature against itself', of art which has lost its belief in reality and in its own truth-claims. When literature undermines its own *raison d'être*, it is, one might say, suicidal. This study will, therefore, not pursue the life of the writer to its end. It will conclude with the death of the artist.

A. *CHANCE*

Chance is an example of objectivity, most precious of aims, not only menaced but definitely compromised. . . . The particular difficulty Mr Conrad has 'elected' to face . . . [is] his so multiplying his creators or, as we are now fond of saying, producers [i.e. narrators], as to make them almost more numerous and quite emphatically more material than the creatures and the production itself in whom and which we by the general law of fiction expect such agents to lose themselves. . . . Marlow's own [omniscience] is a prolonged hovering flight of the subjective over the outstretched ground of the case exposed. We make out this ground but through the shadow cast by the flight . . . [against] the no small menace of intrinsic colour and form and whatever, upon the passive expanse.[45]

The irritated bafflement of Henry James, hardly concealed behind his precious rhetoric and his reluctant tribute to Conrad's artistry, has set the tone for the critical response to *Chance* to this very day. Like James, most critics who have not condemned the novel as a product of Conrad's notorious decline, gallantly attempt to excuse the novelist for his transgression of the Jamesian 'law of fiction', by extricating the tale, as it were, from its multiple frames, by relegating the interfering presence of the narrator to the background, and attending to the story of Flora and Anthony, the 'Damsel' and the 'Knight', in its distilled, objective form.[46]

---

[45] Henry James, 'The New Novel,' in *Notes on Novelists* (London: J. M. Dent & Sons Ltd., 1914), 273–8.

[46] C. B. Cox thus finds Marlow's indirect mode of narration a 'cumbersome and at times absurd' device (*Joseph Conrad: The Modern Imagination* (London: J. M. Dent & Sons, 1974), 123); and Daniel Schwarz writes that 'the almost geometric form threatens to snuff out content. The form, like a series of Chinese boxes, imprisons the characters and mirrors their repression; it is a form that dilutes and undermines passion by setting it at a distance . . . [it] lacks a radial center, a unifying core that informs the various episodes' (*Conrad: The Later Fiction*, 46).

I would suggest that this critical procedure—the attempt to rescue the substance of the work (i.e. the story of Flora and Anthony) from under the shadow of Marlow and the narrators who are perversely more substantial than their material—ought to be reversed; that instead of resisting the thrust of the novel away from the ostensible material and towards the narrators, one should go along with it, and suspend the 'law of fiction', as postulated by James, at least for a while. I believe that the distinction between frame and substance, narrator and protagonist, in this novel is a crucial misconception of its theme, for Marlow is, perhaps, even more than in any of Conrad's previous works, a full-blooded character and, as the following analysis will attempt to establish, the real protagonist of the novel.[47] The exasperated response to the narrative peculiarities of *Chance* is perfectly understandable: Marlow—the narrator who invariably refuses to gratify the desire of his audience (the listeners as well as the readers) for neat endings, for self-contained and fully comprehensible stories, and for facile moralizing—is out-doing himself in this novel. He seems to insist, throughout his narration, on the textual, constructed nature of his task, the 'piecing [together of] bits of disconnected statements' (222), rather than a query for the 'truth'.

The story of Flora and Anthony is, indeed, a patchwork of anecdotes narrated by various 'reciters' as James liked to call them: Flora's story as told to Mrs Fyne, Mrs Fyne's story as told to Marlow, and Franklin's story as told to Powell and transmitted to Marlow. But the seams of this patchwork are not artistically blended to create an illusion of wholeness: the gaps in the story are filled by uninhibited conjecture and imaginative reconstruction on Marlow's part (e.g. the interviews between the governess and Charlie to which there had been no witnesses, the governess's state of mind, Anthony's first view of Flora). Here we have, then, a paradoxical situation: Marlow's virtual omniscience, which is

---

[47] One should note that the critical attitude to the relationship between the narrative frame and the story in *Chance* has not been unanimously unfavourable. The most notable discussions of this relationship have been offered by Ian Watt in 'Conrad, James and *Chance*', in M. Mack and I. Gregor, eds., *Imagined Worlds: Essays in Honour of John Butt* (London: Methuen, 1968), 316; by Royal Roussel in *The Metaphysics of Darkness*, 166–75; and by Gary Geddes in *Conrad's Later Novels*, 25–30.

accounted for by an ingenious system of sub-narrators and coincidences, does not, as one might expect, acquire the appearance of documentary authenticity but, on the contrary, calls attention to itself as an artifact, a collage of fragmented texts.

Marlow's narrative is strewn with expressions which seem to divest it of authority, to deliberately undercut any claim for authenticity and the possession of an objective truth as they constantly remind the reader of the fictionality of the account. His attitude to his material is encapsulated in his ostensibly disparaging comment on young Mr Powell's conception of life: 'to him life, perhaps not so much his own as that of the others, was something still in the nature of a fairy-tale with a "they lived happily ever after" termination. *We are the creatures of our light literature* much more than is generally suspected in a world which prides itself on being scientific and practical.' (288, my emphasis). Marlow's persistent references to the events as the part of a 'story' (309, 311), and his laboured attempts to find a suitable generic label for it, as he tries the definitions of comedy, tragedy, tragicomedy, and farce in turn (53, 55, 177), are powerful antidotes which thwart the comfortable suspension of disbelief we are all too willing to settle into.

Marlow's treatment of the characters is invariably coloured by this view of their essential fictionality, and his persistent reminders that they are, after all, only characters in a story. Giving vent to his contemptuous hostility towards the Fynes, he reduces them to mere constructs of his mind: 'My efforts had invested them with a sort of profundity . . . I saw these two stripped of every vesture it had amused me to put on them for fun' (56). He ridicules their distress after the elopement of Flora and Anthony by a facile literary allusion to 'the affair of the purloined brother' (148); he portrays Flora and her father as 'figures from Dickens' (162); he describes Flora and Anthony as the protagonists of a conventional romance by alluding time and again to the fairy-tale of the Sleeping Beauty (333, 342, 354, 396, 428) and to the story of Cinderella (129).

But it is not only Marlow, the narrator, who insists on the fictionality of his tale. Conrad himself seems to take part in the game of textuality by neatly dividing the story into the section of 'The Damsel' and the section of 'the Knight'. Whereas the reader of a bona fide romance is invited to immerse himself in the world of the work, the reader of *Chance* is constantly reminded of the textual, fictional quality of this world as loudly proclaimed by the generic signals. The dissociation of the novel from the conventions of romance is also implied in Marlow's view of Captain Anthony, another 'creature of light literature'. Marlow believes that the protagonist's excessive idealism, his view of himself as a Knight, and his subsequent attempt to conduct himself in accordance with the chivalric tradition, are at the source of his predicament:

He resembled his father . . . The inarticulate son had set up a standard for himself which that need for embodying in his conduct the dreams, the passion, the impulses the poet puts into arrangement of verses, which are dearer to him than his own self—and may make his own self appear sublime in the eyes of other people, and even in his own eyes. (328)

Reality itself is viewed as a construct rather than a given objective state, an agglomeration of signs without referents. The most notable example of this is the account of de Barral's financial enterprise: 'The fellow had a pretty fancy in names: the "Orb" Deposit Bank, the "Sceptre" Mutual Aid Society, the "Thrift and Independence" Association. Yes, a very pretty taste in names; and nothing else besides' (69); de Barral himself is 'a mere sign, a portent. There was nothing in him. Just at that time the word Thrift was to the fore. You know the power of words. We pass through periods dominated by this or that word—it may be development, or it may be competition. . . . It is the word of the time.' The 'power of words' (74) de Barral harnesses to his 'preposterous chariot' through his advertisements engenders an amazing financial empire. But the collapse of this empire exposes the sham: de Barral's powerful word is a travesty of the primal Word which generated the world, and de Barral himself, the hollow man who had created this cardboard world, is a travesty of the creating Father.

The same hollow or fictitious quality characterizes the lives of the protagonists themselves: 'We live at the mercy of a malevolent word. . . . Flora . . . let herself be carried along by a mysterious force which her person had called into being, as her father had been carried away out of his depth by the unexpected power of successful advertising.' Marlow himself tells the listener how he himself had also once been the victim of the 'malevolent word' (264), and the narrator describes Mr Powell as 'wonderfully amenable to verbal suggestion' (36). The distinction between the word and the world is no longer upheld. Reality is viewed as a construct of language.

In an illuminating article on the differences between the serial version of *Chance* (as published in the Sunday magazine section of the *New York Herald* from 21 January to 30 April 1912) and the book version, Robert Siegle makes some important observations which are worth noting here at some length.[48] Siegle points to passages in the serial version of the novel which overtly draw attention to the reflexive aspect of *Chance*, such as the introduction of the frame narrator as a professional novelist, and Marlow's distinction between the narrator's interest in 'fictional' events as opposed to his own concern with 'real' events. Marlow's 'crusty attitude' to the framer's craft, and his 'denigration of narrative in relation to experience' are also reflected in his reference to the 'somewhat heartless' lookout of the framer-novelist for fictional material.

But Marlow's distinction between the perceptual frameworks for literature and experience is effaced, as Siegle observes, by the frame narrator's description of Marlow himself sitting 'in the shadow thrown across a corner of the room by my big bookcase',[49] a description which has been retained in the book version of the novel as well (see 325, 327). Siegle concludes on a note of 'radical epistemology', arguing that although 'Marlow would like the teleology of tight cosmic plotting, firm narrative control over the unfolding of episodes, and the sense of direction and significance that comes from transcendent purpose', he eventually realizes that his verities, including his belief in the stability of the ethical code of life at sea, are 'fragile fictions', relative and evanescent, that the 'solaces of culture' are fictional texts with 'no ontological standing apart from cultural consensus'.[50]

The main question which emerges from this remarkable analysis of the novel is, why did Conrad choose to omit from the book version of *Chance* precisely those passages which are so significant to a 'textual' reading of the kind offered by Siegle and suggested

---

[48] Robert Siegle, 'The Two Texts of *Chance*,' *Conradiana*, 16/2 (1984): 83–101.

[49] 25 Feb. and 28 Apr. quoted by Siegle, ibid. 84; 18 Feb. issue, discussed by Siegle on 88–9; 19 May, Siegle, ibid. 89.

[50] Siegle, ibid. 96–9. A similar approach is argued by W. W. Bonney in *Thorns and Arabesques: Contexts for Conrad's Fiction* (Baltimore: Johns Hopkins University Press, 1980), 96–107.

by my own earlier comments on the emphatic reflexivity of
Marlow's narrative? Siegle does not address this issue, except at
one point when he suggests that Conrad had omitted the identification of the frame narrator as a novelist because it was 'one twist
too many'.[51] I would suggest that there is another, more complex
reason for this and other omissions.

To understand the shift from the radical reflexivity of the serial
version to the toned-down book version, one must turn the
limelights to Marlow, and examine his development as narrator
and protagonist throughout the novel. The most important characteristics of Marlow's personality as initially reflected in his
narrative are his aestheticism, his callousness, his contempt for the
other characters, and his misogyny. These traits, which have made
him so unpopular with the critics, have been noted by many readers
of the novel, and a few samples would suffice to illustrate them
here.

Marlow's aestheticism is undoubtedly related to the emphasis on
the 'textual' quality of the narrated experience and of reality itself.
He constantly refers to the story in terms of a theatrical production:
he demands to know if he is engaged in 'a farce or a tragedy' in
order 'to regulate [his] feelings' (55). He treats the sight of Mrs
Fyne in distress as an 'admirable' performance: 'I say "admirable"
because it was so characteristic. It was perfect. Nothing short of
genius could have found better. . . . As they say of an artist's work;
this was perfect Fyne. . . . I had a mind to shout "Brava! Brava!"
but I did not do that' (141). He feels a 'certain dramatic fascination'
when he visualizes Flora's story (177), and treats her attempted
suicide as yet another performance, a 'suicide poise' thwarted by
his own voice, since 'she was no longer in proper form for the act'
(203). Anthony is viewed as 'intoxicated with the pity and tenderness of his part' (261), and The Ferndale is described, like the
Fyne's rural cottage, as 'a floating stage of tragi-comedy' (272).

Marlow's refusal to take his characters seriously does not confine
itself to a view of their story as a spectacle held for his entertainment, but sometimes boils over into an almost savage sarcasm,
particularly where the Fynes are concerned; 'the domestic-slave
daughter of Carleon Anthony and the little Fyne of the Civil Service
(that flower of civilization) were not intelligent people' (61); 'A

[51] Siegle, 'The Two Texts of Chance', 85.

discussion in the Fyne menage! How portentous!' (147). His scorn of 'the most virtuous Fyne' (60), or 'Little Fyne' as he often calls him (53), often takes the shape of rather facile puns on his 'pedestrian excellence' (56). Marlow's tendency to be 'amused by the misfortunes of a fellow-creature' (49) is reinforced by his 'aesthetization' of their predicaments, as evidenced in his bursts of outright laughter and uninhibited show of 'mirth' at the Fynes' distress (51, 53, 54).

Marlow's misogyny seems to be another facet of the same frame of mind. He parades his hostility to women as the hallmark of a 'realistic' approach, a judgement which—unlike that of the frame narrator—is not marred by the 'glamorous reticency' of 'masculine chivalry' (53). But the very insistence of his hostile generalizations points to an almost pathological mistrust and resentment of women, a feeling which seems to go much deeper than a denial of the chivalric code:

As to honour—you know—it's a very fine medieval inheritance which women never got hold of. It wasn't theirs. Since it must be laid as a general principle that women always get what they want, we must suppose they didn't want it. In addition they are devoid of decency. I mean masculine decency. (63)

When a woman takes to any sort of unlawful man-trade, there's nothing to beat her in the way of thoroughness. . . . For if we men try to put the spaciousness of all experiences into our reasoning and would fain put the Infinite itself into our love, it isn't, as some writer has remarked, 'It isn't women's doing'. Oh, no. They don't care for these things.(93)

Men do not accumulate hate against each other in tiny amounts, treasuring every pinch carefully till it grows at last into a monstrous and explosive hoard. (110)

I call a woman sincere when she volunteers a statement resembling remotely in form what she really would like to say, what she really thinks ought to be said if it were not for the necessity to spare the stupid sensitivity of men. . . . We could not stand woman speaking the truth. (144, see also 145, 152, 157–9.)

It seems to me that it is at this point that one must make the connection between Marlow the protagonist and Marlow the narrator: for Marlow's arid sarcasm, his jaded aestheticism, and his misogyny are not isolated idiosyncrasies: they are the products of the same state of mind which has produced the peculiar frustrating quality of his narrative, its insistence on the 'textual' quality of reality, and its constant subversion of its own truths.

The Marlow we meet in *Chance* is not the decent, thoroughly dependable character we have met in *Youth* and in *Lord Jim*, or even the more complex and troubled teller of *Heart of Darkness*: he now seems to have completely succumbed to a Nietzschean, relativistic view of human reality, a view of which we had been allowed only momentary glimpses before. He is fully and painfully aware of the essential relativity and fictitiousness of man's 'truths' and values, and the illusions which he must uphold in order to preserve a semblance of order and purpose in an amoral and indifferent cosmos.

It was one of those dewy, clear, starry nights, oppressing our spirit, crushing our pride, by the brilliant evidence of the awful loneliness, of the hopeless obscure insignificance of our globe lost in the splendid revelation of a glittering, soulless universe. (50)

I . . . went out of the cottage to be confronted outside its door by the bespangled, cruel revelation of the Immensity of the Universe. (61)

It was good not to be bothered with what all these things meant in the scheme of creation (if indeed anything had a meaning), or were just piled-up matter without any sense. (337)

Here, again, it is difficult to separate Marlow's cosmic pessimism from that of the author who wrote to his friends:

Understand that thou art nothing, less than a shadow, more insignificant than a drop of water in the ocean, more fleeting than the illusion of a dream . . . The attitude of cold unconcern is the only reasonable one. . . . The mysteries of a universe made of drops of fire and clods of blood do not concern us in the least. The fate of a humanity condemned ultimately to perish from cold is not worth troubling about.[52]

Marlow, so constantly aware of man's utter insignificance in this immensity of matter, cannot relate to human emotions and values as anything but fragile and relative fictions. He scoffs at the 'dithyrambic phraseology for the expression of love' invented by our civilization (234); he questions the validity of any one ethical code, and cynically argues that 'one's very concept of virtue is at the mercy of some felicitous temptation which may be sprung on

[52] Letters to Graham on 14 Dec. 1897, and 14 Jan. 1898, in *Joseph Conrad's Letters to Cunninghame Graham*, 54, 65.

one any day' (54); he mocks the assumptions underlying the relations between the sexes as 'certain well-known, well-established ... almost hackneyed, illusions, without which the average male cannot get on' (94), or as 'the dreams of sentiment-[which] like the consoling mysteries of Faith—are invincible' (206). Experience, for Marlow, is 'always outside of us' (282): it can only become manageable when seen through fictions, as 'each of us arranges the world according to his own notion of the fitness of things' (289).

Marlow is defeated by his Nietzschean outlook. His emotional detachment, his essential isolation, and his misogyny are all the symptoms of a willed withdrawal. The most painful of these symptoms is his retirement from the sea.

Marlow had retired from the sea in a sort of half-hearted fashion some years ago. Mr Powell's comment was: 'Fancied had enough of it?' 'Fancied's the very word to use in this connection,' I observed, remembering the subtly provisional character of Marlow's long sojourn among us. From year to year he dwelt on land as a bird rests on the branch of a tree ... Marlow, lingering on shore, was to me an object of incredulous commiseration like a bird, which, secretly, should have lost its faith in the high virtue of flying. (33–4)

Marlow's former faith in the high virtue of his vocation has apparently been contaminated by the same relativism which afflicts his attitude to the other 'high virtues'. The ethical significance attached to his retirement is strangely echoed by his author, himself a retired seaman:

There is in mankind a bias, a tendency, that drives it towards the cheap, towards the worthless, in letters, in art, in politics, in sentiment, in—by all the gods that sit grinning above—in the very love itself. A trace of the original ape I suppose. To drive it on an upward path you must pat the ape on the back lest it turn and rend you. This is an immoral theory but *I've left my morality on the sea.*[53]

This distinction between the ethics of the land and the ethics of the sea is also made by the protagonists themselves. Marlow's hostility to the land people, where 'no actors [are] too humble and obscure not to have a gallery, that gallery which envenoms the play by stealthy jeers, counsels of anger, amused comments or words of

---

[53] A letter to A. Quiller-Couch on 13 July 1898, in *Collected Letters of Joseph Conrad*, i. 78.

perfidious compassion' (326), is echoed by Anthony who speaks of himself as 'a confirmed enemy of life on shore—a perfect terror to a simple man, what with the fads and proprieties and the ceremonies and affectations' (221, also 372). One must remember, however, that whereas Anthony 'threw himself, figuratively speaking, into the sea' (39), Marlow, likened by the frame narrator to a bird which has 'lost its faith in the high virtue of flying', is out of his element, for 'the sea is the sailor's true element' as the air is the 'true element' of the bird (33–4).

But Conrad could not allow Marlow to remain paralyzed in his relativistic, textual vision for long: he had invested too much of himself in this surrogate. *Chance* is the story of Marlow's recovery. If he is to go back to the sea, his true element, he must regain his lost faith, re-engage in the 'fictions' he has denounced, and become a character—rather than an amused spectator—in his own story. Marlow's gradual recuperation, his increasing involvement in the tale, and the concomitant change in his state of mind, lead to the affirmative note which concludes the novel. The gradual shift in the denotation of 'chance' from an arbitrary and blind 'accident' (36) to an opportunity which has to be seized (446) reflects this process, for it is ultimately Marlow's own chance that is at stake here.

The telling of the tale becomes for Marlow, as it might have been for his author, a therapeutic process, an affirmation of faith. The change is wrought by his encounters, physical and imaginary, with Flora de Barral, who seems to defy the cynicism with which he has tried to shield himself, for 'even in the best armour of steel there are joints a treacherous stroke can always find if chance gives the opportunity' (126). These cracks in Marlow's armour become immediately apparent when his usual sarcasm gives way to sympathy as he describes Flora's 'moral anguish' (188), and her lack of 'footing in this world' (196). His view of the story as a theatrical production is gradually superseded by a genuine emotional response: the 'comic' situation becomes painful (206); curiosity gives way to anxiety, and shame takes the place of his former frivolity (231); he seems to regret his own 'cheap jocularity' and his unsuccessful attempt to 'keep it in the tone of comedy' (236). Marlow gradually comes to recognize his own responsibility for Flora's life, as he moves from the role of a passive observer to that of a participant. Undertaking the task of a mediator between the lovers, he assures Flora of the reality of 'the idea of the son of the poet, the rescuer of the most forlorn damsel of modern times' (238), thus asking her, in fact, to accept the conception of the romance, the 'fiction' he had so vehemently derided before.

Marlow's misogyny is also modified in the course of his narrative until it finally transforms into an attitude which is not unlike the 'masculine chivalry' he has so mockingly diagnosed in the frame narrator: his former diatribes turn into eulogies: 'woman is various indeed' (231); 'A young girl, you know, is something like a temple. . . . The privileged men, the lover, the husband, who are given the key of the sanctuary do not always know how to use it. For myself, without claim, without merit, simply by chance I had been allowed to look through the half-opened door and I had seen the saddest possible desecration' (311); a woman 'is never dense. She's never made of wood through and through as some men are, . . . And that is why so many men are afraid of them' (378). When the frame narrator laughs at Marlow's assertion that 'some women could live by love alone', Marlow replies:

You say I don't know women. Maybe. It's just as well not to come too close to the shrine. But I have a clear notion of *woman*. In all of them, termagant, flirt, crank, washerwoman, blue-stocking, outcast and even in the ordinary fool of the ordinary commerce there is something left, if only a spark. And when there is a spark there can always be a flame. (353)

He has clearly come a long way since the beginning of his tale . . .

To understand the process of Marlow's recovery and his assimilation into the fictional fabric he unfolds, one must examine what I would call the issue of 'surrogacy' in the novel—the marked resemblances between Mr de Barral-Smith and Anthony, between Powell and Anthony, between Powell and Marlow, and between Marlow and Anthony, which make them almost interchangeable in the plot.

Anthony is first described by Powell as a tall, active man, with a 'very red' face under a 'high silk hat' (16). The description is incongruously echoed in the portrayal of de Barral: 'Without removing his eyes from her he took off his hat. It was a tall hat. The hat of the trial. The hat of the thumb-nail sketches in the illustrated papers. . . . De Barral the convict took off the *silk hat* of the financier de Barral and deposited it on the front seat of the cab. . . . *He was red in the face*' (362, my emphases). Flora's estrangement from her father is described as similar to her relationship with Anthony at that time: 'She sank into her place keeping a watchful eye on her companion. He was hardly anything more by this time. Except for her childhood impressions he was just—a man. Almost a stranger. . . . And there was the other too. Also almost a stranger' (366).

Powell, too, tends to see de Barral and Captain Anthony as one and the same person. He recalls that as he walked on deck and peeped down at the Captain's cabin, he had the 'absurd impression that his captain (he was up there, of course) was sitting on both sides of the aftermost skylight at once. He was too preoccupied to reflect on this curious delusion, this phenomenon of seeing double . . .' (276). Both the husband and the father are wearing grey caps which make it impossible to tell them apart from above: 'He had noticed across the skylight a head in a grey cap. But when, after a time, he crossed over to the other side of the deck he discovered that it was not the Captain's head at all' (284–5).

This doubleness or surrogacy can, of course, be accounted for in Freudian terms, as a reflection of the father's Oedipal power over his daughter, and the eventual exchange of the father for the husband brought about by de Barral's suicide. But this is only one link in the chain of 'surrogacies' in which every male character in the novel is mistaken for or substituted by another at some point in the novel.

In an article entitled, 'The Damsel and Her Knights: The Goddess and the Grail in Conrad's *Chance*', Julie M. Johnson convincingly relates the story of the grail to the underlying structure of the novel. Flora, the 'vessel', is the object of the quest of the three knights: Anthony, an idealistic Galahad figure who dies when the quest is completed; Powell, a devoted Perceval figure who sees the grail after Galahad's death and then retires; and Marlow—Bors, who returns to tell the tale to an eager listener.[54] I would argue that the three men, ostensibly so different from each other, assume their roles as Flora's knights by virtue of the 'surrogacy' factor, the qualities which make them interchangeable.

The marked affinity between Powell and Anthony, which turns the younger man into a son-figure for the Captain, prepares the

[54] *Conradiana* 13/3 (1981), 221–8.

ground for the remarriage of Flora, an ending which would otherwise seem to be anticlimactic and sentimental. When Powell notes that 'Captain Anthony was a great reader just about this time; and I, too, I have a great liking for books' (413), one realizes that Powell's amenability to verbal suggestion, which the narrator had previously commented on, parallels Anthony's romantic idealism and his exalted, literary conception of love. Both of them are trying to live up to the fictional ideal of chivalry. Mr Powell's love for Flora, who lights the torch for him both literally and figuratively (318), establishes him as 'a champion of Mrs Anthony' (392). Anthony himself seems to recognize this affinity between himself and the younger man, and when the *Ferndale* sinks he commands him to jump first, saying, 'It isn't my turn. Up with you.' The mistaken identification of Powell with the Captain of the *Ferndale* is the immediate cause of Anthony's death, when he is left behind to sink with his ship (439–40). Flora's remarriage is, therefore, not a mere concession to the need for a happy ending, but an affirmation of the surrogacy which links the two 'knights' to each other and to the ageing, but still enchanting 'damsel'.

The third knight in the story is, of course, Marlow himself. The obvious link between him and the other two knights is their 'common calling', as defined with characteristic solemnity by little Fyne (41). The narrator comments on the 'excellent understanding' which is immediately established between Marlow and Powell, two 'exactly dissimilar' figures, 'one individuality projecting itself in length and the other in breadth, which is already a sufficient ground for irreconcilable difference. . . . Between two such organisms one would not have expected the slightest temperamental accord . . . [But] the men of the sea understand each other very well in their view of earthly things . . .' (32–33). We have already noted that both Anthony and Marlow make an ethical distinction between life on sea and life on shore. Marlow's eventual return to 'his element' will be ratified by an affirmation of his bond with the other two knights.

The most significant bond between these three men is, of course, their love for Flora, for Marlow, too, is strongly attracted to the girl, and affected, like the two romantic knights (whose sentiments he often pretends to mock) by her fate: 'the mouth looked very red in the white face . . . the little pointed chin . . . she was an appealing and—yes—she was a desirable little figure' (201); Marlow's description of Anthony's love for the girl seems to be based on first-hand knowledge:

I don't know in what the sign consisted in this case. It might have been her pallor . . . that white face with eyes like blue gleams of fire and lips like red coals. In certain lights, in certain poises of head it suggested tragic sorrow. . . . Or even just that pointed chin . . . it was the chin's doing; that 'common mortal touch' which stands in such good stead to some women. (217)

In his description of Flora during their last encounter, Marlow uses expressions which the other two have previously employed to describe her: 'Flora came down the garden to meet me, no longer the perversely tempting, sorrowful wisp of white mist . . . Neither did she look like a forsaken elf' (442; see 226 and 424 for the use of these epithets by Anthony and Powell).

The resemblance between Marlow and Powell is enhanced by the similarity of their respective positions in the tale: both are initially curious observers, mere 'chance-comers' (311, 426), 'onlookers' (429), and 'unseen beholders' (430); and both are drawn into the tale by their love for Flora and become active participants as they bring Flora and her 'knight' (Anthony in Powell's case, and Powell in Marlow's case) together. Marlow often attributes his involvement in the story to his curiosity, the 'absurd temptation to remain and see what would come of it', while realizing that all this is 'none of [his] business' (198, see also 40, 48). Powell also refers, albeit in a much more embarrassed manner, to the 'unhealthy curiosity which did away in my case with all the restraints of common decency' (414, see also 280, 296). Both Powell and Marlow share a sense of wonder as to the 'vagaries of fate' (40): Marlow often ruminates on the works of chance, 'that which happens blindly and without intelligent design' (36, see also 99, 126, 312, 376, 437); and Powell marvels, at odd moments of unwonted speculation, at 'the precise workmanship of chance, fate, providence, call it what you will' (411, see also 438).

At the end of the story, Marlow's account of Powell's story, and the frame narrator's account of Marlow's merge, as Powell describes the night of the attempted murder, and the narrator extends the ominous overtones of the description to his nightly session with Marlow: 'Marlow got up to get another cigar. The night was getting on to what I may call its deepest hour, the hour

most favourable to evil purposes of men's hate, despair or greed
. . .; the hour of ill-omened silence and chill and stagnation . . .'
(415). The assimilation of Powell's account into Marlow's narrative is not a mere technical solution: it is an affirmation of their
essential affinity, of the surrogacy which will eventually turn
Marlow into the third knight. The resemblance between Marlow
and Anthony is even more striking. Marlow's conjectures as to
Anthony's life ring with an almost confessional note: we have
already seen that the description of Anthony's love for Flora has
nothing vicarious about it (217), as Marlow seems to share
Anthony's feelings about her. Anthony's description of Flora who
has 'no holding ground on the earth' seems to echo Marlow's plea
for mercy on her behalf: 'if she were given some sort of footing in
this world . . ., she would probably learn to keep a better balance'
(196).

Marlow's descriptions of Anthony's former life, 'a life of solitude
and silence—and desire', before 'chance had thrown the girl in his
way' (328), are apt descriptions of his own life. He can well
understand the 'desire of that man to whom the sea and sky of his
solitary life appeared suddenly incomplete without that glance . . .'
(231). By the end of the story Marlow is stripped of his former
self-sufficiency, and admits that he is lonley (258, 260). Flora had
been 'thrown' in his way before she met Anthony, and he had
missed his chance, but it is precisely this painful admission of
insufficiency and failure which takes him back to the human
element.

Marlow's transformation is complete when he decides to finish
the 'story' in accordance with his newly formulated imperative of
'pairing off', the necessity of the 'embrace', and the 'sacred' call of
life, which is a denial of his former misogyny, self-sufficiency, and
derision of love (426–7). He hires a boat, a 'sloop-rigged three-
tonner' (257), and sets out in pursuit of Mr Powell. The 'happy
ending' which he almost enforces on the characters, the romantic
fiction which he brings into being by his active interference in the
plot, marks the beginning of his own tentative convalescence. He
has become a seaman again.

Marlow's recovery from this emotional paralysis, the correlative of
his unremittingly relativistic conception of the world, is effected,
then, through an elaborate system of surrogacies which assimilate

him into the tale by turning him into the third knight in Flora's tale. But there may be a fourth knight as well: the frame-narrator is also drawn into the tale and materializes before our eyes as another knightly figure as he becomes more and more involved in Flora's story, and is moved by his 'masculine chivalry to protest against Marlow's acerbic treatment of it (283–4). And one is tempted to step overboard, as it were, and name the author himself—who, as we have seen, resembles his protagonists in so many ways—as the fifth knight. For why should Conrad have chosen to eliminate from the book version of *Chance* all the passages which identify the frame-narrator as a writer of fiction, unless he had felt that he, too, was being forcibly drawn into his own fiction?

The multiplication of narrators and the replication of Flora's knights—all surrogate figures for each other—create a spiralling structure which is carried yet further by the recurrence of certain key events in the plot: Flora's suicide attempts are thwarted twice— first by Marlow's voice (43–5), and then by Anthony's interception (214–16). The fatal collision of the *Ferndale* is adumbrated, almost rehearsed for, by the near-collision which Flora and Powell have averted (317–19). Flora's marriage to Anthony following their meeting in the garden (230) is recapitulated at the end, when her interview with Marlow in the garden prepares for her marriage to Powell (442–6). *Chance*, then, is true to the claim of its subtitle: it is 'a story in two parts', a twice (or thrice?) told tale.

This echo-chamber effect, created by the multivocality of the narrative, by the recurrence of key events, and by the endless replication of the 'knights', operates within the story as an integrating force, turning Marlow from an observer to a participant in the tale, and happily concluding Flora's story with a wedding—the proper ending for a romance or a comedy. But the same effect operates at the same time as a reminder of the ultimate textuality of reality. One is reminded again of Conrad's famous image for Marlow's yarns in *Heart of Darkness*: 'to him the meaning of an episode was not inside like a kernel but outside, enveloping the tale which brought it out only as a glow brings out a haze, in the likeness of one of these misty halos that sometimes are made visible by the spectral illumination of moonshine' (*Heart of Darkness*, 48). But it seems that by now the kernel—the solid, comforting, 'one-and-only' truth—is no longer there at all. It has been replaced by an endless reverberation of echoes, a series of shells, frames, and haloes.

B. *VICTORY*

The critical controversy over the artistic merits of *Victory* and its place in Conrad's work has produced a diversity of judgements, ranging from the view that the novel is 'among those of Conrad's works which deserve to be current as representing his claim to classical standing' to the assertion that 'the time has come to drop *Victory* from the Conrad canon'.[55] It seems to me that at least some of the elements which have generated this wide divergence can be resolved by viewing the novel as a product of Conrad's 'textual' mode.

The first chapter opens with the seemingly irrelevant ruminations of the narrator on the relation between diamonds and coal. This introductory passage, atypical of the pace of the rest of the novel in its leisurely, speculative tone, has been taken by critics to establish the theme of doubling in the novel, the resemblance between ostensibly opposite beings like Heyst and 'the plain Mr Jones'.[56] I believe that the theme introduced by this somewhat incongruous opening is more complex than that: coal and diamonds are related to each other not, as one might expect after having read the opening sentence, by an elaborate explanation of the 'very close chemical relation' which links them, but by the fact that 'both these commodities *represent* wealth' (3, my emphasis). The focus, then, is not on a common chemical essence but on the quality of *representation*.

But there is a major difference between these two cases of material substances representing wealth: one can easily understand the practical fascination of coal as a source of energy and heat, but the 'mystical' fascination of diamonds would be much harder to grasp, if it were not for the fact that our civilization has, for no practical reason, chosen to endow these shining pebbles with the power to signify wealth. The relation of the substance to the

---

[55] F. R. Leavis, *The Great Tradition*, 209; A. J. Guerard, *Conrad the Novelist*, 275.

[56] Sharon Kahele and Howard German, 'Conrad's *Victory*: A Reassessment', *Modern Fiction Studies*, 10/1 (1964), 55–72; J. Deurbergue, 'The Opening of *Victory*', *Studies in Joseph Conrad*, 2 (1975), 239–70.

represented quality in the case of coal is metonymic or representative, but in the case of diamonds it is clearly semiotic, i.e. arbitrary
and entirely artificial.

A similar treatment is accorded by the narrator to The Tropical
Belt Company.

The world of finance is a mysterious world in which, incredible as the fact
may appear, evaporation precedes liquidation. First the capital evaporates,
and then the company goes into liquidation. These are very unnatural
physics . . . (3)

This playful inversion of the laws of physics introduces the reader
once again to the major concern of the novel: even the laws of
physics—'discovered' by science and therefore ostensibly objective
and immutable—are presented as a system of signs, human constructs which function by human consent and can be inverted at
will.

As we have already seen, this view of reality as a construct, or—
as the post-modernists would have it—a text, is not atypical of
Conrad, but in *Victory* we meet the first Conrad protagonist who
is so entirely caught up in it that he cannot bring himself to act at
all. An apt diagnosis of Heyst's malady has been offered by H. J.
Laskowski, who rightly relates the protagonist's frame of mind to
the philosophical scepticism of Berkeley and Hume, a 'denial of
what may be called "self" or "mind" if by either of these terms we
mean an abiding human essence' and a ' "skeptical doubt" ' as to
the continued existence of objects when they are not being perceived'. Laskowski diagnoses Heyst as 'a man beset by the skeptical
doubt of Hume, a man who tries to live with a radical awareness
of his own insubstantiality, and the insubstantiality of everything
around him.'[57]

Heyst's 'disenchantment' (65), his view of the world as 'nothing
but an amusing spectacle' (178), his temperamental attitude of 'a
spectator' (185, 196) become not only an epistemological stance
but an ethical position as well. I would suggest that this form of
unbelief is an early version of post-modernist textuality, a view of
the world as an infinite series of signs without an ultimate referent,

---

[57] H. J. Laskowski, '*Esse Est Percipi*: Epistemology and Narrative Method in
Victory', *Conradiana*, 9/3 (1977), 2725–86. For an earlier, similar view of Heyst,
see Donald A. Dike, 'The Tempest of Axel Heyst', *Nineteenth-Century Fiction*, 17/
2 (1962), 95–113.

and a condemnation of essentialism as a falsified conception of life. This view, as reflected in Heyst's relativistic, textual sensibility (which renders the novel extremely vulnerable to deconstruction), is ultimately rejected in *Victory*, at least on the level of the author's conscious and explicit message, on moral grounds.[58]

Axel Heyst is the *fin de siècle* protagonist who realizes that appearances are all that one can ask for or have in this world (204); who scorns life—or rather 'what people call by that name'— for the 'fatal imperfection' of its gifts which, he believes, 'makes of them a delusion and a snare' (212); who has managed to 'refine everything away' by turning the earth to 'a shadow', who has lost 'all belief in realities' (350). In his admission to Lena that he is powerless to protect her (347), that he has 'neither force nor conviction', 'neither strength nor persuasion' to act (350), Heyst himself relates his passivity to his view of reality as a mesh of illusions. His initial response to the pending confrontation with the murderous trio is 'all this is too unreal altogether' (347), a response which he reiterates later in his 'showdown' with Jones: 'you people . . . are divorced from all reality in my eyes' (364). Heyst's inability to suspend his disbelief in the spectacle of life has left him entirely impotent. At the moment when he can easily overcome Jones, his very will is 'dead of weariness' and he moves 'like a prisoner captured by the evil power of a masquerading skeleton out of the grave' (390). The skeleton is not necessarily the spectral figure of Jones staggering at Heyst's side, but that of his father who had, by his negation of life, rendered him unfit for it.

The nature of the Heystian frame of mind, the philosophy of total negation, has been studied in depth by various critics. S. Kahele and Howard German describe him as 'the man whose thinking was devoted to the destruction of illusion', and whose scepticism reflects Conrad's view that ideals are 'inevitably extremely subjective'. Conrad's ambivalence about the role of illusion in the human enterprise—the tension between his Heystian scepticism on the one hand and his realization that illusions are

---

[58] The word 'vulnerability' is used here advisedly, for it seems to me that an interpretation which adheres to the Heystian outlook and chooses to ignore its final condemnation, like that offered by W. Bonney in 'Narrative Perspective in *Victory*: The Thematic Relevance', *The Journal of Narrative Technique*, 5/1 (1975), 24–39, is a denial of the acknowledgement of moral responsibility which is at the core of Conrad's work.

necessary for the survival of humanity on the other (94)—is, they rightly maintain, one of the central dynamic principles of the novel.[59] Another notable study of the Heystian frame of mind is Bruce Johnson's analysis of the novel as an indictment of Schopenhauer's philosophy: 'there can be no doubt that Heyst's skepticism is "metaphysical" and that the elder Heyst's vision of "man's right to absolute moral and intellectual liberty" evolves out of the frightening contingency of man in a universe that has no moral plan'.[60]

The metaphysical nature of Heyst's scepticism is, indeed, irrefutable, but I would suggest that the philosophical prototype of the elder Heyst is Nietzsche rather than Schopenhauer, for while it is true that Nietzsche's metaphysical scepticism evolved out of Schopenhauer's bleak vision, it was he who embraced its logical consequences and declared the 'death of God' in an uninhibited celebration of moral 'perspectivism'.[61] Heyst Sr. cuts a Nietzschean figure in his role as 'a thinker, stylist, and man of the world' (92), a 'destroyer of systems, of hopes, of beliefs' (175). The description of the father's style, 'the broken text of reflections, maxims, short phrases, enigmatical sometimes and sometimes eloquent' (219), is closely reminiscent of the philosopher's notorious aphorisms, and some of the Heystian postulates do, indeed, sound like quotations from Nietzsche: 'the desire is the bed of dreams' (219); 'men live their captivity. To the unknown force of negation they prefer the miserably tumbled bed of their servitude'(220).[62]

Heyst's bleak vision of morality, postulating that 'the so-called wickedness must be, like the so-called virtue, its own reward—to be anything at all' (219), sounds like an echo of Nietzschean gesture beyond Good and Evil, his denial of any transcendental or

---

[59] Kahele and German, 'Conrad's *Victory*', 70, 65.

[60] B. Johnson, *Conrad's Models of Mind*, 160, 165. A similar view is taken by Arnold E. Davidson in *Conrad's Endings: A Study of the Five Major Novels*, UMI Research Press Studies in Modern Literature (Ann Arbor, Mich., 1984). Davidson equates Heyst's physical disarming, the theft of his revolver, to the process of 'metaphysical disarming' set off by Heyst Sr., a process which has robbed reality of its substance for the son (94.).

[61] A recent, much acclaimed study of Nietzsche's work, *Nietzsche: Life as Literature*, by A. Nehamas (Cambridge, Mass.: Harvard University Press, 1986), projects an extremely Heyst-like figure which, I believe, justifies my own treatment of the haunting presence of the father.

[62] For a fuller treatment of the Nietzschean outlook see chapter 1 above, and the inroductory section to this chapter.

inherently valid ethical sanction. It is not surprising, therefore, that the 'plain Mr Jones' is presented as both the father's and the son's double, as it is he, rather than Heyst Jr., who takes the Heystian attitude to its ultimate conclusion.[63] The ethical relativism which emerges from the awareness of the metaphysical void, the sense that, as Johnson puts it, 'there are no sanctions in the artificial fictions of society',[64] opens up a moral abyss down which Heyst the son is forced to look. As he does so, he recognizes a caricatured reflection of himself in the image of Jones.

Another concomitant of the Nietzschean-Heystian world-view is the conception of the world in aesthetic terms, as a spectacle. This typical *fin de siècle* attitude, which finds its paragon in the languid pose of Jones, is also—albeit in a more refined and less ruthless form—at the source of Heyst's conception of the world.[65] The aestheticist dimension in the portrayal of Heyst is mostly evident in Conrad's use of sound and music, which has been largely overlooked even by critics who explore this aspect of the novel. Pater's famous formulation of the aestheticist credo that 'all art constantly aspires to the condition of music' (a reiteration of Schopenhauer's hierarchy of the arts), which reflects the attempt to break away from the concept of mimesis and to work within a perfect system which is entirely self-referential and self-contained, is curiously echoed in the description of Heyst. 'Like most drea-mers, to whom it is given sometimes to hear the music of the spheres, [he] had a taste for silence which he was able to gratify for years. The islands are very quiet' (66).

But Heyst is drawn despite himself out of his insular position into the sordid reality of common humanity by the noise of 'rasped, squeaked, scraped snatches of tunes' played by Zangiacomo's Ladies' Orchestra, 'an instrumental uproar, screaming, grunting, whining, sobbing, scraping, squeaking some kind of lively air' (67–8). Heyst's response to the brutish noise is significant:

---

[63] The justice of Jones's claim to be Heyst's double has been recognized by several critics, including Paul Wiley, *Conrad's Measure of Man*, Kahele and German, 'Conrad's *Victory*', B. Johnson, *Conrad's Models of Mind*, D. A. Dike, 'The Tempest of Axel Heyst', D. Schwarz, *The Later Fiction*, and others.

[64] Bruce Johnson, *Conrad's Models of Mind*, 170.

[65] The relationship between Heyst's outlook and the aesthetic-decadent frame of mind has been noted and discussed in several readings of the novel. Bruce Johnson, *Conrad's Models of Mind*, 43, 160–1; Joseph Martin, 'Conrad and the Aesthetic Movement', *Conradiana*, 3 (1985), 199–213.

In the quick time of that music, in the varied, piercing clamour of the strings . . . there was a suggestion of brutality—something cruel, *sensual* and repulsive. . . . But there is an unholy fascination in systematic noise. He did not flee from it incontinently as one might have expected him to do. He remained, astonished at himself for remaining, since nothing could have been more repulsive to his tastes, more painful to his senses, and, so to speak, more contrary to his genius, than this *rude exhibition of vigour.* The Zangiacomo band was not making music; it was simply murdering silence with *a vulgar, ferocious energy.* (68, my emphases)

It seems to me that the relation posited between crudeness and virility is not accidental: Heyst's hypertrophied cultured sensibility, his taste for the perfect 'music of the spheres' which sends him into a voluntary exile in the realm of silence, is seen by Conrad as a disabling disease which will eventually render the protagonist unfit for survival.

Heyst the son is 'not a fighting man' (9); he is essentially a reader, a man in 'the white drill suit of civilization' (227) with a book in his hand (4 27, 28, 180). Even Lena is ultimately just another 'text' for him: her eyes are 'unreadable' (219), she is 'a script in an unknown language' (222, see also 310, 324). And although she gives him 'a greater sense of his own reality than he had ever known in all his life' (200), it is not yet sufficient for him to recover that dimension of reality which he had renounced. Lena's attempt to reverse Heyst's 'textual' view of life, begins with her request to be named by him:

They call me Alma. . . . Magdelene too. It doesn't matter; you can call me by whatever name you choose. Yes, you give me a name. Think of one you would like the sound of—something quite new. How I should like to forget everything that had gone before, as one forgets a dream that's done with . . . (88)

The power which she grants him to create her anew by naming her, is undoubtedly an Adamic endowment. It is the semi-divine power to create a world with the word, which has been delegated to Adam in the act of naming God's creatures. Lena later reinforces her proffered gift when she tells her lover: 'Do you know, it seems to me, somehow, that if you were to stop thinking of me I shouldn't be in the world at all . . . I can only be what you think I am' (187). But Heyst cannot take the gift of creation. He has lost his belief in the power of the word to create a world, and Lena seems to despair of her role as an Eve to his Adam when she asks him: 'Do you believe that I exist?' (247) It seems that he does not.

Heyst's failure to take up the Adamic role is closely related to the lethal scepticism of his father who had tried to silence the 'imperative echoes' of 'the oldest voice in the world'. It is this oldest voice which had uttered the words of creation, which had fathered the 'original Adam', the 'primeval ancestor' to whom Heyst the son would like to relate himself (173). The doctrine of 'universal unbelief' (199) and 'universal nothingness (219) embraced by Heyst Sr. reverses the Adamic endowment in its view of human reality as a hollow construct. He leaves his son with a conception of a world 'perhaps not substantial enough to grasp' (176), with a legacy of counterfeit coins.

In an illuminating analysis of this relationship between the Adamic voice and the voice of Heyst Sr., Tony Tanner rightly juxtaposes the imperatives of the two fathers, the 'double voice of the dual father'. The Adamic voice commands Heyst to 'copulate and multiply' and the voice of the dead father tells him to deny his sexuality, to abstain. Tanner describes the father as 'the ghost voice of books', who had tried 'to dominate and master the world with the word', and contrasts Lena's physical, literal presence, her 'living voice', with the dead 'sense' of the father's presence.[66] I believe that this juxtaposition of the father's word with Lena's voice underscores the proposed diagnosis of the pathological textuality which afflicts the protagonist.

The wider cultural implications of *Victory*, its critique of the ethical relativism and the scepticism of the post-Nietzschean world which engendered the aestheticist-decadent outlook, and its hostile anticipation of some post-modernist concepts, call for a view of the story of Axel Heyst as a study case of crumbling civilization. This aspect of the novel has been recognized by several critics.[67] The view of the sophisticated and highly civilized as foredoomed by definition, of hypercerebration and reflection as inimically hostile to instinctual life forces is, indeed, symptomatic of the age.

---

[66] Tony Tanner, 'Joseph Conrad and the Last Gentleman', *Critical Quarterly*, 28/2 (1986), 133.

[67] See Paul L. Wiley, *Conrad's Measure of Man*, 151; D. Schwarz, *Conrad: The Later Fiction*, 60–1, 66; Stanley Renner, 'The Garden of Civilization: Conrad, Huxley and the Ethics of Evolution', *Conradiana*, 7/2 (1975), 61–75; Geddes, *Conrad's Later Novels*, 58.

This attitude is succinctly formulated in *The Modern Temper* by Joseph Wood Krutch who regards 'the detachment of mind from its function [i.e. physical survival] which makes philosophy possible' as a 'vital liability', because 'intelligence which is detached, skeptical, ironic . . . puts the man or the race which possess it at a disadvantage in dealing with those whose intelligence serves their purpose'. He concludes—like Nietzsche, Spengler, and other prophets of doom—that 'civilizations die from philosophical calm, irony and the sense of fair play quite as surely as they die of debauchery'.[68]

However one may object to or wish to modify this prognosis, it is certainly true in the case of Axel Heyst, the urbane, ironic, ultra-civilized specimen of a dying race. Living amongst the overgrown ruins of the commercial Western enterprise, in the shadow of the gigantic blackboard featuring the initials of the evaporated company, he is, indeed, a 'man of the last hour' or 'the hour before last' (359) rather than the 'original Adam' (173). It is Wang, the man who cultivates the vegetable garden and uses his intelligence as an instrument for survival, who is the true descendent of the first man. If there is one sense in which Heyst does share something with the original Adam, it is the fact of the fall, but whereas the first fall was occasioned by the first man's need to eat of the tree of knowledge, his weary descendant is already carrying the seed of that life-denying fruit of knowledge—left to him as a legacy from his father—within him, as he tried to reinstate himself in the Garden.

Another relevant aspect of *Victory* is the plurality of its textual affinities. The novel has been successfully and convincingly shown to be related to various biblical passages, to *The Tempest*, to *Hamlet*, to *Macbeth*, and to the *Aeneid*.[69] As the literary models suggested by the critics cited below are all substantiated by weighty

---

[68] Joseph Wood Krutch, *The Modern Temper*, 44, 43, 45.

[69] Wilfred S. Dowden, *Joseph Conrad: The Imaged Style* (Nashville: Vanderbilt University Press, 1970), 156–66; Dwight Purdy, *Joseph Conrad's Bible* (Norman: University of Oklahoma Press, 1984), 118–44; David Lodge, 'Conrad's *Victory* and *The Tempest*: An Amplification', *Modern Language Review*, 59 (1964), 195–9; Donald A. Dike, 'The Tempest of Axel Heyst'; A. Gillon, 'Joseph Conrad and Shakespeare, part Four: A Reinterpretation of *Victory*', *Conradiana* 8/1 (1975), 61–75; T. Tanner, 'Gentlemen and Gossip: Aspects of Evolution and Language in Conrad's *Victory*', *L'Époque Conradienne* (May 1981), 1–56; C. Watts, 'Reflections on *Victory*', *Conradiana*, 15/1 (1983), 73–9.

evidence in the novel, there emerges a baffling range of texts all claiming to be the literary progenitors of this work. Which, then, is the prototext to which *Victory* should be related? The answer, I believe, should be, 'all of them'. The blatant textuality of this novel, the fact that it parades itself as a literary text by numerous allusions to other texts, is a significant correlative of the protagonist's frame of mind. For Heyst the reader, a man who views reality as a spectacle or a mesh of appearances, is so afflicted with this textual or literary view of life, that he can never suspend his disbelief and respond to the drama of reality as if it were real indeed.

An interesting symptom of this state of mind which generates a view of reality as a system of references without referents appears in the use of the monetary analogy in the novel. Heyst explains his father's disillusionment in terms of counterfeit coins:

I suppose he began like other people; took fine words for good, ringing coin and noble ideas for valuable bank notes. . . . Later he discovered— how am I to explain it to you? Suppose the world were a factory and all mankind workmen in it. Well, he discovered that the wages were not good enough. That they were paid in counterfeit money. (195–6)

A strikingly similar analogy has been made by Hans Vaihinger in *The Philosophy of 'As If'*.

We hardly notice that we are acting on a double stage—our own inner world (which, of course, we objectify as the world of sense-perception) and also an entirely different and external world. There are then exchange centers, where the values of one world are changed into those of the other and the active intercourse between both worlds is made possible, where the light paper currency of thought is exchanged for the heavy coin of reality, and where on the other hand the heavy metal of reality is exchanged for a lighter currency which nevertheless facilitates intercourse.

The difficulty . . . lies entirely in the reduction of one system to another, in effecting the exchange. Large quantities of false paper-money, many false ideas, that cannot be changed into material values, find their way into circulation; the nominal value of paper money is not always paid, but the price which rules on the market . . . [But] all higher speculation and the whole of our intricate system of exchange are only possible by this expedient and by these fictional values.

'Fictional value' is the name given in political economy to paper-money and such ideas as, for instance, the pound sterling, etc. The paper is regarded as if it had the value of metal . . . Our analogy thus has a real basis. . . . Concepts too are merely conventional signs. . . . In every instance it is the fictive function that is here at workd.[70]

But Heyst's analogy, seemingly straightforward and simple, has yet another twist, of which he—like many professed disciples of Saussure—seems to be oblivious. If all mankind are workmen in the 'factory', then there is no sense in which one can talk of counterfeit money because the value of currency is determined by human consent. Bank notes have no intrinsic value beyond the paper they are printed on. They acquire value when a significant group of people decides that these particular pieces of paper represent something else, something tangible and 'real', like land or sheep. Language functions in much the same way, on the basis of common consent. When a group of people accept a certain sound combination as a signifier, it becomes a living word.

Thus when Heyst talks of his father's 'living word' (196), he is, in a sense, using the very counterfeit money he despises, for once he has decided to break through the barrier of silence in which he had cloistered himself, he must share the basic assumptions that are common to mankind, he must believe that there is something real to be represented in order for any communication to take place at all. His agony at the thought of Lena's response to Schomberg's allegations against him is also embedded in a recognition of the inevitability of representation: 'you thought that there was no smoke without fire!' For a man to whom *all* is smoke without fire, the discovery of the 'power of words' (214) is shattering indeed.

This last point is related to two fault-lines which have served as the arena for the critical debate about the literary value of the novel and which, I believe, are closely related to each other. The first problem is the generic transition from the realistic mode of Part I to an allegorical mode which eventually seems to take over the rest of the work. This ambivalent generic identity has generated an opposition between two mutually exclusive approaches to the novel. Hewitt, Moser, and Guerard view the novel as a realistic work that fails partly because of the insistent allegorical dimension which precludes realistic psychological characterization, whereas Paul Wiley, John Palmer, and others celebrate the allegorical

---

[70] Vaihinger, The Philosophy of 'As If', 159–60.

dimension and the rich symbolism of the novel.[71] There have been some attempts to accommodate the generic transition, notably by R. W. B. Lewis who modifies the allegorical element and prefers to call it an 'allegorical swelling', or Gary Geddes who argues that the pervading irony in the novel acts as a 'built-in antidote or counter-weight to its allegorizing tendencies'.[72] I would suggest a different, perhaps less apologetic way of accommodating the seemingly incongruent generic mix in the novel, and relate it to the second, ostensibly technical difficulty—the narrative discontinuity.

The blatant inconsistency of the narrative mode, the abandon-ment of the first-person narrator of Part I, his replacement by an omniscient narrative voice in Part II, when the action moves to Samburan, and his eventual reinstatement at the very end, after Heyst's death, has been regarded by critics as yet another of the novel's failures, an awkward handling of the physical removal of the protagonists away from the first narrator's territory to an isolated island. It is only in the more recent readings of the novel (like those offered by Gary Geddes and William Bonney) that serious attempts to account for this narrative transition as a correlative of a thematic shift have been made.

I believe that both these targets of critical disapproval—the generic shift and the narrative discontinuity—reflect the basic dynamism of the novel. These two 'aesthetic' ruptures should be viewed in a Bakhtinian light, as the projections of the protagonist's frame of mind, the fault-lines within his consciousness. Both the allegorical mode and the omniscient narrative voice belong to a metaphysically integrated conception of the world: the allegory depends for its viability on an a priori clear-cut conceptual system, just as the omniscient narrative voice is premised on a clear notion of authority. One can easily see why allegory as a genre and omniscience as a narrative mode are not favoured in the literature produced in the age of relativism after the disintegration of metaphysics and the death of God. What we have in Part II of the novel, then, is a transition to a different premise, or at least an

[71] Guerard, *Conrad the Novelist*; Hewitt, *Conrad: A Reassessment;* Moser, *Achievement and Decline;* P. Wiley, *Conrad's Measure of Man*; John A. Palmer, *Joseph Conrad's Fiction* (Ithaca, NY: Cornell University Press, 1968), 166–97.

[72] R. W. B. Lewis, 'The Current of Conrad's *Victory*' in F. R. Karl (ed.), *Joseph Conrad: A Collection of Criticism* (New York: McGraw-Hill Book Company, 1975), 101–19; G. Geddes, *Conrad's Later Novels*.

attempt to suspend the radical, essentially modern scepticism of the first-person narrator which is but a reflection of the Heystian frame of mind. In Part II Heyst is given the opportunity to cast himself into the allegory, or into the Eden myth: he may be able to redeem himself by suspending his disbelief and acting out his part in the allegory.

The significant use of religious terminology can also be viewed in the same context. The volcano which is Heyst's closest neighbour and which resembles the intermittent glow of his cigar, is 'a pillar of smoke by day and a loom of fire at night' (168). This is an obvious reference to the pillar of alternating smoke and fire which had led the Israelites on their way to the promised land, whose immediate significance is, of course, heavily ironic: in Heyst's world there can be no promised land, and his 'pilgrimage' is indeed 'aimless' (31). Heyst's eventual choice of death by fire may, then, be construed at least as an attempt to redeem the value of that debased religious currency, to reinstate the metaphysical frame-work which makes the allegory viable. Heyst's references to the deluge, the destruction of a corrupt civilization (191), and his playful attitude to the notion of Providence (199, 359), of 'retribu-tion' (354), can also be seen in the same light as the foredoomed attempts of the protagonist to restore the lost metphysical dimension.

It seems to me that the transition to the allegorical mode is effective in its very crudity, for it is Heyst himself who posits the allegory in his search for a textual or literary model to his reality. It is Heyst himself who presents the trio as 'evil intelligence', 'instinctive savagery', and 'brute force' (329). But the self-con-sciousness of the spectator-participant, who tried to define the generic category of the spectacle divests the allegory of its primal power which depends on a system of beliefs and cannot function in the absence of a coherent metaphysical view. For Heyst, the man who cannot believe, 'good' and 'evil' are but 'optical delusions' like hope or fellowship or love (see 80, 82).[73] The allegory remains a quaint artistic spectacle, because Heyst cannot bring himself to act upon it as an Everyman would have done.

---

[73] The concept of 'human optics' may have been derived from Nietzsche. 'We speak as though there were really existing things . . . But real things exist only for human optics: and from this we cannot escape' (quoted by Vaihinger, *The Philosophy of 'As If'* 348).

The discontinuity of the narrative mode can also be accounted for by this wavering of the novel between the poles of disbelief and willed belief, between the Heystian temperament and the desire to negate the 'universal nothingness' (219) with an act of creation. The narrator of the first part embodies, as observed by W. Bonney, 'a placid model of Old Heyst' in his static detachment, his pervasive irony, and his refusal to commit himself and engage in an intimate contact with the protagonists.[74] He persistently—and for the most part without any apparent relevance—calls attention to his use of words: his somewhat crude puns on 'forced' and 'forcible' (5), on the bald 'top' of Heyst's head and the 'tip-top' house of the Tesman Brothers (7), enhance the sense of a 'free play of meaning', as does his gossipy speculative manner of introducing the protagonists. This self-reflexive quality of the narrative is yet another symptom of the 'textual' state of mind, the conception of all human enterprise as an illusory construct.

The transition to the omniscient mode, like the allegorical shift, affords the protagonist a temporary sanctuary by transporting him to Samburan, out of the relativizing voice of the first-person narrator. But Heyst's scepticism is incurable. The tentative sanctuary with which Conrad has provided him is not strong enough to withstand the corrosive voice of his father. As the story reverts to the realistic mode and the first-person narrator takes over once more, one realizes that the victory of Lena's life-giving powers, a victory which Heyst seems to have finally conceded in the verbal affirmation with which he concludes his life, is yet another illusion. The last word is 'nothing'.

There remains, of course, the question of the artistic merit of the novel. Rather than join the controversy on the side of either the realistic or the allegorical readings, I would suggest that if the novel does not 'work', it is not because of any technical or stylistic defects. The failure here is a failure of vision, the work of a writer who, like his protagonist, cannot will himself into a belief in the power of words, who, like his protagonist, has come to suspect language as counterfeit coins. When Axel Heyst tells Lena of 'the man with the quill pen in his hand' who is 'responsible for [his] existence' (195), he points to the portrait of his father. But the man who has, in fact, created Heyst with the quill pen in his hand and

---

[74] W. Bonney, 'Narrative Perspectives in *Victory*', 30.

is thus responsible for his existence is, of course, Conrad himself, the author of Heyst's tale. The ambivalence of the attribution, the deliberate fusion of parental authority and authorial responsibility is, I believe, at the core of *Victory*, for it is Conrad's own failure, as well as that of his protagonist, to fend off the Heystian element in himself which underlies the peculiar generic conflict in the novel, the narrative discontinuity, and the ambiguity of the denouement.

The close affinity between the Conradian temperament and that of his protagonist is evident to any reader of Conrad's letters. The most thorough discussions of this resemblance are offered by Daniel Schwarz, who rightly describes Heyst as 'a double for part of Conrad's temperament', and by Douglas D. Park, who describes Conrad's own scepticism as 'a temperamental condition', a consciousness which 'undermines all perception' and which 'ultimately turns against itself. It dissolves its own surfaces, rationalizations, impulses, emotions, until nothing is left but a paralyzed complexity.' Conrad's Heystian sensibility is evident, as Park shows, in his letters to Marguerite Poradowska and to Edward Garnett, where he confesses—like his protagonist—to having lost all sense of reality. A similar line is followed by Gary Geddes, who also quotes the letters to Garnett, Cunninghame Graham, and others in support of the correlation between Conrad's outlook and that of his protagonist, and aptly underscores some phrases that 'might have been lifted directly from the writings of Heyst's father'.[75]

The significance of Heyst Sr's attempt to silence 'the oldest voice in the world' has already been discussed. The analogy between the primal act of creation—that of the primal voice which had created the world with his word—and the creative power of the artist is obvious: had Conrad accepted the Heyst imperative to 'look on—make no sound' (175), he would have been, like his protagonist, another exile in the realm of silence. His manifest disobedience is, in itself, a kind of victory, a declaration of faith in the power of the word to create a world.

---

[75] Schwarz, *Conrad: The Later Fiction*, 69; Douglas B. Park, 'Conrad's *Victory*; The Anatomy of a Pose', *Nineteenth-Century Fiction*, 31/2 (1976), 151–2; Geddes, *Conrad's Later Novels*, 55–6.

C. *THE ARROW OF GOLD*

The Arrow of Gold is one of Conrad's least controversial novels. Critics are virtually unanimous in their verdict on its poor quality, and the most notable studies of Conrad have chosen either to avoid any discussion of this work, or to relegate it to chapters bearing titles such as 'The Exhaustion of Creative Energy', 'The Exhausted Self', and 'The Collapse of Form'.[76] These summary discussions deal, for the most part, with the obvious failings of *The Arrow*: its inflated rhetoric, the failure to dramatize characters and emotions, the apparent lack of narrative control, and the ineffectiveness of its symbolism. The purpose of the present chapter is not to redeem the novel from literary disrepute or to offer another detailed analysis of this admittedly problematic work, but to diagnose its failure as a reflection of an unresolved generic ambiguity, and to examine its symptomatic relevance to the failure of textuality and to Conrad's conception of himself in relation to his art.

The Arrow proclaims itself as a romance by an overwhelming deployment of markers or signals which set the terms of the generic contract between the reader and the writer. These generic signals (which operate, as we shall see, through patterns of action, characterization, and recurrent motifs) tend to trivialize and deflate the story. They establish a process of 'familiarization', a framework of aesthetic and normative assumptions, resulting in an almost anaesthetic effect on the reader who, following their implicit directive, settles into a reading of the story as a typical romance.

Love and Adventure, the two essential ingredients of romance, dominate the action in the novel, and the plot can be summarized as a version of classical knight-errantry: Monsieur George, a brave young seaman, sets out on a perilous adventure for the sake of Rita, the 'woman of all times' (67), rescues her from the villainies of Ortega, and carries her off to a secluded mountain resort where his courage and devotion are amply rewarded. This reading of the novel as a romance which is predicated on the chivalric rescue of a damsel in distress is further reinforced by patterns of characterization that follow the 'general dialectic structure' of romance.

---

[76] Thomas Moser, *Achievement and Decline*, 179–212; Leo Gurko, *Joseph Conrad: Giant in Exile*, 224–40; Daniel R. Schwarz, *Conrad: The Later Fiction*, 125–38.

Characters tend to be either for or against the quest. If they assist it they are idealized as simply gallant or pure; if they obstruct it they are caricatured as simply villainous or cowardly. Hence every typical character in romance tends to have his moral opposite confronting him, like black and white pieces in a chess game.[77]

Monsieur George, the young, arduous, and honest protagonist, is opposed by Captain Blunt, the 'black knight', a polished, blasé man-of-the-world, 'the last of his race' (176), who suffers from a mysterious insomnia. The other villain, Ortega, and Rita's sister, Thérèse, assume the roles of the 'evil magician and the witch . . . who seem to have a suggestion of erotic perversion about them'.[78] Ortega's murderous ravings of lust throw Rita into a state of paralysing fear (328), and Thérèse, albeit morbidly pious and sanctimonious, seems to have a predatory affection for young men (121, 160). Appropriately enough, Ortega and Thérèse elope when their designs upon Rita's person and fortune are thwarted. These two sinister figures are opposed by Dominic and Rose who are neatly fitted into the 'moral antithesis' underlying the characterization in the romance as 'faithful companions' of 'shadow figures' of the protagonists. Another characteristic romance figure is Mills in the role of the 'wise old man' who withdraws from the scene but 'seems to affect the action he watches over'.[79] Another important feature of romance is its distinct propensity towards social snobbery.

Naive romance confines itself largely to royal families; sentimental romance gives us patterns of aristocratic courage and courtesy, and much of it adopts a 'blood will tell' convention, the association of moral virtue and social rank implied in the word 'noble'.[80]

Gillian Beer relates this aristocratic bias of romance to the wish-fulfilment aspect of the genre, viewing it as a residue of the childish need for a sense of omnipotence.[81] Rita's mysterious affiliation to Don Carlos, the Royal Pretender, is an obvious case in point. This

---

[77] Northrop Frye, *Anatomy of Criticism* (Princeton: Princeton University Press, 1957), 195.

[78] Ibid. 196.

[79] Ibid. 195–6.

[80] Northrop Frye, *The Secular Script*, 161.

[81] Gillian Beer, *The Romance*, The Critical Idiom Series no. 10 (London: Methuen, 1970), 3.

fairy-tale quality of romance is marked not only by its pervasive social snobbery, but also by 'an extraordinarily persistent nostalgia, its search for some kind of imaginative golden age in time or space',[82] a mood which is manifest in *The Arrow* with its recurrent emphasis on the characters' youth and innocence and the Arcadian aura which surrounds them.[83] In his analysis of the patterns of action in the romance, Frye attributes the success of the hero to luck, 'a current of energy which is partly from him and partly outside him', and cites the case of Ulysses, the prototype of the romance hero, as an example of the protagonist's loss of his luck.[84] The fact that M. George is known in Marseilles as 'young Ulysses' (14) and the recurrent references to his good luck or to his loss of it (223, 256–7) operate by allusion to his literary prototype as yet another generic signal, another arrow pointing to romance as the appropriate frame for reading the novel.

But the arrow is a double-edged one. The generic conventions to which *The Arrow* appears to adhere, which would induce a normally competent reader to relate it to the sphere of romance, are constantly undermined and violated by a process of 'defamiliarization', a series of striking and blatant transgressions of the generic code. The first and most obvious of these transgressions is embodied in the narrative frame, the two Notes enclosing M. George's narrative.

In the First Note the anonymous editor introduces the young hero as viewed by Mills: 'A young gentleman who had arrived furnished with proper credentials and who apparently was doing his best to waste his life in an eccentric fashion. *He pretended rather absurdly to be a seaman himself.* (5, my emphasis.) The suggestion that M. George is not, in fact, the experienced seaman that he pretends to be undermines his later description as 'young Ulysses'. The account of M. George's involvement with the Carlist cause is also presented somewhat differently from his own version of it:

They [Mills and Blunt] decided that he should be drawn into the affair if it could be done. . . . Thus lightly was the notorious (and at the same time

---

[82] Frye, *Anatomy of Criticism.*

[83] The Arcadian motifs in The Arrow are discussed by Harold E. Toliver in 'Conrad's *Arrow of Gold* and the Pastoral Tradition', *Modern Fiction Studies*, 8 (1962), 148–58.

[84] Frye, *The Secular Script*, 67.

mysterious) Monsieur George brought into the world; out of the contact of two minds which did not give a single thought to his flesh and blood. (5–6)

George's later presentation of himself as a chivalrous knight is thus overshadowed by the reader's knowledge that he had, in fact, been cleverly manipulated into this heroic posture.

The Second Note takes up the story after the kiss which finalizes Rita's surrender to M. George's love. The famous kiss, 'the thing itself' (336), could easily have been the last scene of a traditional romance, a gesture which marks the end of strife and adventure and the beginning of the happily-ever-after phase in which the reader of romance had little or no interest. But the frame-narrator of *The Arrow* goes beyond the sanctioned boundaries of the genre in a passage which is worth quoting at some length:

The narrative of our man goes on for some six months more, from this, the last night of the Carnival season up to and beyond the season of roses. *The tone of it is much less of exultation than might have been expected.* . . .

It is to be remarked that this period is characterized more by a deep and joyous tenderness than by sheer passion. All fierceness of spirit seems to have *burnt itself out* in their preliminary struggles against each other and themselves. . . . Both show themselves amazingly ingenuous in the practice of sentiment. . . . In the unreserved and instant sharing of all thoughts . . . we see the naiveness of a children's foolhardy adventure. This unreserve expressed for him the truth of the situation. With her it may have been different. *It might have been assumed; yet nobody is altogether a comedian; and even comedians themselves have got to believe the part they play.* But if in this she was a comedienne then it was but a great achievement of her ineradicable honesty. Having once renounced her honourable scruple *she took good care that he should taste no flavour of misgivings in the cup.*

[As to Rose] the girl could not have been very reassured by what she saw. . . . (337–9, my emphases)

This long passage with its peculiar overtone of disillusionment, its sceptical attitude to love, and its suggestions of pretence and hidden regrets in the lovers' relationship, operates as a blatant breach of the generic contract which M. George's narrative seemed to have established, for 'in traditional romance no one is ever disillusioned'[85] and the supreme value and power of love must never be questioned.

The denouement of the story is brutally anticlimatic. M. George is severely wounded in a duel with Captain Blunt. Upon his recovery he finds out that Rita has left him. Mills's cryptic explanation of her departure, 'she has sacrificed [the chance of finding love] . . . to the integrity of your life' (350), is far from convincing, and M. George's easy resignation to the ultimate separation from 'the woman of all times' (67) is difficult to reconcile with his former passion for her. Mills's comment on Rita's exit sounds like en epitaph to romance: 'You know that this world is not a world for lovers . . . No, a world of lovers would be impossible' (350). The account of M. George's surprisingly fast emotional recovery is also couched in ambiguous terms:

He went to [the sea] . . . as soon as he had strength enough to feel the crushing weight of his loss (or his gain) fully, and discovered that he could bear it without flinching . . . He tells his correspondent that *if he had been more romantic he would never have looked at any other woman*. But on the contrary. No face worthy of attention escaped him. (351, my emphasis)

Critics and reviewers who read *The Arrow* as a romance have registered some bafflement in their discussion of these strangely dissonant Notes: Walter de la Mare qualifies his generous review of the novel with the comment that the Second Note is 'a chilling dissipating douche to the story's romance. Here and there in its telling the power of the magician [i.e. Conrad] wanes'.[86] An unsigned review of the novel in the *Nation* describes the Notes as 'a very prickly hedge against the reader's entrance to the enchanted castle.'[87] These and other similar comments on the Notes postulate a division between M. George's story and the frame narrative, in an attempt to preserve a coherent view of the story as a romance. I would argue against the validity of this double view, because even if—in spite of Conrad's insistence that 'these notes are material to the comprehension of the experience related in the narrative' (p. vii)—the Notes might be regarded as an appendage to the story,

[85] Beer, *The Romance*, 40.
[86] *The Times Literary Supplement*, 7 Aug. 1919, 422; repr. in Norman Sherry (ed.), *Joseph Conrad: The Critical Heritage* (London: Routledge & Kegan Paul, 1973), 320.
[87] *The Nation*, 6 Sept. 1919, 680–2; repr. in *The Critical Heritage*, 327.

an outsider's view expressed by a jaded and cynical narrator, there are other dissonant elements that operate within M. George's narrative itself in violation of the ostensible generic contract.

The story is presumably told after a long interval in a letter written by M. George to a childhood friend, but the self-consciousness of the narrator seems to be more than an optical effect of time; it is a force which can thwart and paralyse the action itself, an undercurrent of wry scepticism which undermines the ostensible romance. Both he and Rita are possessed by a sense of their own unreality; both seem to suspect that their own existence is predicated upon a fictional—and fictitious—model. The First Note introduces M. George as a fictional entity, a figure born out of the contact of two minds (6). His own account does nothing to dispel this aura of fictitiousness which surrounds him; his very name is assumed, and the note of self-conscious mockery he adopts in referring to it points to a latent rift between his assumed identity and his 'real', unknown self. George's claim to the title 'young Ulysses' is invalidated not only by the First Note but by his own story as well:

The tentative period was over; all our arrangements had been perfected ... Our friends, mostly bought for cash and therefore valuable, had acquired confidence in us ... They gave to Dominic all their respect and to me a great show of deference; for I had all the money, while they thought that Dominic had all the sense. (125)

The self-conscious attitude of the protagonist and his doubts about his own identity make for a narrative which oscillates between a passionate affirmation of the code of romance upon which the protagonist's assumed identity is modelled, and a sceptical attitude, punctuated by self-inflicted stabs of irony, which deflate the rhetoric of passion. A symptomatic passage describes M. George's despair after a quarrel with Rita. The suicidal tone of his thoughts is played off against his careful management of his morning toilet before the mirror:

Love for Rita ... if it was love I asked myself despairingly, while I brushed my hair before a glass. ... All that appertained to her haunted me with the same awful intimacy. ... 'Heavens! Am I as crazy as Thérèse?' I asked myself with a passing chill of fear while occupied in equalizing the end of my neck-tie. About the time I finished with my neck-tie I had done with life too. 'Why don't I drop dead now?' I asked myself peevishly, taking a clean handkerchief out of the drawer and stuffing it in my pocket. (163–5)

Rita, too, suffers from a constant 'sense of unreality' (55). She, too, had chosen a name for herself because 'one must have a name' (108), and although she is presented as the moving force behind the Carlist adventure, a muse whose 'spirit hovers upon the waters of Legitimacy' (242), she professes not to have her heart at stake (101), and does not seem to have much faith in the Royalist cause, which will 'crumble into dust before long . . .' (104).

George and Rita are both play-acting in a stage romance, but their consciousness of being on stage, as it were, spoils the act itself. The narrative is studded with masks, disguises, costumes, and other stage properties which the narrator ostensibly relates to the 'others'. George's story begins in the season of the carnival:

The Carnival time was drawing to an end. Everybody, high and low, was anxious to have the last fling. Companies of masks with linked arms and whooping like red Indians swept the streets in crazy rushes. There was a touch of bedlam in all this. I was neither masked, nor disguised, nor yelling, nor in any way in harmony with the bedlam element of life. (7–8)

It ends twelve months later on the last evening of the carnival:

The same masks, the same yells, the same mad rushes, the same bedlam of disguised humanity blowing about the streets in the great gusts of mistral that seemed to make them dance like dead leaves on an earth where all joy is watched by death. (263)

George's description of the others is invariably couched in theatrical imagery:

The others, including Mills, sat like a lot of deaf and dumb people. No. It was something more detached. They sat like a superior lot of wax-works, with the fixed but indetermined facial expression and with that odd air wax figures have of being aware of their existence being nothing but a sham. I was the exception. (69)

Don Carlos is, according to M. George, just 'a man attending to his business of being a Pretender . . . the obvious romance for the use of royalists' (7). The hair of the Republican journalist is like 'a very expensive wig in the window of a hair dresser' (71), and his eyes seem to have been 'borrowed from some idiot for the purpose of that visit' (73).

Captain Blunt, M. George's opponent, is the most obviously threatrical figure in the cast. He introduces himself as a man who lives by his sword (14), 'Américain, catholic et gentilhomme' (18). But this 'romantic aura' (15) is not quite genuine; he seems to be overplaying his part:

I was struck on closer view by the perfect correctness of his personality. Clothes, slight figure, clear-cut, thin, sun-tanned face, pose, all this was so good that it was saved from the danger of banality only by the mobile black eyes ... Another thing was that, viewed as an officer in mufti, he did not look sufficiently professional. That imperfection was interesting, too. (12–13)

Captain Blunt's manner of world-weary indifference 'may have been put on, for the whole personality was not clearly definable' and his smile is 'a flash of white teeth ... strangely without any character of its own ...' (23–4). Even his account of Rita's life is rendered in theatrical terms: 'Mr Blunt ... passed on to what he called the second act ...' (41). But Blunt's hollowness and the suggestion of shamming that accentuates the description of his personality are projected on the narrator himself. M. George is introduced to his opponent by Mills, who tells the Captain that George is a seaman 'in the same sense' that Blunt is a military man (14). This introduction is somewhat ambiguous in view of the First Note where George's identity as a seaman is described as an absurd pretence, and of George's own description of Blunt as a pretender. When Mrs Blunt later suggests that George resembles her son in many ways, she might be less mistaken than he would like to admit: 'I am aware that you are much younger, but the similitudes of opinions, origins and perhaps at bottom, faintly, of character, of chivalrous devotion ...' (175). The fact that both of them are in the service of the Royal Pretender is not accidental.

If Captain Blunt is M. George's shadowy *alter ego* as well as his opponent, Rita's counterpart is a tailor's 'dummy, without head or hands but with beautifully shaped limbs' (21), which had served Allegre as a model for the *Byzantine Empress* and *The Girl in the Hat*, for which he drew his inspiration from Rita's face. Both George and Blunt seem to relate to the dummy as a surrogate of Rita herself: when Blunt talks of her his dark eyes flash 'fatally ... in the direction of the shy dummy' (58). George describes it as 'pitiful and headless in its attitude of alarmed chastity' (48), and later draws some comfort from its presence in his rooms in Rita's absence:

I knew its history. It was not an ordinary dummy. . . . The knowledge of its origin, the contempt of Captain Blunt's references to it, with Thérèse's shocked dislike of the dummy, invested that summary reproduction with a sort of charm, gave me a faint and miserable illusion of the original. . . . I felt positively friendly to it. (240–1).

The relationship between the lovers is invested with the same illusory quality. The most ardent professions of love are riddled with doubts about the reality of the beloved one:

That image which others see and call by your name—how am I to know that it is anything else but an enchanting mist? You have always eluded me except in one or two moments which seem still more dream-like than the rest. Since I came into this room you have done nothing to destroy my conviction of your unreality apart from myself. . . . Is it because you suspect that apart from me you are but a mere phantom . . .? (296–7)

The same ambiguity which infects the lovers' relationship is reflected in the narrator's use of imagery. The arrow of gold, ostensibly used in its traditional function as an emblem of love in the romance (262, 267, 312), is wrenched out of this context and turns into a 'philistinish conception' (255), and a 'poor philistinish ornament' (332), in the lovers' own words. The romantic figures in the tapestry of Rita's drawing room, 'slender women with butterfly wings and lean youths with narrow birds' wings' are alternately 'a display of fancy, a sign of grace' and 'the delirious fantasy of some enriched shopkeeper' (214). These and other sardonic references to the romantic décor of the drawing room [88] disrupt the illusion of romance and suggest that the protagonists themselves might be a winged youth and a butterfly woman mutely engaged in an empty, decorative pose.

Some of the subversive elements in *The Arrow* have been noted by those critics whose readings of the novel are predicated on its proclaimed generic affinity with the romance. The dissonance created by these elements has produced interpretations which relegate the 'anti-romance' factor to the 'others', the forces of evil

---

[88] See also 218–20.

which confront the protagonists, while insisting on the pure romantic quality of the protagonists themselves.[89] I believe that the inadequacy of such readings—convenient as they are—has been sufficiently established in my analysis of the schizoid quality of the protagonists themselves, and the ambiguity of their relationship.

I would suggest that the ostensibly deconstructed dynamics of the novel, its blatant violation of its own elaborate generic framework, can best be accounted for in relation to Conrad's autobiographical works, *The Mirror of the Sea* and *A Personal Record*. The relationship between *The Arrow*, with the quasi-autobiographical status conferred on it by the author, and the factual history of Conrad's life has been a constant source of puzzlement to Conrad's biographers, but the customary division between biographical and literary research has not proved conducive to an integrated view of this issue.[90] My own feeling is that the full complexity of this relationship can only be understood when one views the generic ambiguity in the novel as an unconscious reflection and a product of the divided psyche of its author.

Conrad himself had insisted that the novel was an authentic autobiography. The *Tremolino* episode in Conrad's manifestly autobiographical work, *The Mirror of the Sea*, written thirteen years before *The Arrow*, contains some remarkable parallels with the novel: the gunrunning for the Carlists, the historical identity of the characters, the suggestions of a romantic rivalry between Blunt and George, and the failure of the last venture. In the copy of *The Arrow* he gave to Richard Curle, Conrad wrote, 'all the persons are authentic and the facts are as stated',[91] an avowal which he later reiterated in his letters to Sir Sidney Colvin and in the Author's Note he wrote for the novel in 1920. Conrad had probably

---

[89] See Paul L. Wiley in *Conrad's Measure of Man*, 162–72, repr. in R. W. Stallman, ed. *The Art of Joseph Conrad: A Critical Symposium* (East Lansing: Michigan State University Press, 1960), 317–22; Michael H. Bengal, 'The Ideals of Despair: A View of Joseph Conrad's *The Arrow of Gold*', *Conradiana*, 3/3 (1971–2), 37–40; Harold E. Toliver, 'Conrad's *Arrow of Gold*', 149; and Robert Chianese, 'Existence and Essence in Conrad's *Arrow of Gold*', *Conradiana*, 9/2 (1977), 148–58.

[90] Albert J. Guerard had somewhat slightingly relegated it to the 'gossip of biographers' (*Conrad the Novelist*, 284), and this seems to have been the attitude of other Conrad scholars as well.

[91] Quoted by Jocelyn Baines in *Joseph Conrad: A Critical Biography* (London: Weidenfeld & Nicolson, 1960), 50.

presented the novel in the same light to his wife, Jessie, and to his
first biographer, Gerard Jean-Aubry, who uninhibitedly drew the
material for his biography from the novel itself, asserting that
'though certain revelations made there are veiled, though the
chronology is uncertain, the facts recounted there may be considered true'.[92]

Conrad's later biographers were rather more circumspect in their
reliance on Conrad's own source materials. Jocelyn Baines,
R. Tennant, F. Karl, and Z. Najder have all produced conclusive
evidence in support of their view that *The Arrow* could not possibly
have had the authenticity that Conrad had claimed for it.[93] There
are some major chronological discrepancies between Conrad's
account of the Carlist activities and the historical evidence about
them; there is no evidence of the existence of Rita or of any one
likely prototype of her; and finally, the letters sent by Conrad's
uncle, Tadeusz Bobrowski, to Stephan Buszczynski, a close friend
of the family, and to Conrad himself, clearly indicate that Conrad
was not wounded in a romantic duel, but shot himself in the chest
in a suicide attempt.

Why, then, had Conrad felt the need to mislead his wife, his
friends, his biographer, and his readers about the autobiographical
authenticity of the novel? I believe that—notwithstanding the
considerable factual discrepancies between Conrad's life in Marseilles and the events described in the novel—*The Arrow* is indeed
an important autobiographical document. It exposes the psyche of
its author and sheds some light on the dynamics of his work in
ways which were probably only dimly suspected by Conrad and
entirely out of his control. In his Author's Note to *The Arrow*,
Conrad wrote, 'the subject of this book I had been carrying about
with me for many years, *not so much a possession of my memory
as an inherent part of myself*' (vii–viii, my emphasis). This peculiar
distinction between 'memory' and 'self' suggests that Conrad might
have suspected that he was telling a truth about himself, a truth
which had little to do with the objective facts of his biography.

---

[92] Gerard Jean-Aubry, *The Sea Dreamer* (New York: Doubleday, 1957), 68.
The Sea Dreamer is an elaboration of Jean-Aubry's earlier biography, *Joseph
Conrad: Life and Letters* (Garden City, NY: Doubleday, 1927).
[93] Baines, *Joseph Conrad: A Critical Biography*; Roger Tennant, *Joseph Conrad*
(London: Sheldon Press, 1981), 229–34; Frederic Karl, *Joseph Conrad: The Three
Lives*, 156–78; Zdzislaw Najder, *Joseph Conrad: A Chronicle*, 47–53.

In his semi-biographical study of Conrad's short stories, Edward Said focuses on Conrad's 'problem of self-definition', his desire 'to make a character of and for himself', and his need for 'a role to play so that he could locate himself solidly in existence'.[94] Conrad's concept of character refers, according to Said, 'not only to the character or personage created by an author for his fiction, but also [to] our private notion of ourselves to which we hold in tenacious desperation'.[95] The resemblance between Conrad and his protagonist in their need for an adequate pose, a private as well as a public persona, is striking indeed.

A close reading of Conrad's 'real' autobiographical works, those 'masterpieces of evasion' as Said rightly calls them, would reveal that apart from the obvious parallels of action that one might expect to find in a novel which is consciously modelled on an earlier account, there are other, more subtle echoes of Conrad's autobiographical works in *The Arrow*. Conrad's initiation into the life of a seaman as recounted in *The Mirror* is couched in the imagery of romance: the memory of the gales is 'welcome in dignified austerity, as you would remember with pleasure the noble features of a stranger with whom you crossed swords once in a knightly encounter and are never to see again' (76); the quay is 'the place where one beheld the aristocracy of ships ... a noble gathering of the fairest and swiftest, each bearing at the bow the carved emblem of her name as in a gallery of plaster-casts, figures of women with mural crowns, women with flowing robes ...; heads of men helmeted or bare; full lengths of warriors, of kings, of statesmen, of lords and princesses ...' (130).

Conrad's self-concept, like that of his fictional counterpart is modelled on the figure of Ulysses, the prototype of romance:

Happy he who, like Ulysses, has made an adventurous voyage; ... for it is we alone who, swayed by the audacity of our minds and the tremors of our hearts, are the sole artisans of all the wonder and romance of the world.(151)

---

[94] Edward Said, *Joseph Conrad and the Fiction of Autobiography*, 10–12. The obvious weakness of Said's work is its reliance on Jean-Aubry's version of Conrad's life, which leads him to interpret *The Arrow* as one of the author's 'plain narratives of fact' (72), but I believe that his view of Conrad's inner life is, on the whole, illuminating.

[95] Ibid. 37.

All unversed in the arts of the willy Greek, the deceiver of gods, the lover of strange women, the evoker of bloodthirsty shades, I yet longed for the beginning of my own obscure Odyssey. (154)

But the *Tremolino* episode, the most romantic of all and the ostensible biographical source of *The Arrow*, witnesses a disturbing shift in the narrative pose, an intrusion of self-consciousness, doubt, and scepticism into the heart of the romance. The presiding spirit is no longer Ulysses, but 'that most excellent cavalier Don Quixote de la Mancha' (155), and the story is coloured by the imagery of illusion which operates as a subversive element in *The Arrow* as well; the 'royalist gang' appears 'clear-cut and very small, with affected voices and stiff gestures, like a procession of rigid marionettes upon a toy stage' (176); the ladies concerned are 'all sorts of ladies, some old enough to know better than to put their trust in princes, others young and full of illusions'. Rita is described as 'one of these last . . .' (160). As we can see, the literary schizophrenia which underlies the fictional work operates in the ostensible memoirs in the same manner.

Conrad's ambivalent conception of romance as a genre is also evident in *A Personal Record*, another autobiographical work, which is not overtly concerned with the same period in his life. In explaining the nature of the urge which had driven him to leave his country and expose himself to the censure of his compatriots, Conrad invokes once again the figure of Cervantes's hero:

The barber and the priest, backed by the whole opinion of the village, condemned justly the conduct of the ingenious hidalgo. . . . His was a very noble, a very unselfish fantasy, fit for nothing except to raise the envy of baser mortals. But there is more than one aspect to the charm of that exalted and dangerous figure. He, too, had his frailties. After reading so many books he desired naively to escape with his very body from the intolerable reality of things. (36)

This patron saint whom Conrad had adopted for himself makes another appearance in a conversation of the young man with his tutor, who is trying to dissuade him from going to sea. Realizing that his young pupil is determined to fulfil his dream, the tutor calls him 'an incorrigible, hopeless Don Quixote', and Conrad reports having felt 'vaguely flattered at the name of the immortal knight turning up in connection with my own folly . . .' (44).

This invocation of Don Quixote is ambiguous in itself: it can be viewed either as a celebration of Romanticism, an assertion of the power of imagination and of inward vision over external reality, or as a corrosive attack on the futile idealism of the chivalric tradition.[96] Both these attitudes to the Romantic tradition are, as we have seen, evident in Conrad's work (most notably in *Lord Jim*, which is predicated on these conflicting views), and may have been a reflection of Conrad's ambiguity about his father, Apollo Korzeniowski, a paragon of the Romantic ideal. The ambivalence of the Quixotic invocation is compounded by Conrad's admission, 'mine was not the stuff that the protectors of forlorn damsels, the redressers of the world's wrongs are made of' (*A Personal Record*, 44).

The precarious sense of identity which afflicts M. George is evident in Conrad's letters as well. His view of himself as Punch, 'his spine broken in two, his nose on the floor between his feet; his legs and arms flung out stiffly in that attitude of profound despair' and his not entirely comical definition of himself as 'the absent one', as well as his explicit admission that 'one's own personality is only a ridiculous and aimless masquerade of something hopelessly unknown',[97] point to his deep psychological affinity with his *poseur*-protagonists.

The best illustration of this affinity is the clear echo of Conrad's inscription on a photograph of himself sent to his grandmother, Teophila Bobrowska, in 1863 concluding with 'Pole-Catholic and Szlachcic, Konrad',[98] in Captain Blunt's introduction of himself as 'Américain, catholic, et gentilhomme' (18). When one recalls that Blunt is, in fact, M. George's double as well as his rival, there emerges a kaleidoscopic pattern in which both these protagonists and the author mirror and reflect on each other as in an echo-chamber where one can no longer distinguish the fictional from the real.

When we turn back from Conrad's autobiographical works to *The Arrow*, it seems that the failure of the novel as a romance derives, paradoxically enough, from its essential truthfulness: Conrad's character is trying, like the author himself in his autobiographies, to construe his life and his character in terms of romance, and

[96] Beer, *The Romance*, 39–45.
[97] Letters to Marguerite Poradowska on 16 Oct. 1891, and 10 June 1890; letter to Garnett on 23 Mar. 1896. In *Collected Letters*, ed. Karl and Davies, i.
[98] Najder, *Joseph Conrad: A Chronicle* 18.

to make up for his precarious sense of identity by modelling himself, as it were, on the prototype of a fictional genre. The subversive elements in M. George's narrative—his self-consciousness, the suggestions of his and Rita's insubstantiality, the symbolic ambiguity of the trappings of romance, the ubiquity of masks and disguises in his story, and the inevitable failure of his pose as a romance hero—reflect the ambivalence of his author, a *homo duplex* who never fully resolved these conflicting attitudes in himself.

Bibliography

CONRAD'S WORKS

The Uniform Edition. London: J. M. Dent & Sons, 1923–8.

CRITICAL EDITIONS OF CONRAD'S WORKS

CARABINE, KEITH, ed. and intr., *Nostromo*. The World's Classics. Oxford University Press, 1984.

COX, C. B., ed., *Conrad: 'Heart of Darkness', 'Nostromo' and 'Under Western Eyes'*. Casebook series. London: Macmillan Publishers, 1981.

MOSER, THOMAS C., ed., *The Norton Critical Edition of 'Lord Jim'*. New York: W. W. Norton & Company, Inc., 1968.

These critical editions were used in this study for editorial material only. All references to Conrad's works follow the Dent Uniform Edition.

CONRAD'S LETTERS

BLACKBURN, WILLIAM, ed., *Joseph Conrad: Letters to William Blackwood and David S. Meldrum*. Durham, NC: Duke University Press, 1958.

CURLE, RICHARD, ed., *Conrad to a Friend: 150 Selected Letters from Joseph Conrad to Richard Curle*. London: Sampson Low, Marston & Co., 1928.

GARNETT, EDWARD, ed., *Letters from Conrad 1885–1924*. London: Nonesuch Press, 1928.

JEAN-AUBRY, GERARD, *Joseph Conrad: Life and Letters*. Garden City, NY: Doubleday, 1927.

KARL, FREDERICK, and DAVIES, LAURENCE, *The Collected Letters of Joseph Conrad*. Vol. i: 1861–97; Vol ii: 1898–1902. Cambridge: Cambridge University Press, 1983, 1986.

NAJDER, ZDZISLAW, ed., *Conrad's Polish Background: Letters to and from Polish Friends*, trans. Halina Carroll. London: Oxford University Press, 1964.

WATTS, C. T., ed., *Joseph Conrad's Letters to Cunninghame Graham*. Cambridge: Cambridge University Press, 1969.

BIOGRAPHIES

ALLEN, JERRY, *The Sea Years of Joseph Conrad*. New York: Doubleday, 1965.

BAINES, JOCELYN, *Joseph Conrad: A Critical Biography*. London: Weidenfeld & Nicolson, 1960. 2nd edn., 1969.

KARL, FREDERICK, R., *Joseph Conrad: The Three Lives*. London: Faber & Faber, 1979.

JEAN-AUBRY, GERARD, *The Sea Dreamer*. New York: Doubleday, 1957.

MEYER, BERNARD C. *Joseph Conrad: A Psychoanalytic Biography*. Princeton: Princeton University Press, 1967.

NAJDER, ZDZISLAW. *Joseph Conrad: A Chronicle*, trans. Halina Carroll-Najder. Cambridge: Cambridge University Press, 1983.

TENNANT, ROGER, *Joseph Conrad*. London: Sheldon Press, 1981.

BIBLIOGRAPHIES

EHRSAM, T. G., *A Bibliography of Joseph Conrad*. Metuchen, NJ: Scarecrow Press, 1969.

TEETS, BRUCE, E., and GERBER, HELMUT, ed., *Joseph Conrad: An Annotated Bibliography of Writings about Him*. De Kalb, Ill.: Northern Illinois University Press, 1971.

DONALD RUDE, 'Conrad Bibliography: A Continuing Checklist'. *Conradiana*, 3/2 (1972), 111–16; *Conradiana*, 3/3 (1971), 60–5; *Conradiana*, 4/1 (1972), 77–82; *Conradiana*, 4/2 (1972), 75–9; *Conradiana*, 4/3 (1972), 62–6; *Conradiana*, 5/3 (1973), 79–83; *Conradiana*, 7/2 (1975), 189–99; *Conradiana*, 7/3 (1975), 283–92; *Conradiana*, 8/3 (1976), 277–89; *Conradiana*, 9/3 (1977), 295–307; *Conradiana*, 10/3 (1978), 205–9; *Conradiana*, 11/1 (1979), 91–100; *Conradiana*, 12/2 (1980), 135–46.

HIGDON, DAVID LEON, 'Conrad in the Eighties: A Bibliography and Some Observations', *Conradiana*, 13/3 (1985), 214–49.

BOOKS ON CONRAD

BERTHOUD, JACQUES, *Joseph Conrad: The Major Phase*. Cambridge: Cambridge University Press, 1978.

BONNEY, W. W., *Thorns and Arabesques: Contexts for Conrad's Fiction*. Baltimore: Johns Hopkins University Press, 1980.

COX, C. B., *Joseph Conrad: The Modern Imagination*. London: J. M. Dent & Sons, 1974,

CRANKSHAW, EDWARD, *Joseph Conrad: Some Aspects of the Art of the Novel*. First published in 1936. 2nd edn., London: Macmillan Press Ltd., 1976.

CURLE, RICHARD, *The Last Twelve Years of Joseph Conrad*. London: Sampson, Law, Marston, 1928.

DALESKI, H. M., *Joseph Conrad: The Way of Dispossession*. London: Faber & Faber, 1977.

DARRAS, JACQUES, *Joseph Conrad and the West: Signs of Empire*, trans. Anne Luyat and Jacques Darras. London: Macmillan Press, Ltd., 1982.

DAVIDSON, ARNOLD, E. *Conrad's Endings: A Study of the Five Major Novels*. Ann Arbor, Mich.: UMI Research Press, 1984.

DOWDEN, WILFRED S., *Joseph Conrad: The Imaged Style*. Nashville: Vanderbilt University Press, 1970.

FLEISHMAN, AVROM, *Conrad's Politics*. Baltimore: Johns Hopkins University Press, 1967.

GEDDES, GARY, *Conrad's Later Novels*. Montreal: McGill-Queen's University Press, 1980.

GILLON, ADAM, *Conrad and Shakespeare*. New York: Astra Books, 1976.

GLASSMAN, PETER, J., *Language and Being: Joseph Conrad and the Literature of Personality*. New York: Columbia University Press, 1976.

GUERARD, ALBERT, J., *Conrad the Novelist*. Cambridge, Mass.: Harvard University Press, 1958.

GURKO, LEO, *Joseph Conrad: Giant in Exile*. New York: Macmillan Publishing Co., 1962.

HAWTHORN, JEREMY, *Joseph Conrad: Language and Fictional Self-Consciousness*. London: Edward Arnold, 1979.

HAY, ELOISE KNAPP, *The Political Novels of Joseph Conrad*. Chicago: University of Chicago Press, 1963.

HEWITT, DOUGLAS, *Joseph Conrad: A Reassessment*. 1952. 3rd edn., London: Bowes & Bowes, 1975.

HUNTER, ALLAN, *Joseph Conrad and the Ethics of Darwinism*. London: Croom Helm, 1983.

JOHNSON, BRUCE, *Conrad's Models of Mind*. Minneapolis: University of Minnesota Press, 1971.

JONES, MICHAEL P., *Conrad's Heroism: A Paradise Lost*. Ann Arbor, Mich.: UMI Research Press, 1985.

KARL, F. R., ed., *Joseph Conrad: A Collection of Criticism*. New York: McGraw-Hill Book Co., 1975.

KIRSCHNER, PAUL, *Conrad: The Psychologist as Artist*. Edinburgh: Oliver & Boyd, 1968.

MCCLURE, JOHN A., *Kipling and Conrad: The Colonial Fiction*. Cambridge, Mass: Harvard University Press, 1981.

MORF, G., *The Polish Heritage of Joseph Conrad*. London: Sampson, Low, Marston, 1929.

MORF, G., *The Polish Shades and Ghosts of Joseph Conrad*. New York: Astra Books, 1976.

MOSER, THOMAS C., *Joseph Conrad: Achievement and Decline*. Hamden, Conn.: Archon Books, 1966.

MURFIN, ROSS C., ed. and intr., *Conrad Revisited: Essays for the Eighties*. Alabama: University of Alabama Press, 1985.

NETTELS, ELSA, *James and Conrad*. Athens, Ga.: University of Georgia Press, 1977.

O'HANLON, REDMOND, *Joseph Conrad and Charles Darwin*. Edinburgh: Salamander Press, 1984.

PALMER, JOHN A., *Joseph Conrad's Fiction*. Ithaca, NY: Cornell University Press, 1968.

PARRY, BENITA, *Conrad and Imperialism: Ideological Boundaries and Visionary Frontiers*. London: Macmillan Press Ltd., 1983.

PETTERSSON, TORSTEN, *Consciousness and Time: A Study in the Philosphy and Narrative Technique of Joseph Conrad*. Abo: Abo Akademi, 1982.

PURDY, DWIGHT H., *Joseph Conrad's Bible*. Norman, Okla.: University of Oklahoma Press, 1984.

ROSENFIELD, CLAIRE, *Paradise of Snakes: An Archetypal Analysis of Conrad's Political Novels*. Chicago: University of Chicago Press, 1967.

ROUSSEL, ROYAL, *The Metaphysics of Darkness: A Study in the Unity and Development of Conrad's Fiction*. Baltimore: Johns Hopkins Press, 1971.

SAID, EDWARD, *Joseph Conrad and the Fiction of Autobiography*. Cambridge, Mass.: Harvard University Press, 1966.

SAVESON, JOHN E., *Joseph Conrad: The Making of a Moralist*. Amsterdam: Rodopi NV, 1972.

SCHWARZ DANIEL *Conrad: 'Almayer's Folly' to 'Under Western Eyes'*. London: Macmillan, 1980.

—— *Conrad: The Later Fiction*. London: Macmillan, 1982.

SENN, WERNER, *Conrad's Narrative Voice: Stylistic Aspects of His Fiction*. Berne: A. Francke AG Verlag, 1980.

SHERRY, NORMAN, *Conrad's Eastern World*. Cambridge: Cambridge University Press, 1966.

—— *Conrad's Western World*. Cambridge: Cambridge University Press, 1971.

—— ed., *Joseph Conrad: The Critical Heritage*. London: Routledge & Kegan Paul, 1973.

—— ed., *Joseph Conrad: A Commemoration*. London: Macmillan, 1977.

STALLMAN, ROBERT W., ed., *The Art of Joseph Conrad: A Critical Symposium*. East Lansing, Mich.: Michigan State UP, 1960.

TANNER, TONY, *Conrad: 'Lord Jim'*. Studies in English Literature no. 12, ed. David Daiches. London: Edward Arnold, 1963.

THORBURN, DAVID, *Conrad's Romanticism*. New Haven, Conn.: Yale University Press, 1974.

VERLEUN, JAN, *Patna and Patusan Perspectives: A Study of the Function of the Minor Characters in Joseph Conrad's 'Lord Jim'*. Groningen: Bouma's Boekhuis, 1979.

WATT, IAN, *Conrad in the Nineteenth Century*. London: Chatto & Windus, 1980.

WATTS, CEDRIC T., *Conrad's 'Heart of Darkness'*. Milan: Mursia International, 1977.

—— *A Preface to Conrad* London: Longman, 1982.

—— *The Deceptive Text: An Introduction to Covert Plots*. Sussex: Harvester Press, 1984.

WILEY, PAUL L., *Conrad's Measure of Man*. Madison: University of Wisconsin Press, 1954.

WRIGHT, WALTER F., *Romance and Tragedy in Joseph Conrad*. Lincoln, Neb.: University of Nebraska Press, 1949.

ARTICLES AND CHAPTERS IN BOOKS

BATCHELOR, JOHN, *The Edwardian Novelists*. London: Duckworth & Co., 1982, 27–91.

BENGAL, MICHAEL H., 'The Ideals of Despair: A View of Joseph Conrad's *The Arrow of Gold*', *Conradiana*, 3/3 (1971–2): 37–40.

BEVAN, ERNST, Jr., '*Nostromo*: The Permanence of the Past'. *Conradiana*, 10/1 (1978), 63–71.

BONNEY, WILLIAM W., 'Narrative Perspectives in *Victory*: The Thematic Relevance', *Journal of Narrative Technique*, 5/1 (1975), 24–39.

—— '"Eastern Logic Under My Western Eyes": Conrad's Schopenhauer and the Orient', *Conradiana*, 10/2 (1978), 225–52.

BUSZA, ANDRZEJ, 'Conrad's Polish Literary Background and Some Illustrations of the Influence of Polish Literature on His Work', *Antemurale*, 10 (1966), 109–256.

—— 'Rhetoric and Ideology in Conrad's *Under Western Eyes*', in N. Sherry, ed., *A Commemoration*, 105–17.

CASERIO, R., '*The Rescue* and the *Ring of Meaning*', in R. C. Murfin, ed., *Conrad Revisited*, 125–49.

CHEATHAM, GEORGE, 'The Absence of God in *Heart of Darkness*', *Studies in the Novel*, 18/3 (1986), 304–13.

CHIANESE, ROBERT, 'Existence and Essence in Conrad's *Arrow of Gold*'. *Conradiana* 9/2 (1977), 148–58.

COATES, PAUL, *The Realist Fantasy: Fiction and Reality since 'Clarissa'*. London: Macmillan, 1983, 114–30.

CREWS, FREDERICK C., 'Conrad's Anxiety—and Ours', in *Out of My System: Psychoanalysis, Ideology, and Critical Method*. New York, Oxford University Press, 1975, 41–62.

DE LA MARE, WALTER, an unsigned review of *The Arrow of Gold*. *The Times Literary Supplement*, 7 Aug. 1919, repr. in N. Sherry ed., *Joseph Conrad: A Commemoration*, 316–20.

DEURBERGUE, J., 'The Opening of *Victory*', *Studies in Joseph Conrad*, 2 (1975), 239–70.

DIKE, DONALD A., 'The Tempest of Axel Heyst'. *Nineteenth-Century Fiction*, 17/2 (1962), 95–113.

EAGLETON, TERRY, 'Joseph Conrad and *Under Western Eyes*', in *Exiles and Émigrés*. London: Chatto & Windus, 1970, 21–32.

EMMET, VICTOR J., 'The Aesthetics of Anti-Imperialism: Ironic Distortions of the Vergilian Epic Mode in Conrad's *Nostromo*', *Studies in the Novel*, 4/3 (Autumn 1972), 459–72.

EVANS, ROBERT O., 'Conrad's Underworld'. *Modern Fiction Studies*, 2 (1956), 56–62.

FEDER, LILLIAN, 'Marlow's Descent into Hell'. *Nineteenth-Century Fiction*, 9/4 (1955), 280–92.

FLEISHMAN, A., 'Speech and Writing in *Under Western Eyes*', in N. Sherry, ed., *Joseph Conrad: A Commemoration*, 119–28.

FORSTER, E. M., 'Joseph Conrad: A Note'. *Abinger Harvest*. First published in 1936. Harmondsworth: Penguin, 1967.

GILLIAM, H., 'Vision in Conrad's *Under Western Eyes*', Texas Studies in Literature and Language, 19/3 (1977), 24–41.

—— 'The Daemonic in *Under Western Eyes*', *Conradiana*, 9/2 (1977), 219–36.

—— 'Russia and the West in Conrad's *Under Western Eyes*', *Studies in the Novel*, 10/2 (1978), 218–23.

GILLON, ADAM, 'Joseph Conrad and Shakespeare, Part Four: A Reinterpretation of *Victory*'. *Conradiana*, 8/1 (1975), 61–75.

GOSE, ELLIOT B. Jr., 'Pure Exercise of Imagination. Archetypal Symbolism in *Lord Jim*', *PMLA*, 79 (Mar. 1964), 137–47.

GROSS, SEYMOUR L., 'A Further Note on the Function of the Frame in "Heart of Darkness"', *Modern Fiction Studies*, 3 (1957), 167–70.

GUETTI, JAMES, *The Limits of Metaphor: A Study of Melville, Conrad and Faulkner*. Ithaca, NY: Cornell University Press, 1967, 46–148.

HAWKINS, HUNT, 'Conrad's Critique of Imperialism in *Heart of Darkness*', *PMLA*, 94/2 (1979), 286–99.

HERBERT, WRAY, C., 'Conrad's Psychic Landscape: The Mythic Element in *Karain*. *Conradiana*, 8/3 (1976), 225–32.

HOUGH, GRAHAM, '*Chance* and Joseph Conrad', in *Image and Experience: Studies in a Literary Revolution* London: Gerald Duckworth & Co., 1960, 211–22.

JAMES HENRY, 'The New Novel', *Notes on Novelists*. London: J. M. Dent & Sons, 1914, 273–8.

JAMESON, FREDRIC, 'Romance and Reification: Plot Construction and Ideological Closure in Joseph Conrad', *The Political Unconscious: Narrative as a Socially Symbolic Act.* London: Methuen, 1981, 206–80.

JENKINS, GARETH, 'Conrad's *Nostromo* and History', *Literature and History* [vol. 3], 6 (Autumn 1977), 138–78.

JOHNSON, JULIE M., 'The Damsel and Her Knights: The Goddess and the Grail in Conrad's *Chance*'. *Conradiana*, 13/3 (1981), 221–8.

JONES, MICHAEL P., 'A Paradise Lost: Conrad and the Romantic Sensibility', *Critical Quarterly*, 18/4 (1976), 37–49.

KAHELE, SHARON, and GERMAN, HOWARD, 'Conrad's *Victory*: A Reassessment', *Modern Fiction Studies*, 10/1 (1964), 55–72.

KERMODE, FRANK, 'Secrets and Narrative Sequence', *Critical Inquiry*, 7(1980), 83–101. Repr. in *Essays on Fiction.* London: Routledge & Kegan Paul, 133–54.

KNOWLES, OWEN, 'The Year's Work in Conrad Studies, 1985: A Survey of Periodical Literature', *The Conradian*, 2/1 (1986), 57–71.

KRIEGER, MURRAY, *The Tragic Vision.* New York: Holt, Rinehart, and Winston, 1960, 1–22, 179–94.

LASKOWSKI, HENRY J., '*Esse Est Percipi*: Epistemology and Narrative Method in *Victory*', *Conradiana*, 9/3 (1977), 275–86.

LEAVIS, F. R., *The Great Tradition.* 1948. London: Chatto & Windus, 1979, 173–226.

LEITER, LOUIS H., 'Echo Structures: Conrad's *The Secret Sharer*', *Twentieth-Century Literature*, 5/4 (1960), 159–75.

LEVENSON, MICHAEL, *A Genealogy of Modernism: A Study of English Literary Doctrine 1908–1922.* Cambridge: Cambridge University Press, 1984, 1–36.

—— 'The Value of Facts in the *Heart of Darkness*', *Nineteenth-Century Fiction*, 40/3 (1985), 261–80.

LEWIS, R. W. B., 'The Current of Conrad's *Victory*', in F. R. Karl, ed., *A Collection of Criticism*, 101–19.

LODGE, DAVID, 'Conrad's *Victory* and The Tempest; An Amplification', *Modern Language Review*, 59/2 (1964), 195–9.

MCALINDON, T., '*Nostromo*: Conrad's Organicist Philosophy of History', *Mosaic*, 15/3 (1982), 27–41.

MARTIN, JOSEPH, 'Conrad and the Aesthetic Movement', *Conradiana*, 17/3 (1985), 199–213.

MARTIN, W. R., 'Charting Conrad's Costaguana', *Conradiana*, 8/2 (1976), 163–7.

MATLAW, R. E., 'Dostoevskij [*sic*] and Conrad's Political Novels', *American Contributions to the Fifth International Congress of Slavists*, vol. i. The Hague: Mouton, 1963, 213–33.

MILLER, J. HILLIS, *Poets of Reality: Six Twentieth Century Writers.* Cambridge, Mass.: Harvard University Press, 1965, 13–67.

MILLER, J. HILLIS, *Fiction and Repetition*. Oxford: Basil Blackwell, 1982, 22–41.

—— 'Heart of Darkness Revisited', in R. C. Murfin, ed., *Conrad Revisited*, 31–50.

MILLER, KARL, *Doubles: Studies in Literary History*. Oxford: Oxford University Press, 1985, 245–66.

NAJDER, ZDZISLAW, 'Conrad in his Historical Perspective', *English Literature in Transition*, 14/3 (1971), 157–166.

PARK, DOUGLAS B., 'Conrad's *Victory*: The Anatomy of a Pose', *Nineteenth-Century Fiction*, 31/2 (1976), 150–69.

PECORA, VINCENT, 'Heart of Darkness and the Phenomenology of Voice', *ELH*, 52 (1985), 993–1011.

PRICE, MARTIN, 'Conrad; The Limits of Irony', *Forms of Life: Character and Moral Imagination in the Novel*. New Haven: Yale University Press, 1983, 235–66.

PURDY, DWIGHT H., 'Creature and Creator in *Under Western Eyes*', *Conradiana*, 8/3 (1976), 241–6.

—— '"Peace that Passeth Understanding": The Professor's English Bible in *Under Western Eyes*', *Conradiana*, 13/1 (1981), 83–93.

RAY, MARTIN, 'Conrad and Decoud', *The Polish Review*, 29/3 (1984), 53-64.

RENNER, STANLEY, 'The Garden of Civilization: Conrad, Huxley and the Ethics of Evolution', *Conradiana*, 7/2 (1975), 61–75.

ROSENFIELD, CLAIRE, 'An Archetypal Analysis of Conrad's *Nostromo*', *Texas Studies in Literature and Language*, 3/4 (1962), 510–34.

RUTHVEN, K. K., 'The Savage God: Conrad and Lawrence', *Critical Quarterly*, 10/1, 2 (1968), 39–54. Repr. in C. B. Cox, ed., *Conrad: 'Heart of Darkness', 'Nostromo' and 'Under Western Eyes'*, 78–84.

SAID, EDWARD W., 'Conrad and Nietzsche', in N. Sherry, ed., *Joseph Conrad: A Commemoration*, 65–76.

—— *Beginnings: Intention and Method*. Baltimore: Johns Hopkins University Press, 1975, 100–37.

SAVESON, JOHN E., 'The Moral Discovery of *Under Western Eyes*', *Criticism*, 14/1 (1972), 32–48.

SCHLEIFER, R., 'Public and Private Narrative in *Under Western Eyes*'. *Conradiana*, 9/3 (1977), 232–54.

SECOR, ROBERT, 'The Function of the Narrator in *Under Western Eyes*', *Conradiana*, 3/1 (1970–1), 27–38.

SIEGLE, ROBERT, 'The Two Texts of *Chance*', *Conradiana*, 16/2 (1984), 83–101.

SPATT, HARTLEY S., 'Nostromo's Chronology: The Shaping of History', *Conradiana*, 8/1 (1976), 37–46.

STEIN, WILLIAM BYSSHE, 'The Lotus Posture and *Heart of Darkness*', *Modern Fiction Studies*, 2 (1956), 235–7.

STEINER, JOAN E., 'Modern Pharisees and False Apostles: Ironic New Testament Parallels in Conrad's "Heart of Darkness"', *Nineteenth-Century Fiction*, 37/1 (1982), 75–96.

SZITTYA, PENN R., 'Metafiction: The Double Narration in *Under Western Eyes*'. *ELH*, 48 (1981), 817–40.

TANNER, J. E., 'The Chronology and the Enigmatic End of *Lord Jim*'. *Nineteenth-Century Fiction*, 21/4 (1967), 369–80.

TANNER, TONY, 'Nightmare and Complacency: Razumov and the Western Eye', *Critical Quarterly*, 4/3 (1962), 197–214. Repr. in C. B. Cox, ed., *Conrad: 'Heart of Darkness', 'Nostromo' and 'Under Western Eyes'*, 163–85.

—— 'Butterflies and Beetles—Conrad's Two Truths', *Chicago Review*, 16 (Winter–Spring 1963): 123–40. Repr. in Thomas C. Moser, ed., Norton Critical Edition of *Lord Jim*. New York: W. W. Norton & Company, Inc., 1968, 447–62.

—— '"Gnawed Bones" and "Artless Tales"—Eating and Narration in Conrad', *The Partisan Review*, 45/1 (1978), 94–107.

—— 'Gentlemen and Gossip: Aspects of Evolution and Language in Conrad's *Victory*', *L'Époque Conradienne* (May 1981), 1-56.

—— 'Joseph Conrad and the Last Gentleman', *Critical Quarterly*, 28/2 (1986), 109–42.

TILLYARD, E. M. W., *The Epic Strain in the English Novel*. London: Chatto & Windus, 1967, 126–67.

TOLIVER, HAROLD E., 'Conrad's *Arrow of Gold* and the Pastoral Tradition', *Modern Fiction Studies*, 8 (1962), 148–58.

VAN GHENT, DOROTHY, *The English Novel: Form and Function*. New York: Rinehart and Co., 1953, 229–44. Repr. in Norton Edition of *Lord Jim*, 376–89.

VERLEUN, J., 'The Changing Face of Charlie Marlow, Part I', *The Conradian*, 8/2 (1983), 21–7.

—— 'The Changing Face of Charlie Marlow, Part II', *The Conradian*, 9/1 (1984), 15–24.

WARREN, ROBERT PENN, '*Nostromo*', *The Sewanee Review*, 59 (1951), 363–91. Repr. as the Introduction to the Modern Library Edition of *Nostromo*.

WATT, IAN, 'Story and Idea in Conrad's *The Shadow-Line*', *Critical Quarterly*, 2/2 (1960), 133–48.

—— 'Conrad, James, and *Chance*', in M. Mack and I. Gregor, eds., *Imagined Worlds: Essays in Honour of John Butt*. London: Methuen, 1968, 301–22.

—— '*Heart of Darkness* and Nineteenth-Century Thought', *The Partisan Review*, 45/1 (1978), 108–19.

WATTS, C. T., 'Conrad's Absurdist Techniques: A Terminology', *Conradiana*, 9/2 (1977), 141–8.

WATTS, C. T., 'The Mirror-tale: An Ethico-structural Analysis of Conrad's "The Secret Sharer"', *Critical Quarterly*, 19/3 (1977), 25–37.
—— 'Reflections on *Victory*', *Conradiana*, 15/1 (1983), 73–9.
WHEELER, M. 'Russia and Russians in the Works of Conrad', *Conradiana*, 12/1 (1980), 23–36.
WHITE, ALLON, *The Uses of Obscurity: The Fiction of Early Modernism*. London: Routledge & Kegan Paul, 1981, 108–29.
WILLIAMS, RAYMOND, *The English Novel from Dickens to Lawrence*. St Albans: Paladin, 1974, 114–25.

BACKGROUND READING

BABBITT, IRVING, *Rousseau and Romanticism*. Boston: Houghton Mifflin Co., 1919.
BAKHTIN, MIKHAIL M., *The Dialogic Imagination*, ed. Michael Holquist, trans. Caryl Emerson and Michael Holquist. Austin, Tex.: University of Texas Press, 1981.
—— *Problems of Dostoevsky's Poetics*, trans. R. W. Rostel. Ann Arbor, Mich.: Ardis, 1973. Also ed. and trans. Caryl Emerson. Minneapolis: University of Minnesota Press, 1984.
BARTHES, ROLAND, *Mythologies*. First published in Paris, 1957. London: Jonathan Cape Ltd., 1972.
BEER, GILLIAN, *The Romance*. The Critical Idiom Series no. 10. London: Methuen, 1970.
BELL, DAVID, 'Philosophy', in Cox and Dyson, ed., *The Twentieth-Century Mind*, 174–224.
BERLIN, SIR ISAIAH, 'Two Concepts of Liberty'. Inaugural lecture as Chichele Professor of Social and Political Theory. Oxford: Clarendon Press, 1958. Repr. in *Four Essays on Liberty*. Oxford: Oxford University Press, 1969, 118–72.
—— Foreword to F. Meineke, *Historicism: The Rise of a New Historical Outlook*. First published in 1959. Trans. J. E. Anderson. London: Routledge & Kegan Paul, 1972, ix–xvi.
BLOOM HAROLD, *The Ringers in the Tower: Studies in Romantic Tradition*. Chicago: University of Chicago Press, 1971.
BRADBURY, MALCOM, and MACFARLANE, JAMES, eds. *Modernism*. First published in 1974. Sussex: Harvester Press Ltd., 1978.
—— 'The Name and Nature of Modernism', in *Modernism*, 19–55.
BUBER, MARTIN, 'Religion and Ethics', *The Eclipse of God*. London: Victor Gollancz Ltd., 1953, 123–46.
BURKE, KENNETH, *A Grammar of Motives* (Englewood Cliffs, NJ: Prentice-Hall, 1954), 508.
CASSIRER, ERNST, *The Philosophy of Symbolic Forms*, 3 vols., trans R. Manheim. New Haven: Yale University Press, 1955, vol. ii.

—— *Symbol, Myth, and Culture: Essays and Lectures by Ernst Casssirer 1935–1945*, ed., Donald Philip Verene. New Haven, Conn.: Yale University Press, 1979.

CLARK, KATERINA and HOLQUIST MICHAEL, *Mikhail Bakhtin*. Cambridge, Mass.: Harvard University Press, 1984.

COX, C. B. and DYSON, A. E., eds. *The Twentieth-Century Mind*. 3 vols. London: Oxford University Press, 1972, vol. i: 1900–1918.

CULLER, JONATHAN, *Structuralist Poetics*. London: Routledge & Kegan Paul, 1975.

DELBANCO, NICOLAS, *Group Portrait*. London: Faber & Faber, 1982.

DOSTOEVSKY, FYODOR, *Crime and Punishment*. First published in 1866. Trans. and intr. David Magarshack. Harmondsworth: Penguin Books, 1951.

—— *The Devils [The Possessed]*. First published in 1871. Trans and intr. David Magarshack. Harmondsworth: Penguin Books, 1953.

DUBROW, HEATHER, *Genre*. The Critical Idiom Series no. 42. London: Metheun, 1982.

ELIADE, MIRCEA, *Myth and Reality*. World perspectives. London: George Allen & Unwin Ltd., 1964.

ELLMANN, RICHARD, *Golden Codgers: Biographical Speculations*. Oxford: Oxford University Press, 1973.

FOWLER, ALASTAIR, *Kinds of Literature*. Oxford: Oxford University Press, 1982. Paperback edition, 1957.

FRYE, NORTHROP, *Anatomy of Criticism*. Princeton: Princeton University Press, 1957.

—— *The Secular Script: A Study of the Structure of Romance*. Cambridge, Mass.: Harvard University Press, 1976.

—— *The Great Code: The Bible and Literature*. First published in 1981. London: Ark Paperbacks, 1983.

GRAFF, GERALD, *Literature against Itself: Literary Ideas in Modern Society*. Chicago: University of Chicago Press, 1979.

GOULD, ERIC, *Mythical Intentions in Modern Literature*. Princeton: Princeton University Press, 1981.

HARTMAN, Geoffrey, *Beyond Formalism*. New Haven, Conn.: Yale University Press, 1970.

HELLER, ERICH, *The Disinherited Mind*. 4th edn. First published in 1952. London: Bowes & Bowes, 1975.

HINRICHS, CARL, Introduction to F. Meineke, *Historicism: The Rise of a New Historical Outlook*. First published in 1959. Trans. By J. E. Anderson. London: Routledge & Kegan Paul, 1972, xvii–liii.

HUGHES, H. STUART, *Oswald Spengler*. Twentieth-Centurary Library. London: Charles Scribner's Sons, 1952.

—— *Consciousness and Society: The Reorientation of European Social Thought 1890–1930*. London: McGibbon & Kee, 1959.

HYNES, SAMUEL, *The Edwardian Turn of Mind*. Princeton: Princeton University Press, 1968.

IGGERS, GEORG G., 'Historicism', *The Dictionary of the History of Ideas*. New York: Charles Scribner's Sons, 1973, 456–64.

KERMODE, FRANK, *The Sense of an Ending*. New York: Oxford University Press, 1967.

KIRK, G. S. *Myth*, Cambridge: Cambridge University Press, 1970.

KOLAKOWSKI, LEZSEK, *The Presence of Myth*. First published in 1966. Trans. Into Hebrew by Eliezar Ha'cohen. Tel-Aviv: Sifriyat Poalim, 1971.

—— 'Modernity on Endless Trial', *Encounter*, 66/3 (Mar. 1986), 8–12.

KRUTCH, JOSEPH WOOD, *The Modern Temper*, London: Jonathan Cape, 1930.

LANGER, SUSANNE, K., *Philosophy in a New Key: A Study of the Symbolism of Reason, Rite and Art*. 3rd edn. First published in 1942. Cambridge, Mass.: Harvard University Press, 1969.

LESTER, JOHN A., Jr., *Journey through Despair: Transformations in British Literary Culture 1880–1914*. Princeton: Princeton University Press, 1968.

LEWIS, C. S., 'De descriptione temporum'. An Inaugrual lecture at Cambridge, 1954. Repr. In *They Asked for a Paper*. London: Geoffrey Bles, 1962, 9–25.

LUKACS, GEORG, *The Theory of the Novel*. First published in 1920. Trans. Anna Bostock. London: Merlin Press, 1971.

MCFARLANE, JAMES, 'The Mind of Modernism', in Bradbury and McFarlane, eds., *Modernism*, 71–93.

MACINTYRE, ALASDAIR, *After Virtue: A Study in Moral Theory*. First published in 1981. 2nd edn. London: Duckworth, 1985.

MALINOWSKI, BRONISLAW, *Myth in Primitive Psychology*. New York: W. W. Norton & Co., 1926. Repr. In *Magic, Science, and Religion*. New York: W. W. Norton & Co., 1955.

MASUR, GERHARD, *Prophets of Yesterday: Studies in European Culture 1890–1914*. London: Weidenfeld & Nicolson, 1963.

MILLER, JOSEPH HILLIS, *The Disappearance of God*. First published in 1963. 2nd edn. Cambridge, Mass.: Harvard University Press, 1975.

—— 'Stevens' Rock and Criticism as Cure', *Georgia Review*, 30 (1976), 5–33, 330–48.

NEHAMAS, A., *Nietzsche: Life as Literature*. Cambridge, Mass.: Harvard University Press, 1986.

NIETZSCHE, FRIEDRICH, *The Gay Science*. First published in 1882. Trans. Walter Kaufmann. New York: Vintage Books, 1974.

—— *Beyond Good and Evil: Prelude to a Philosophy of the Future*. First published in 1886. Trans. Walter Kaufmann. New York: Vintage Books, 1966.

—— *Twilight of the Idols* and *The Anti-Christ*. First published in 1889, 1895. Trans. and intr. R. J. Hollingdale. Harmondsworth: Penguin Books, 1968.

—— *A Nietzsche Reader*. Sel. trans. and intr. R. J. Hollingdale. Harmondsworth: Penguin Books, 1977.

ORTEGA Y GASSET, JOSÉ, *The Modern Theme*. A series of lectures delivered in 1921–2. Trans. J. Cleugh. London: W. C. Daniel Co., 1931.

RICOEUR, PAUL, 'Myth and History', *The Encyclopedia of Religion*, ed. M. Eliade. New York: Macmillan, 1987, 272–82.

ROSE, JONATHAN, *The Edwardian Temperament*. Athens, Ohio: Ohio University Press, 1986.

SCHMITT, CARL, *Political Romanticism*. First published in 1919. Trans. Guy Oakes. Cambridge, Mass: MIT Press, 1986.

SCHORSKE, CARL E., *Fin-de-Siècle Vienna*. First published in 1961. London: Weidenfeld & Nicolson, 1980.

STERN, F., *The Politics of Cultural Despair*. Berkeley: University of California Press, 1961. Introduction, xi–xxx.

STERN, J. P., *Nietzsche*. Fontana Modern Masters, ed. Frank Kermode. London: Fontana Press Ltd., 1978.

STONE, NORMAN, *Europe Transformed: 1878–1919*. Fontana History of Europe. London: Fontana Press Ltd., 1983.

THATCHER, DAVID, *Nietzsche in England 1890–1914: The Growth of a Reputation*. Toronto: University of Toronto Press, 1970.

TODOROV, TZVETAN, *Literature and its Theorists*. London. Routledge & Kegan Paul, 1988, chap. 5.

—— *Mikhail Bakhtin: The Dialogic Principle*, trans. Wlad Godzich, *Theory and History of Literature*, vol. xiii. Manchester: Manchester University Press, 1984.

TRILLING, LIONEL, 'On the Teaching of Modern Literature', *Beyond Culture: Essays in Literature and Learning*. London: Secker & Warburg, 1966, 3–30.

VAIHINGER, HANS, *The Philosophy of 'As If': A System of the Theoretical, Practical and Religious Fictions of Mankind*. First published in Berlin, 1911. Trans. C. K. Ogden. First published in English in 1924. London: Routledge & Kegan Paul, 1952.

Index

References in bold are to sections dealing exclusively with a specific work